Corners *and* Curves

45 Granny Square patterns for crocheters ready to play with colours, corners, and curves.

by Shelley Husband

Copyright © 2024 by Shelley Husband

All rights reserved. No part of this publication may be reproduced or transmitted by any means, electronic, photocopying or otherwise without prior written permission of the author.

ISBN: 978-0-6486053-4-8

Charts made by Amy Gunderson

Email: kinglouiespizza@gmail.com

Ravelry ID: AmyGunderson

Graphic Design by Michelle Lorimer

Email: hello@michellelorimer.com

Technical Editing by Kelly Lonergan

Email: kelly@hazennainspired.com

Project Photography by Jo O'Keefe

Email: jookeefe@hotmail.com

Instagram: missfarmerjojo

Photos taken at Sommarhus Port Fairy

https://linktr.ee/Sommarhus_PortFairy

Other Photography by Shelley Husband

First edition 2024

Published by Shelley Husband

PO Box 11

Narrawong VIC 3285

Australia

shelleyhusbandcrochet.com

0824

Contents

Welcome to Corners and Curves	5
Supplies and Knowledge	6
Pattern Index	16
Small Patterns	18
Medium Patterns	66
Large Patterns	116
Extensions	158
Projects	166
Projects to Make	168
Design Your Own Projects	196
Yardage and Stitch Counts	200
Glossary	202
Yarn Information	204
Helpful Links	206
Thank You	207
About the Author	208
Other Books by Shelley Husband	209

Welcome
to Corners and Curves

Designing new granny squares has given me a lot of happiness for many years. And others too, going by the projects and stories shared with me. I am so pleased I can continue my fun and yours with my tenth book!

So, welcome back, if you've crocheted with me before. Or, if it's your first foray into my world of granny squares, a heartfelt hello and welcome. I hope you enjoy cornering some curves with me.

When making granny squares, there is a special moment of glee when squaring off a circle. The thrill when you get around the circle and you have the right number of stitches to square off. I see it all the time in workshops. It's an oft celebrated moment.

That is what this collection of granny squares is all about – circles going square.

There are 45 moments of triumph for you in this book, with three different sized squares and oh so many options. So grab a refreshing brew, read on and start planning your Corners and Curves Granny Square play.

Supplies and Knowledge

The supplies needed to crochet are pretty minimal. Apart from scissors and a yarn needle, all you really need is a crochet hook and some yarn.

Supplies

Yarn

You can use yarn of any fibre and weight to make these patterns.

I have provided you with the amount and type of yarn I used to make each granny square in three yarn weights, and the same information for each project.

If you change yarn and hook size, and/or have a different crochet style to me, your yarn needs will be different.

The best way to estimate your yarn needs if using a different yarn is to compare the metres per gram ratio of the yarn I used to the yarn you wish to use. If there are less metres per gram, you will need more. If there are more metres per gram, you will need less.

Your desires for the end product should guide your yarn choice, along with your budget, access to different yarns and your personal preferences.

Hook

I have shared the hook size I used for each yarn weight and project. You are not bound by that. If you prefer more drape, use a larger hook. If you prefer a tighter fabric, use a smaller hook.

You will see in some of the projects, I have used a different hook size to what would usually be recommended for the yarn weights. Think about what you want your finished project to be and let that guide your hook size choice.

Again, using a different hook size will change the amount of yarn needed. A larger hook means you will need more yarn and a smaller hook means you will need less.

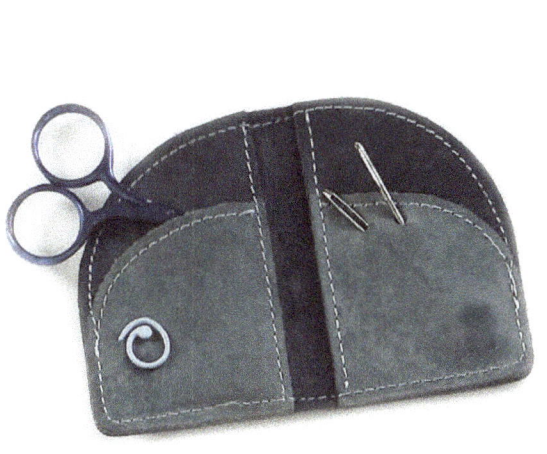

Knowledge

This book has been written for those who know how to read a pattern or chart. If you know how to do the most common crochet stitches and are willing to play with new combinations of stitches and techniques, you will be able to tackle any pattern in this book.

I have included a difficulty rating for each granny square pattern.

easiest ───────────────▶ most interesting

I have ordered the granny square patterns in each section to start with the easiest ones, progressing to the most interesting at the end of each section.

Reading the patterns

How to read the written patterns

The abbreviations of all the stitches and techniques used in the patterns are explained in full in the Glossary on page 202.

Here's an excerpt from the Ecliptic pattern on page 24:

R4: ch3 (stch), tr in same st as ss, *tr in next 2 sts**, 2tr in next st*, rep from * to * 10x & * to ** 1x, join with ss to 3rd ch of stch. {48 sts}

And another from the Radiance Squared pattern on page 100:

R11: dc in same st as ss, *10x [ch1, skip 1 st, dc in next st], ch1, skip 1 st**, (dc, ch2, dc) in next st*, rep from * to * 2x & * to ** 1x, dc in same st as first st, ch1, join with dc to first st. {12 sts, 11 1-ch sps on each side; 4 2-ch cnr sps}

Asterisks and repeats

After the beginning of round instructions, the first single asterisk indicates the start of a repeat and the second single asterisk indicates the end of a full repeat. The double asterisks indicate the end of a partial repeat. Ignore the asterisks and follow the instructions until you get to "rep". That is your cue to go back to the first single asterisk and redo the pattern repeat as many times in full and partially as instructed.

After the repeats, I tell you how to finish off the round.

Brackets

(xxxx) are stitches and/or chain spaces that are either to be all worked in the one stitch or space as indicated, or a set of stitches and/or chain spaces to be skipped.

[xxxx] indicate a small set of stitches and/or chain spaces to be repeated within a full pattern repeat. These brackets will be preceded with a number and x to indicate how many times to work the small repeat.

{xxxx} contain the stitch count for each round. For a square shape, it states how many stitches are along each side between the corners and describes the corners. If the pattern begins as a shape with no corners, then it describes how many stitches in total make up that round.

Things to note

When chains count as stitches

At the start of rounds, if a number of chains is followed by **(stch)** (starting chain), that means those chains count as the first stitch. The starting chains are included in the stitch count as the first stitch.

Here's an excerpt from the Coffer pattern on page 22:

R1: **ch3 (stch)**, 11tr, join with ss to 3rd ch of stch. {12 sts}

The chain three is counted as a stitch in the stitch count.

If there are a number of chains at the beginning of a round not followed by (stch), these chains are not included in the stitch count.

Here's an excerpt from the HAL 9000 pattern on page 84:

R1: **ch1**, 10dc, join with ss to first st. {10 sts}

The ch1 at the start is not included in the stitch count. It is there to make it easier find the first stitch to join into.

Slip stitches

If there is a slip stitch at the beginning of a round, it is not included in the stitch count. The slip stitch joins are not included in the stitch count. However, if there is a slip stitch within a pattern repeat, it is included in the stitch count.

Here's an excerpt from the Zinderella pattern on page 112:

R3: dc in same st as ss, *ch2, **ss in flo** of next st of R1, ch2, skip 1 st**, dc in next st*, rep from * to * 8x & * to ** 1x, **join with ss** to first st. {20 sts, 20 2-ch sps}

The "ss in flo" are included in the stitch count, but the "join with ss" slip stitch is not.

Which round to work into

If the instructions don't specify a round to work into or skip, it is assumed you work into or skip the stitches of the previous round. If you need to work into stitches of rounds other than the previous round, it will be stated in the instructions.

Here's an excerpt from the Stellate pattern on page 62:

R5: ch3 (stch), *5tr **in R3 st** behind 5-ch sp, skip 5-ch sp**, **tr in next st**, rep from * to * 6x & * to ** 1x, join with ss to 3rd ch of stch. {48 sts}

The 5tr are worked in a Round 3 stitch as specified. The "tr in next st" is worked into a Round 4 stitch (the previous round) as it is not specified.

Seamless tips

To avoid having a visible seam where the rounds begin and end, I end each round in the middle of a corner. In the case of a square with 2-chain corner spaces, the round will end with the instruction to chain 1 and join with a double crochet. That double crochet takes the place of the second chain and places your hook in exactly the right spot to begin the next round, with no need to slip stitch or work backwards. Depending on the pattern, you may be instructed to work a stitch over that joining stitch.

Treat the joining stitch as the second chain of the 2-chain corner space and work over it as if it were a chain space. If the corners of the pattern are longer chain loops, the final number of chains to be worked and the joining stitch will be different. For example, if a round has corners of 4-chain spaces, it may end with chain 1, join with a treble crochet. A round with 3-chain corner spaces may end with chain 1, join with a half treble crochet. Check the Helpful Links on page 206 for a more detailed explanation of this technique.

Insert hook like this to work over joining stitch

dc worked over joining dc

false st and a tr worked over joining dc

Another trick to make your crochet look seamless is to work a false stitch instead of a starting chain. While I state the standard starting chain at the beginning of rounds, (e.g. ch3 to take the place of a treble crochet), I rarely use starting chains when crocheting. Instead, I use a false stitch. You can find a link to a video of it on my YouTube Channel on the Helpful Links page.

Blocking

Blocking is a way to make your crochet sing. Some patterns require a good blocking to sit flat and square. It's part of the process and does not take long to do.

You don't need anything fancy to block. A folded towel works well. I use foam mats intended for temporary flooring. These are handy to block large blankets too.

Your fibre choice will determine which blocking method works best.

Steam blocking is fine for most fibres. Natural wool suits wet blocking best. If making with wool, I generally steam block the squares as I make them, and wet block the final project.

Steam blocking

Block each square by pinning it out and squirting it with steam. An iron or garment steamer works fine. Some squares will only need a pin in each corner, while others will need some along the edges and in the centre to correct any swirl or distortion.

Wet blocking

Some fibres will block best after washing according to yarn label instructions and pinning out while wet to dry.

To wet block, add some wool wash to tepid water, dunk your project into the water, squeezing the water through gently. Let it soak for 15 minutes or so. Remove from the water, gently squeezing. Roll between towels to remove more water. Lay out flat to dry. Pin corners and edges if needed.

SUPPLIES AND KNOWLEDGE

Joining

There are many ways to join granny squares. I like to keep it simple, so the granny squares are the main attraction.

I used three slightly different joining methods to make the projects in this book. Each of them is done with the right sides held together so the join is on the back.

All these methods work well when joining granny squares with different stitch counts and strips of different sized granny squares.

How to join granny squares with different stitch counts

When joining squares with different stitch counts, as many times as needed, use the same stitch on the smaller stitch count square while using a new stitch on the larger stitch count square.

For example, consider joining Begirt and Betwixt. Begirt has 23 stitches on each side while Betwixt has 18. So, five times as you join, use the same stitch twice on Betwixt while always using a new stitch on Begirt. Spread the places you work the double stitch out along the side.

This will work regardless of the stitch count difference, as long as the squares are the same physical size. There is a very large stitch count difference between some of the largest squares in this book. Two squares have 35 stitches on each side and one has 52 stitches – a difference of 17 stitches - and the joining works just fine as the squares are the same size.

On page 200, there is a table listing all the patterns in this book with their stitch counts.

Begirt (left) has 23 stitches along the side, whereas Betwixt has 18.

SUPPLIES AND KNOWLEDGE

How to join projects using different sized squares

The best way to tackle the joining when using different sized squares is to lay your squares out and look for strips that can be made, and then blocks. Start with squares of the same size that are next to each other. Make blocks with your strips and join the blocks together.

How I joined the Compendium blankets

I joined strips of each of the three sizes of squares first. **(yellow)**

Then I joined the medium and small square strips, and added the large square strips last. **(light blue)**

To help keep the joining even, add stitch markers to your strips and blocks. For example **(dark blue)**:

- where joins meet on both strips
- halfway through a square to a join on a strip.

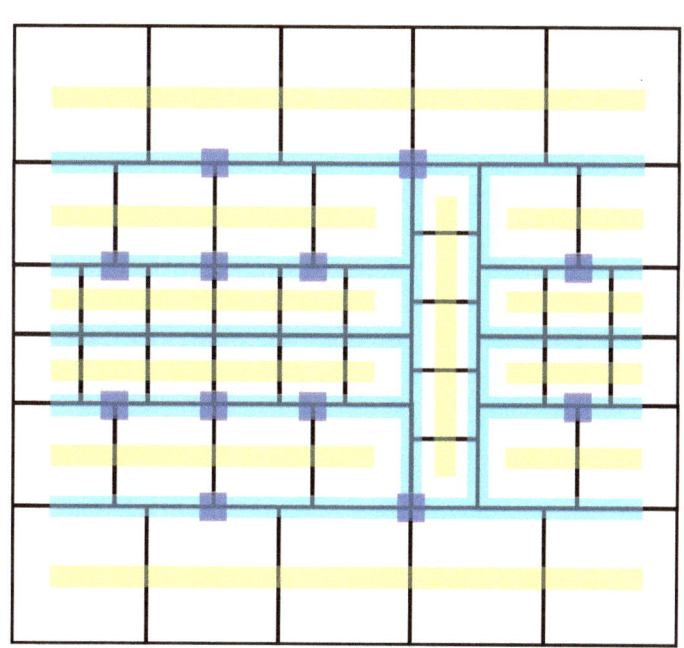

SUPPLIES AND KNOWLEDGE

Joining methods

dc on back join

Hold squares right sides together, attach joining yarn with a standing double crochet to both 2-chain corner spaces of each square at the same time. Work a double crochet into both loops of both squares all the way along, end with a double crochet in both 2-chain corner spaces. Fasten off.

dc on back though blo join

Worked the same for the dc on back join, but when working along the edges of the squares, use the back loops only.

Whip stitch on back through blo

Cut a long length of yarn and thread it onto a yarn needle. Holding the squares right sides together, sew from one to the other, starting with a single strand of a chain on each square, then using the blo of each stitch of both squares, ending with a single strand of a chain of each square. Fasten off.

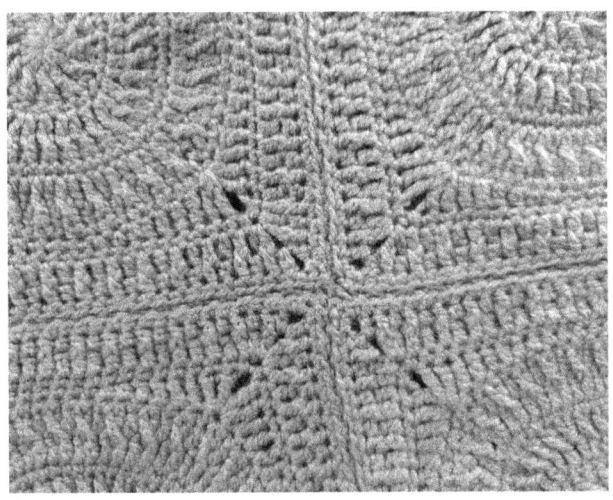

A note about sizing

You may find some of your squares are a little different in size to others in the same size group. There are many reasons for this, from crochet style of certain stitches to changing hook size and yarn weight from what I used.

It's easy to deal with size differences.

If the difference is small, say less than half an inch, blocking to size should suffice. Joining will help even the sizing as well.

For larger differences, you have options.

To add size, either add an extra round or two of double crochet, or change the last round stitch to a taller one.

To reduce size, in some patterns it will be easy to leave off the last round. For others you may need to change the last round's stitch to a shorter one.

Pattern Index

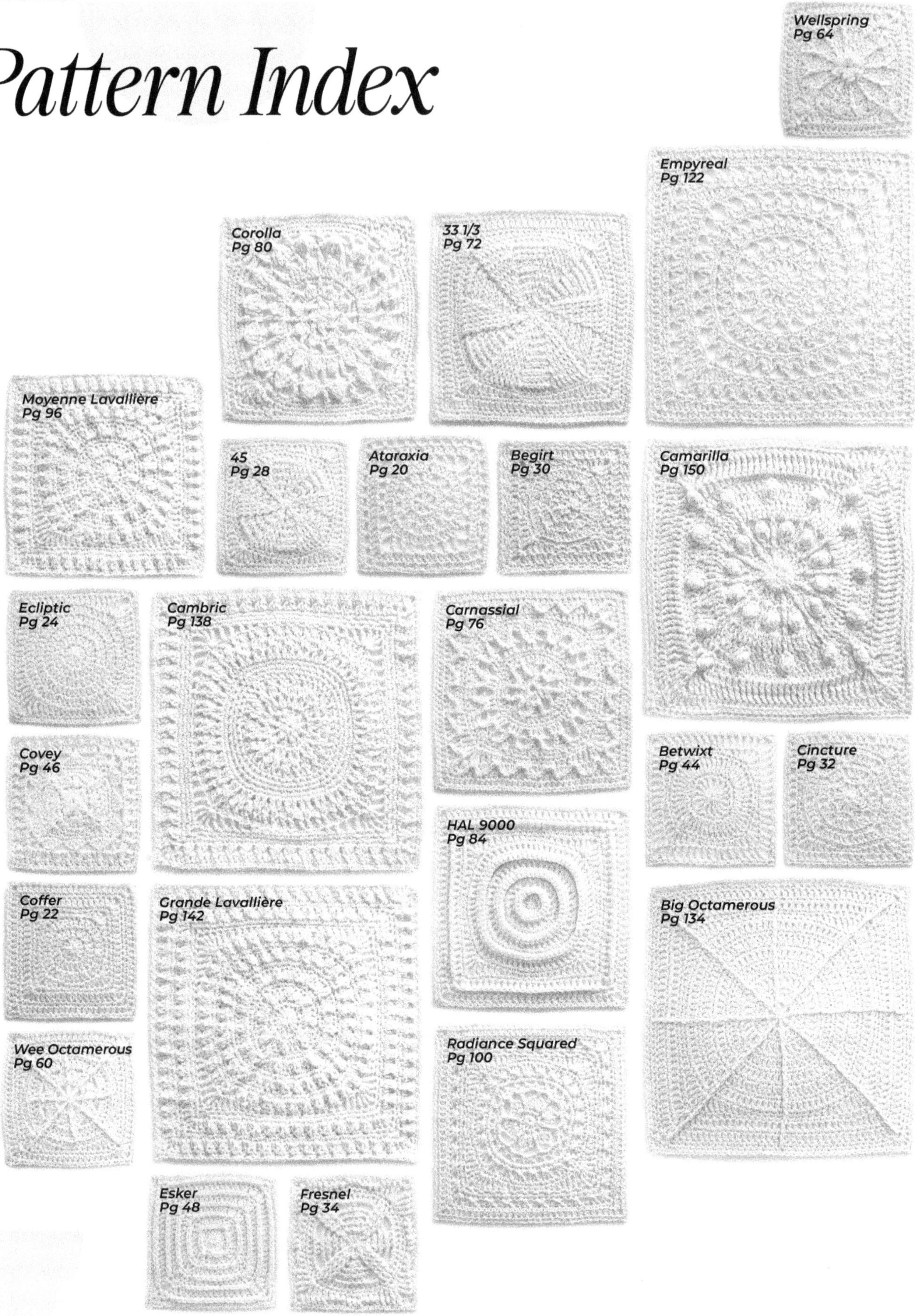

- Wellspring Pg 64
- Empyreal Pg 122
- Corolla Pg 80
- 33 1/3 Pg 72
- Moyenne Lavallière Pg 96
- 45 Pg 28
- Ataraxia Pg 20
- Begirt Pg 30
- Camarilla Pg 150
- Ecliptic Pg 24
- Cambric Pg 138
- Carnassial Pg 76
- Covey Pg 46
- Betwixt Pg 44
- Cincture Pg 32
- Coffer Pg 22
- Grande Lavallière Pg 142
- HAL 9000 Pg 84
- Big Octamerous Pg 134
- Wee Octamerous Pg 60
- Radiance Squared Pg 100
- Esker Pg 48
- Fresnel Pg 34

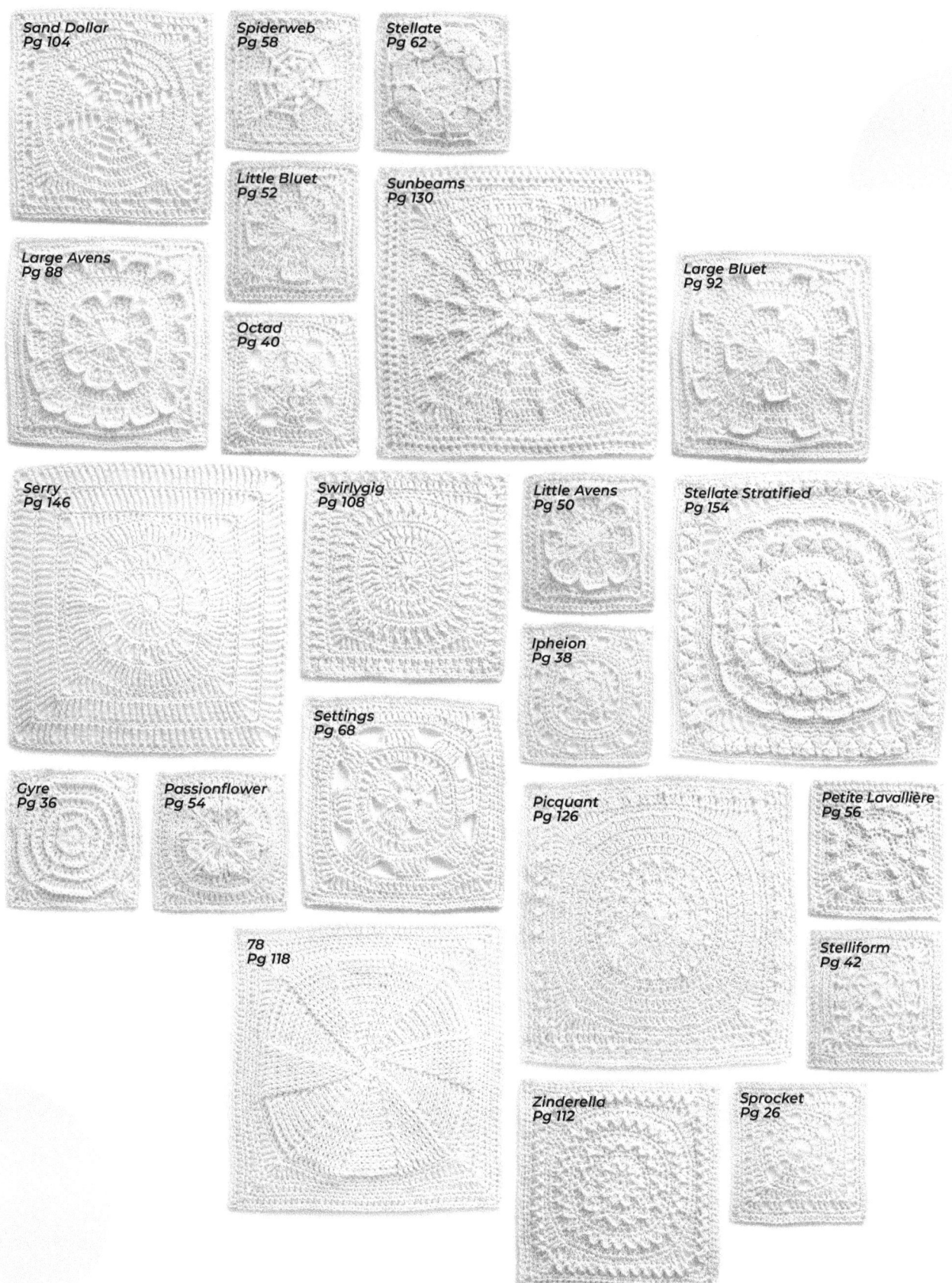

PATTERN INDEX • 17

Small

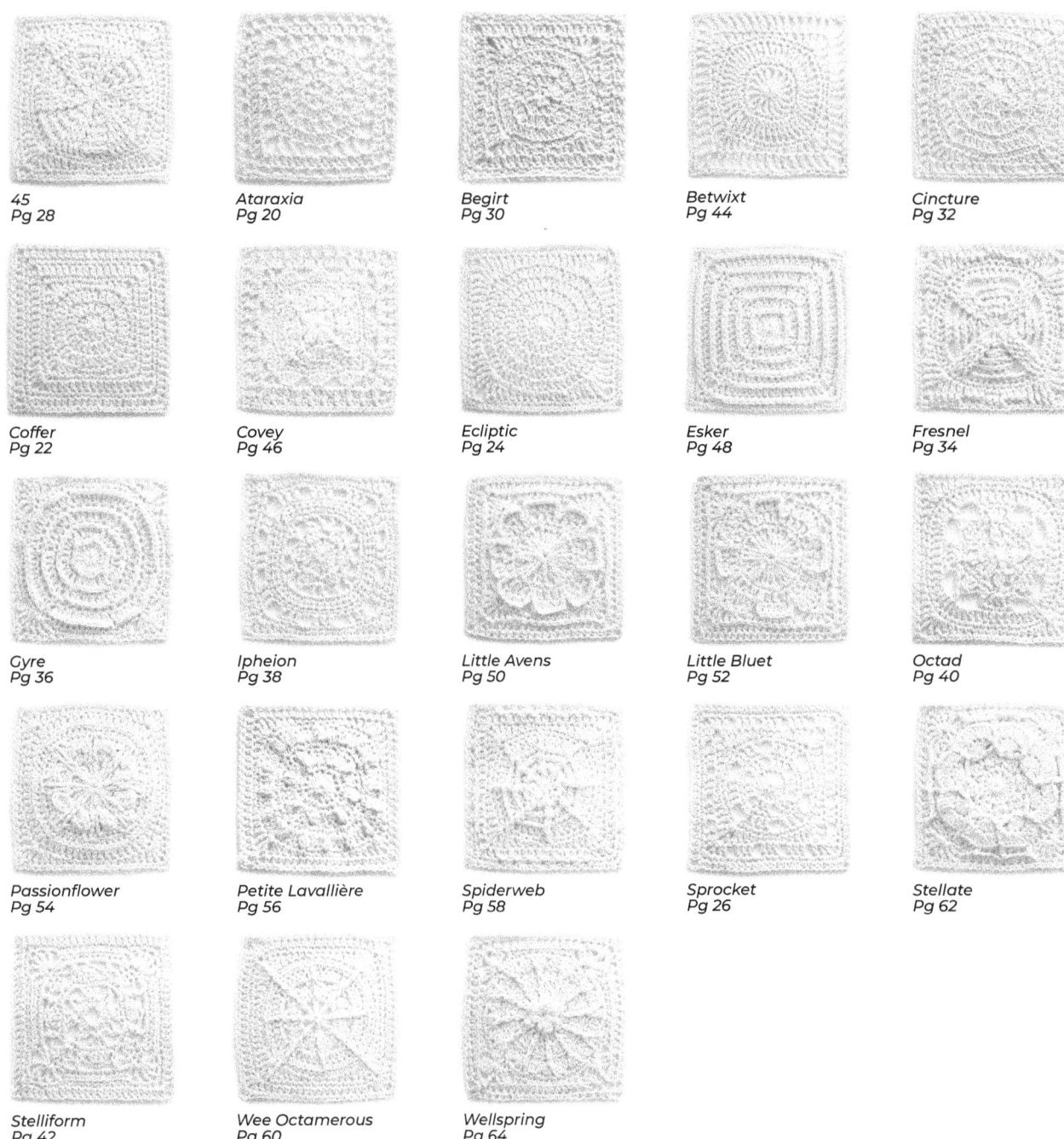

45 Pg 28	*Ataraxia* Pg 20	*Begirt* Pg 30	*Betwixt* Pg 44	*Cincture* Pg 32
Coffer Pg 22	*Covey* Pg 46	*Ecliptic* Pg 24	*Esker* Pg 48	*Fresnel* Pg 34
Gyre Pg 36	*Ipheion* Pg 38	*Little Avens* Pg 50	*Little Bluet* Pg 52	*Octad* Pg 40
Passionflower Pg 54	*Petite Lavallière* Pg 56	*Spiderweb* Pg 58	*Sprocket* Pg 26	*Stellate* Pg 62
Stelliform Pg 42	*Wee Octamerous* Pg 60	*Wellspring* Pg 64		

18 • **SMALL PATTERNS**

Here's a guide to the expected finished size of the squares made with different yarn weights and hook sizes. The amount of yarn listed on each pattern page is based on using the medium weight yarn and corresponding hook size. The amount of yarn needed for the other yarn weights is listed on page 200.

Hook	3.5 mm hook	4.5 mm hook	5.5 mm hook
Yarn	4 ply/sock/fingering	8 ply/DK/light worsted	10 ply/aran/worsted
Size	5"	6"	7"

SMALL PATTERNS

Ataraxia

I may be stretching it a bit far with this one. Ataraxia is a philosophical term meaning freedom from worry and anxiety - completely tranquil. I am sure this one won't cause you stress.

 31 m / 34 yd

Begin with mc.

R1: ch3 (stch), *ch1**, tr*, rep from * to * 4x & * to ** 1x, join with ss to 3rd ch of stch. {6 sts, 6 1-ch sps}

R2: ch3 (stch), tr in same st as ss, *2tr in 1-ch sp**, 2tr in next st*, rep from * to * 4x & * to ** 1x, join with ss to 3rd ch of stch. {24 sts}

R3: ch3 (stch), tr in same st as ss, *ch1, skip 1 st**, 2tr in next st*, rep from * to *10x & * to ** 1x, join with ss to 3rd ch of stch. {24 sts, 12 1-ch sps}

R4: ch3 (stch), tr in next st, *2tr in 1-ch sp**, tr in next 2 sts*, rep from * to *10x & * to ** 1x, join with ss to 3rd ch of stch. {48 sts}

R5: ch4 (stch), *ch1, skip 1 st, hdtr in next st, ch1, skip 1 st, tr in next st, ch1, skip 1 st, htr in next st, ch1, skip 1 st, tr in next st, ch1, skip 1 st, hdtr in next st, ch1, skip 1 st**, (dtr, ch3, dtr) in next st*, rep from * to * 2x & * to ** 1x, dtr in same st as first st, ch1, join with htr to 4th ch of stch. {7 sts, 6 1-ch sps on each side; 4 3-ch cnr sps}

R6: ch3 (stch), tr over joining htr, *6x [tr in next st, tr in 1-ch sp], tr in next st**, (2tr, ch2, 2tr) in 3-ch cnr sp*, rep from * to * 2x & * to ** 1x, 2tr in same sp as first sts, ch1, join with dc to 3rd ch of stch. {17 sts on each side; 4 2-ch cnr sps}

R7: ch2 (stch), *8x [ch1, skip 1 st, htr in next st], ch1, skip 1 st**, (htr, ch2, htr) in 2-ch cnr sp*, rep from * to * 2x & * to ** 1x, htr in same sp as first st, ch1, join with dc to 2nd ch of stch. {10 sts, 9 1-ch sps on each side; 4 2-ch cnr sps}

R8: dc over joining dc, *9x [dc in next st, dc in 1-ch sp], dc in next st**, (dc, ch2, dc) in 2-ch cnr sp*, rep from * to * 2x & * to ** 1x, dc in same sp as first st, ch2, join with ss to first st. Fasten off. {21 sts on each side; 4 2-ch cnr sps}

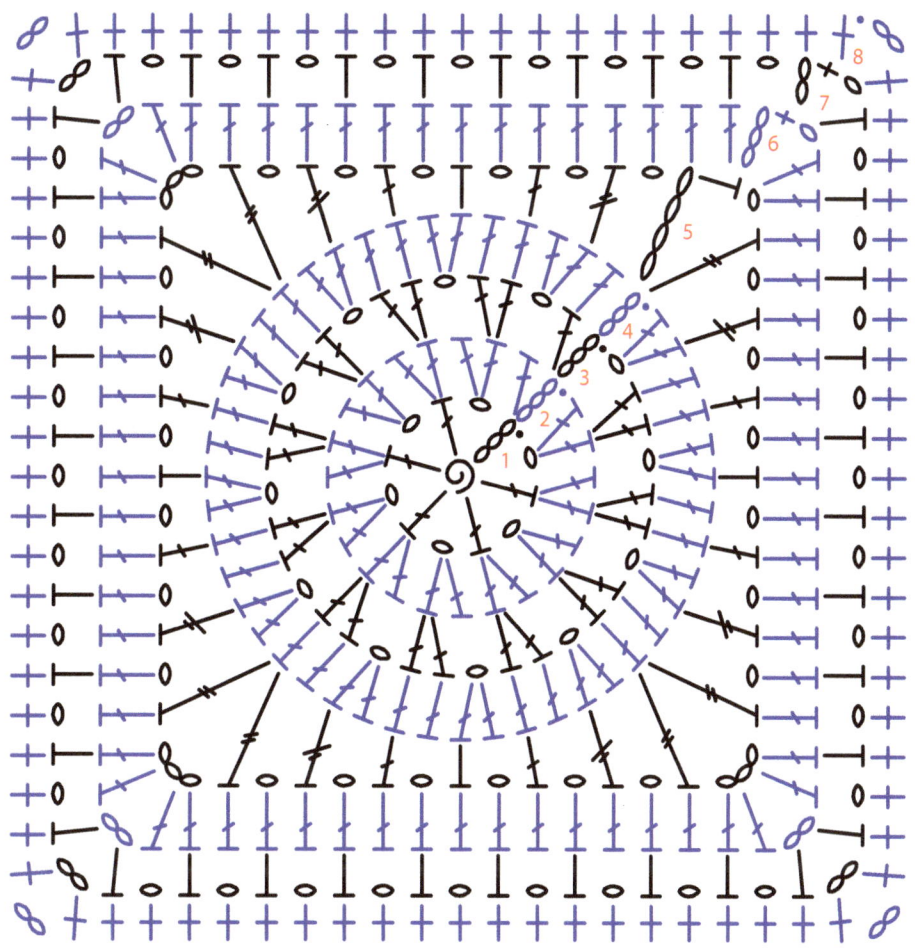

Kim

Kym

SMALL PATTERNS • 21

Coffer

A coffer is a box or chest for holding valuables. Our pattern appears to have layers of boxes keeping the circle safe.

 35 m / 38 yd

Begin with mc.

R1: ch3 (stch), 11tr, join with ss to 3rd ch of stch. {12 sts}

R2: ch3 (stch), tr in same st as ss, 2tr in next 11 sts, join with ss to 3rd ch of stch. {24 sts}

R3: ch3 (stch), tr in same st as ss, *tr in next st**, 2tr in next st*, rep from * to * 10x & * to ** 1x, join with ss to 3rd ch of stch. {36 sts}

R4: ch3 (stch), tr in same st as ss, *htr in next 2 sts, dc in next 4 sts, htr in next 2 sts**, (2tr, ch2, 2tr) in next st*, rep from * to * 2x & * to ** 1x, 2tr in same st as first sts, ch1, join with dc to 3rd ch of stch. {12 sts on each side; 4 2-ch cnr sps}

R5: dc over joining dc, *dc in next 12 sts**, (dc, ch2, dc) in 2-ch sp*, rep from * to * 2x & * to ** 1x, dc in same sp as first st, ch1, join with dc to first st. {14 sts on each side; 4 2-ch cnr sps}

R6: ch3 (stch), *tr in next 14 sts**, (tr, ch2, tr) in 2-ch sp*, rep from * to * 2x & * to ** 1x, tr in same sp as first st, ch1, join with dc to 3rd ch of stch. {16 sts on each side; 4 2-ch cnr sps}

R7: dc over joining dc, *dc in next 16 sts**, (dc, ch2, dc) in 2-ch sp*, rep from * to * 2x & * to ** 1x, dc in same sp as first st, ch1, join with dc to first st. {18 sts on each side; 4 2-ch cnr sps}

R8: ch2 (stch), *htr in next 18 sts**, (htr, ch2, htr) in 2-ch sp*, rep from * to * 2x & * to ** 1x, htr in same sp as first st, ch1, join with dc to 2nd ch of stch. {20 sts on each side; 4 2-ch cnr sps}

R9: dc over joining dc, *dc in next 20 sts**, (dc, ch2, dc) in 2-ch sp*, rep from * to * 2x & * to ** 1x, dc in same sp as first st, ch2, join with ss to first st. Fasten off. {22 sts on each side; 4 2-ch cnr sps}

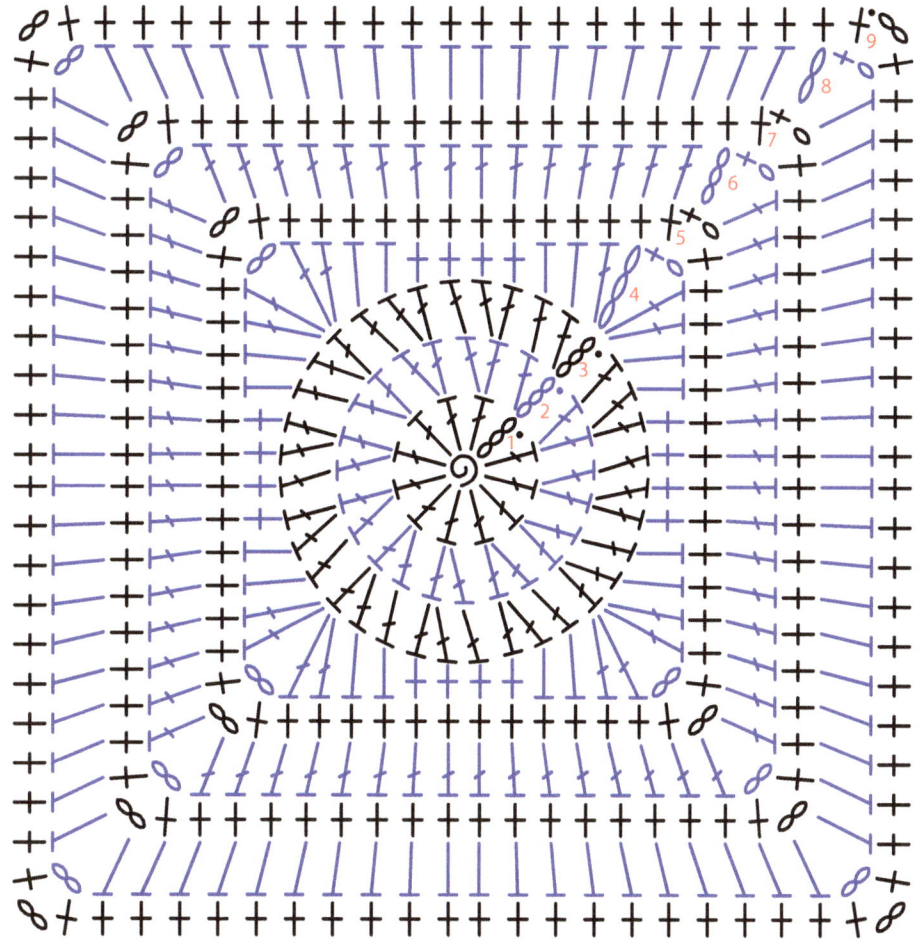

Kim *Kym*

SMALL PATTERNS

Ecliptic

Ecliptic describes the orbital plane of Earth around the Sun. A large circle if you will. Just like this pattern.

 37 m / 40 yd

Begin with mc.

R1: ch3 (stch), 11tr, join with ss to 3rd ch of stch. {12 sts}

R2: ch3 (stch), tr in same st as ss, 2tr in next 11 sts, join with ss to 3rd ch of stch. {24 sts}

R3: ch3 (stch), tr in same st as ss, *tr in next st**, 2tr in next st*, rep from * to * 10x & * to ** 1x, join with ss to 3rd ch of stch. {36 sts}

R4: ch3 (stch), tr in same st as ss, *tr in next 2 sts**, 2tr in next st*, rep from * to * 10x & * to ** 1x, join with ss to 3rd ch of stch. {48 sts}

R5: ch3 (stch), tr in same st as ss, *tr in next 3 sts**, 2tr in next st*, rep from * to * 10x & * to ** 1x, join with ss to 3rd ch of stch. {60 sts}

R6: ch5 (stch), trtr in same st as ss, *dtr in next 2 sts, hdtr in next 2 sts, tr in next 2 sts, htr in next 2 sts, tr in next 2 sts, hdtr in next 2 sts, dtr in next 2 sts**, (2trtr, ch2, 2trtr) in next st*, rep from * to * 2x & * to ** 1x, 2trtr in same st as first sts, ch1, join with dc to 5th ch of stch. {18 sts on each side; 4 2-ch cnr sps}

R7: dc over joining dc, *dc in next 18 sts**, (dc, ch2, dc) in 2-ch sp*, rep from * to * 2x & * to ** 1x, dc in same sp as first st, ch1, join with dc to first st. {20 sts on each side; 4 2-ch cnr sps}

R8: dc over joining dc, *dc in next 20 sts**, (dc, ch2, dc) in 2-ch sp*, rep from * to * 2x & * to ** 1x, dc in same sp as first st, ch2, join with ss to first st. Fasten off. {22 sts on each side; 4 2-ch cnr sps}

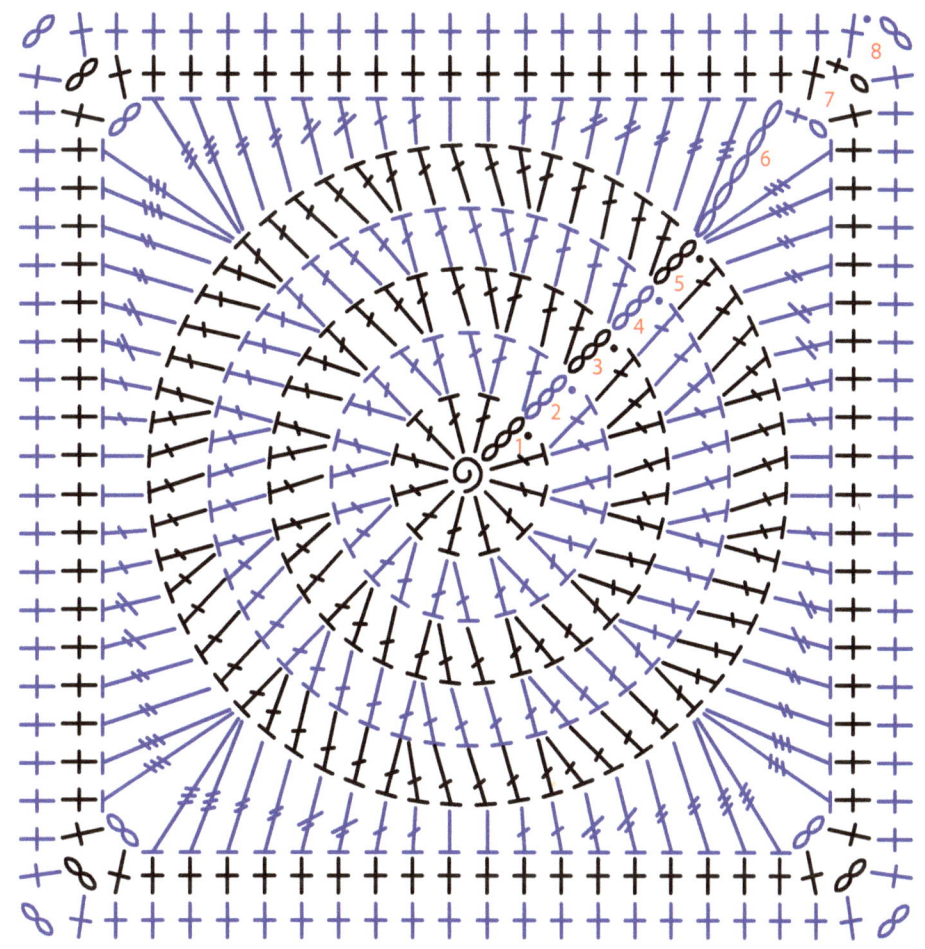

Kim

Kym

SMALL PATTERNS

Sprocket

As this one is quite chain cog wheel-like, sprocket seemed to fit.

 34 m / 38 yd

Begin with mc.

R1: ch3 (stch), 17tr, join with ss to 3rd ch of stch. {18 sts}

R2: ch3 (stch), tr in next 2 sts, *ch2**, tr in next 3 sts*, rep from * to * 4x & * to ** 1x, join with ss to 3rd ch of stch. {18 sts, 6 2-ch sps}

R3: dc in same st as ss, dc in next 2 sts, *2dc in 2-ch sp**, dc in next 3 sts*, rep from * to * 4x & * to ** 1x, join with ss to first st. {30 sts}

R4: ch3 (stch), tr in next 3 sts, *ch3, skip 1 st**, tr in next 4 sts*, rep from * to * 4x & * to ** 1x, join with ss to 3rd ch of stch. {24 sts, 6 3-ch sps}

R5: dc in same st as ss, *2dc in next 2 sts, dc in next st, 2dc in 3-ch sp**, dc in next st*, rep from * to * 4x & * to ** 1x, join with ss to first st. {48 sts}

R6: ch4 (stch), hdtr in same st as ss, *tr in next 2 sts, htr in next 2 sts, dc in next 3 sts, htr in next 2 sts, tr in next 2 sts**, (hdtr, dtr, ch2, dtr, hdtr) in next st*, rep from * to * 2x & * to ** 1x, (hdtr, dtr) in same st as first sts, ch1, join with dc to 4th ch of stch. {15 sts on each side; 4 2-ch cnr sps}

R7: ch3 (stch), tr over joining dc, *tr in next st, 3x [ch1, skip 1 st, tr in next 3 sts], ch1, skip 1 st, tr in next st**, (2tr, ch2, 2tr) in 2-ch cnr sp*, rep from * to * 2x & * to ** 1x, 2tr in same sp as first sts, ch1, join with dc to 3rd ch of stch. {15 sts, 4 1-ch sps on each side; 4 2-ch cnr sps}

R8: dc over joining dc, *4x [dc in next 3 sts, dc in 1-ch sp], dc in next 3 sts**, (dc, ch2, dc) in 2-ch cnr sp*, rep from * to * 2x & * to ** 1x, dc in same sp as first st, ch1, join with dc to first st. {21 sts on each side; 4 2-ch cnr sps}

R9: ch2 (stch), *htr in next 21 sts**, (htr, ch2, htr) in 2-ch cnr sp*, rep from * to * 2x & * to ** 1x, htr in same sp as first st, ch2, join with ss to 2nd ch of stch. Fasten off. {23 sts on each side; 4 2-ch cnr sps}

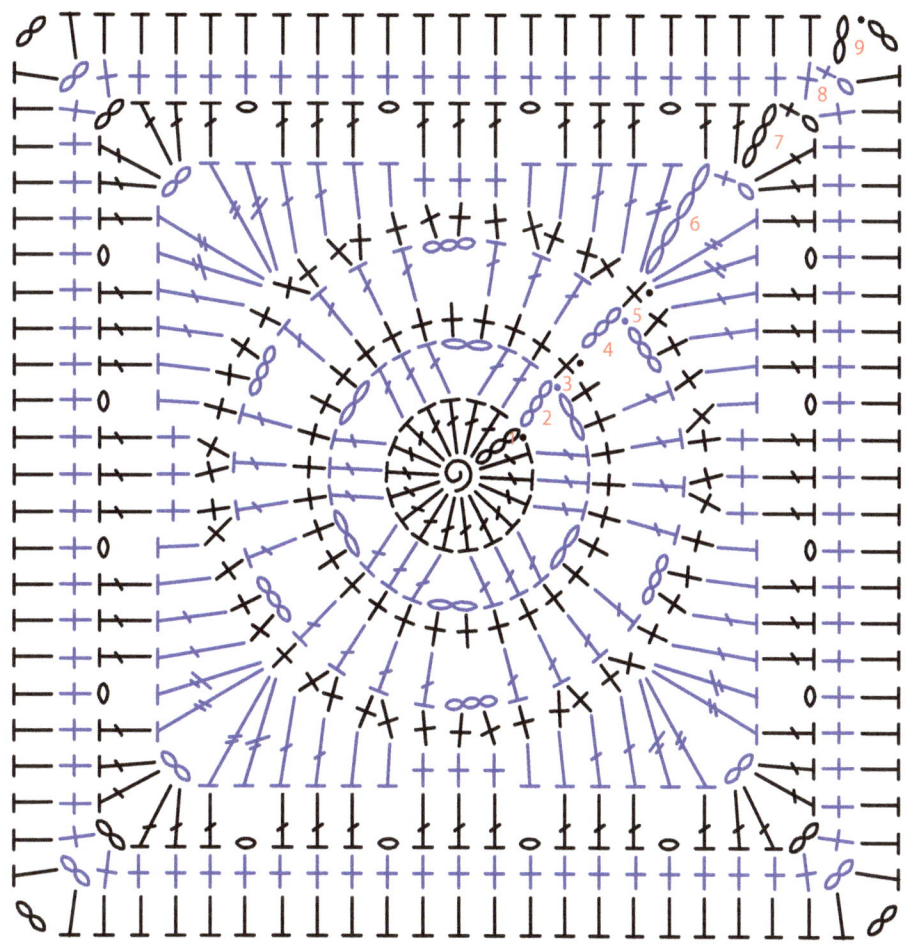

Kim

Kym

SMALL PATTERNS • 27

45

Reminiscent of a good old vinyl single - hence 45. Do you remember the first one you bought?

 44 m / 48 yd

Begin with mc.

R1: ch3 (stch), 11tr, join with ss to 3rd ch of stch. {12 sts}

R2: ch3 (stch), fptr around same st as ss, *(tr in, bptr around) next st**, (tr in, fptr around) next st*, rep from * to * 4x & * to ** 1x, join with ss to 3rd ch of stch. {24 sts}

R3: ch3 (stch), fptr around same st as ss, fptr around next st, *(tr in, bptr around) next st, bptr around next st**, (tr in, fptr around) next st, fptr around next st*, rep from * to * 4x & * to ** 1x, join with ss to 3rd ch of stch. {36 sts}

R4: ch3 (stch), fptr around same st as ss, fptr around next 2 sts, *(tr in, bptr around) next st, bptr around next 2 sts**, (tr in, fptr around) next st, fptr around next 2 sts*, rep from * to * 4x & * to ** 1x, join with ss to 3rd ch of stch. {48 sts}

R5: ch3 (stch), fptr around same st as ss, fptr around next 3 sts, *(tr in, bptr around) next st, bptr around next 3 sts**, (tr in, fptr around) next st, fptr around next 3 sts*, rep from * to * 4x & * to ** 1x, join with ss to 3rd ch of stch. {60 sts}

R6: fptr around same st as ss, fptr around next 4 sts, *bptr around next 5 sts**, fptr around next 5 sts*, rep from * to * 4x & * to ** 1x, join with ss to first st. {60 sts}

R7: dc in same st as ss, dc in next 59 sts, join with ss to first st. {60 sts}

R8: ch4 (stch), 2hdtr in same st as ss, *tr in next 3 sts, htr in next 3 sts, dc in next 2 sts, htr in next 3 sts, tr in next 3 sts**, (2hdtr, dtr, 2hdtr) in next st*, rep from * to * 2x & * to ** 1x, 2hdtr in same st as first sts, join with ss to 4th ch of stch. {14 sts on each side; 4 5-st cnrs}

R9: dc in same st as ss, *dc in next 18 sts**, (dc, ch2, dc) in next st*, rep from * to * 2x & * to ** 1x, dc in same st as first st, ch1, join with dc to first st. {20 sts on each side; 4 2-ch cnr sps}

R10: dc over joining dc, *dc in next 20 sts**, (dc, ch2, dc) in 2-ch cnr sp*, rep from * to * 2x & * to ** 1x, dc in same sp as first st, ch2, join with ss to first st. Fasten off. {22 sts on each side; 4 2-ch cnr sps}

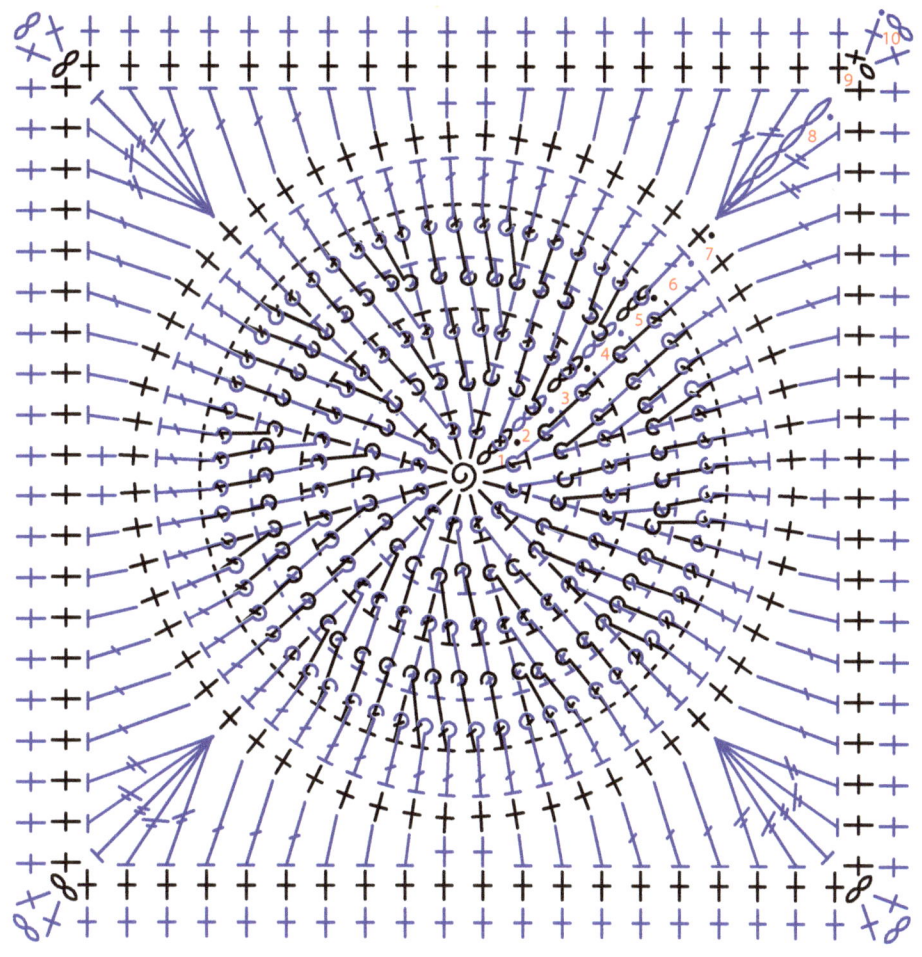

Kim

Kim

Kim

Kym

SMALL PATTERNS • 29

Begirt

"Our home is girt by sea". The only time "girt" is used in a sentence is in the Australian National Anthem. Such a weird word meaning encircled. So this one is begirt with the lines around the circles.

 36 m / 39 yd

Begin with mc.

R1: ch1, 16dc, join with ss to first st. {16 sts}

R2: ch3 (stch), *tr in blo of next st**, tr in next st*, rep from * to * 6x & * to ** 1x, join with ss to 3rd ch of stch. {16 sts}

R3: ch3 (stch), tr in same st as ss, *2tr in blo of next st**, 2tr in next st*, rep from * to * 6x & * to ** 1x, join with ss to 3rd ch of stch. {32 sts}

R4: ch3 (stch), tr in same st as ss, tr in next st, *2tr in blo of next st, tr in blo of next st**, 2tr in next st, tr in next st*, rep from * to * 6x & * to ** 1x, join with ss to 3rd ch of stch. {48 sts}

R5: dc in same st as ss, *dc in blo of next 11 sts**, dc in next st*, rep from * to * 2x & * to ** 1x, join with ss to first st. {48 sts}

R6: ch4 (stch), dtr in same st as ss, *tr in blo of next st, tr in next st, htr in blo of next st, htr in next st, dc in blo of next st, dc in next st, dc in blo of next st, htr in next st, htr in blo of next st, tr in next st, tr in blo of next st**, (2dtr, ch2, 2dtr) in next st*, rep from * to * 2x & * to ** 1x, 2dtr in same st as first sts, ch1, join with dc to 4th ch of stch. {15 sts on each side; 4 2-ch cnr sps}

R7: ch3 (stch), tr over joining dc, *7x [tr in blo of next st, tr in next st], tr in blo of next st**, (2tr, ch2, 2tr) in 2-ch cnr sp*, rep from * to * 2x & * to ** 1x, 2tr in same sp as first sts, ch1, join with dc to 3rd ch of stch. {19 sts on each side; 4 2-ch cnr sps}

R8: dc over joining dc, *9x [dc in blo of next st, dc in next st], dc in blo of next st**, (dc, ch2, dc) in 2-ch cnr sp*, rep from * to * 2x & * to ** 1x, dc in same sp as first st, ch1, join with dc to first st. {21 sts on each side; 4 2-ch cnr sps}

R9: dc over joining dc, *10x [dc in next st, dc in blo of next st], dc in next st**, (dc, ch2, dc) in 2-ch cnr sp*, rep from * to * 2x & * to ** 1x, dc in same sp as first st, ch2, join with ss to first st. Fasten off. {23 sts on each side; 4 2-ch cnr sps}

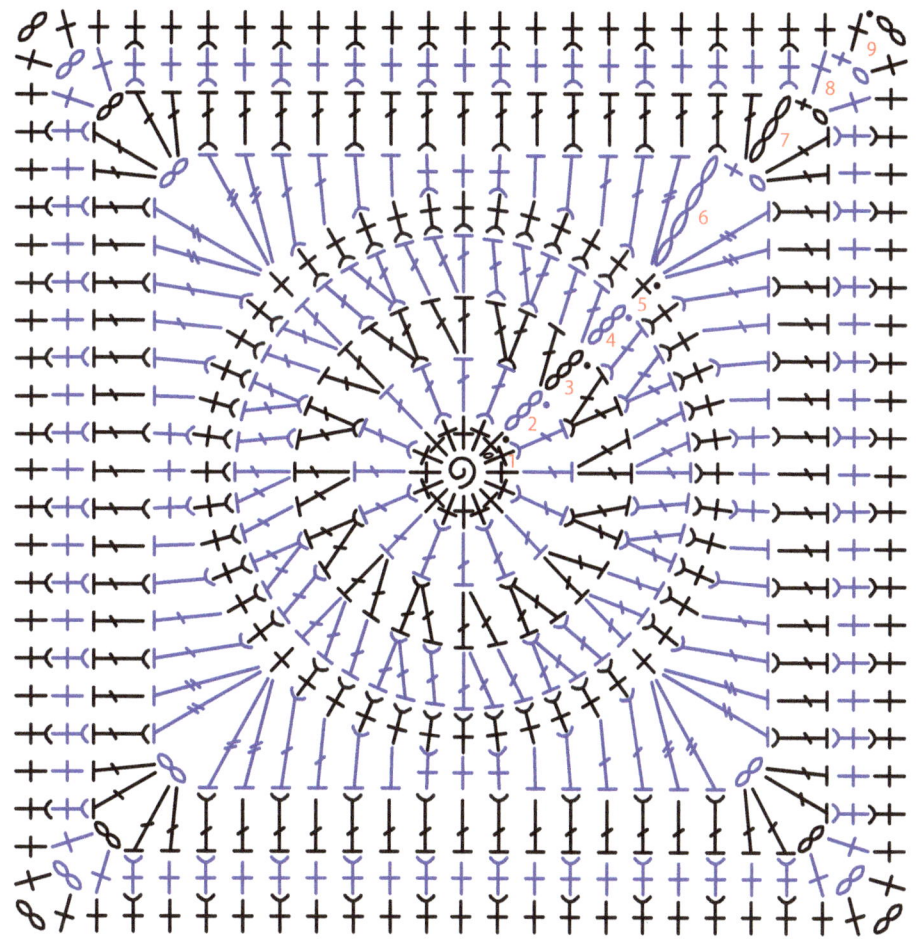

Kim

Kym

SMALL PATTERNS • 31

Cincture

A cincture is a belt or girdle. Our circles are surrounded by lines that put me in mind of belts.

 31 m / 34 yd

Begin with mc.

R1: ch3 (stch), tr, *ch1, 2tr*, rep from * to * 6x, join with dc to 3rd ch of stch. {16 sts, 8 1-ch sps}

R2: dc over joining dc, *dc in blo of next 2 sts**, dc in 1-ch sp*, rep from * to * 6x & * to ** 1x, join with ss to first st. {24 sts}

R3: ss to next st, ch3 (stch), tr in same st as ss, 2tr in next st, *ch1, skip 1 st, 2tr in next 2 sts*, rep from * to * 6x, join with dc to 3rd ch of stch. {32 sts, 8 1-ch sps}

R4: dc over joining dc, *dc in blo of next 4 sts**, dc in 1-ch sp*, rep from * to * 6x & * to ** 1x, join with ss to first st. {40 sts}

R5: ss to next st, ch3 (stch), tr in same st as ss, tr in next 2 sts, 2tr in next st, *ch1, skip 1 st, 2tr in next st, tr in next 2 sts, 2tr in next st*, rep from * to * 6x, join with dc to 3rd ch of stch. {48 sts, 8 1-ch sps}

R6: dc over joining dc, *dc in blo of next 6 sts**, dc in 1-ch sp*, rep from * to * 6x & * to ** 1x, join with ss to first st. {56 sts}

R7: ch4 (stch), hdtr in same st as ss, *tr in next 2 sts, htr in next 2 sts, dc in next 5 sts, htr in next 2 sts, tr in next 2 sts**, (hdtr, dtr, hdtr) in next st*, rep from * to * 2x & * to ** 1x, hdtr in same st as first sts, join with ss to 4th ch of stch. {13 sts on each side; 4 3-st cnrs}

R8: ch3 (stch), tr in same st as ss, *3x [tr in next 3 sts, ch1, skip 1 st], tr in next 3 sts**, (tr, hdtr, tr) in next st*, rep from * to * 2x & * to ** 1x, tr in same st as first sts, join with ss to 3rd ch of stch. {12 sts, 3 1-ch sps on each side; 4 3-st cnrs}

R9: dc in same st as ss, *dc in blo of next 4 sts, 2x [dc in 1-ch sp, dc in blo of next 3 sts], dc in 1-ch sp, dc in blo of next 4 sts**, (dc, ch2, dc) in next st*, rep from * to * 2x & * to ** 1x, dc in same st as first st, ch2, join with ss to first st. Fasten off. {19 sts on each side; 4 2-ch cnr sps}

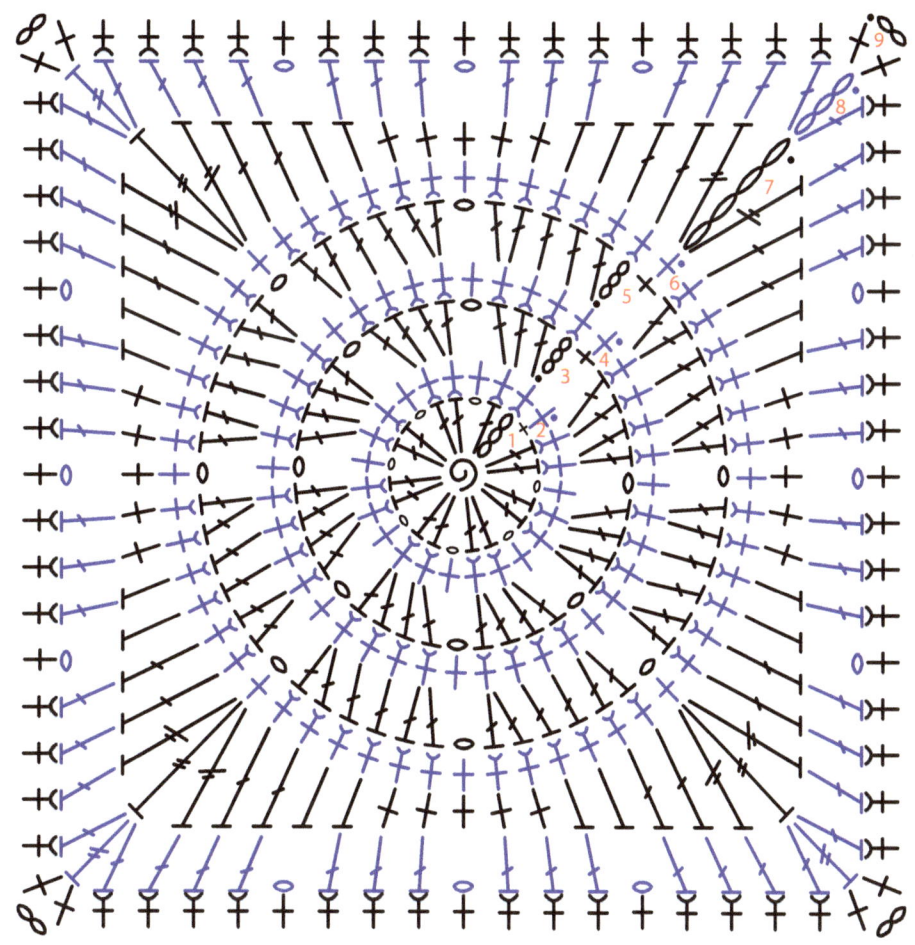

Kim

SMALL PATTERNS • 33

Fresnel

A Fresnel Lens is the faceted thick glass lens once used in lighthouses. The shapes created by the stitches remind me of that.

 42 m / 46 yd

Begin with mc.

R1: ch3 (stch), 23tr, join with ss to 3rd ch of stch. {24 sts} Leave an approx. 1 cm hole when pulling mc closed.

R2: fptr around same st as ss, fptr around next st, *ch1, bptr around next 3 sts, ch1**, fptr around next 3 sts*, rep from * to * 2x & * to ** 1x, fptr around next st, join with ss to first st. {24 sts, 8 1-ch sps} Pull mc fully closed.

R3: fptr around same st as ss, fptr around next st, *ch2, bptr around next 3 sts, ch2**, fptr around next 3 sts*, rep from * to * 2x & * to ** 1x, fptr around next st, join with ss to first st. {24 sts, 8 2-ch sps}

R4: fptr around same st as ss, fptr around next st, *ch3, bptr around next 3 sts, ch3**, fptr around next 3 sts*, rep from * to * 2x & * to ** 1x, fptr around next st, join with ss to first st. {24 sts, 8 3-ch sps}

R5: fptr around same st as ss, fptr around next st, *ch4, bptr around next 3 sts, ch4**, fptr around next 3 sts*, rep from * to * 2x & * to ** 1x, fptr around next st, join with ss to first st. {24 sts, 8 4-ch sps}

R6: fptr around same st as ss, fptr around next st, *4htr in 4-ch sp, bptr around next 3 sts, 4htr in 4-ch sp**, fptr around next 3 sts*, rep from * to * 2x & * to ** 1x, fptr around next st, join with ss to first st. {56 sts}

R7: ch4 (stch), dtr in same st as ss, *tr in next 2 sts, htr in next 3 sts, dc in next 3 sts, htr in next 3 sts, tr in next 2 sts**, (2dtr, ch2, 2dtr) in next st*, rep from * to * 2x & * to ** 1x, 2dtr in same st as first sts, ch1, join with dc to 4th ch of stch. {17 sts on each side; 4 2-ch cnr sps}

R8: ch2 (stch), *fptr around next 4 sts, bptr around next 3 sts, fptr around next 3 sts, bptr around next 3 sts, fptr around next 4 sts**, (htr, ch2, htr) in 2-ch cnr sp*, rep from * to * 2x & * to ** 1x, htr in same sp as first st, ch1, join with dc to 2nd ch of stch. {19 sts on each side; 4 2-ch cnr sps}

R9: dc over joining dc, *dc in next 19 sts**, (dc, ch2, dc) in 2-ch cnr sp*, rep from * to * 2x & * to ** 1x, dc in same sp as first st, ch2, join with ss to first st. Fasten off. {21 sts on each side; 4 2-ch cnr sps}

Kim *Kym*

SMALL PATTERNS • 35

Gyre

Do you see the swirling vortex?

 42 m / 46 yd

Begin with mc.

R1: ch3 (stch), 2tr, *ch1, 3tr*, rep from * to * 4x, join with dc to 3rd ch of stch. {18 sts, 6 1-ch sps}

R2: dc over joining dc, *bphtr around next 3 sts**, dc in 1-ch sp*, rep from * to * 4x & * to ** 1x, join with ss to first st. {24 sts}

R3: ch3 (stch), tr in next st, *2tr in next st**, tr in next 3 sts*, rep from * to * 4x & * to ** 1x, tr in next st, join with ss to 3rd ch of stch. {30 sts}

R4: dc in same st as ss, *bphtr around next 4 sts**, dc in next st*, rep from * to * 4x & * to ** 1x, join with ss to first st. {30 sts}

R5: ch3 (stch), *2tr in next st, tr in next 2 sts, 2tr in next st**, tr in next st*, rep from * to * 4x & * to ** 1x, join with ss to 3rd ch of stch. {42 sts}

R6: dc in same st as ss, *bphtr around next 6 sts**, dc in next st*, rep from * to * 4x & * to ** 1x, join with ss to first st. {42 sts}

R7: ch3 (stch), *2tr in next 6 sts**, tr in next st*, rep from * to * 4x & * to ** 1x, join with ss to 3rd ch of stch. {78 sts}

R8: 2dc in same st as ss, *bphtr around next 12 sts**, 2dc in next st*, rep from * to * 4x & * to ** 1x, join with ss to first st. {84 sts}

R9: ch4 (stch), 3dtr in same st as ss, *skip 3 sts, dc in next 14 sts, skip 3 sts**, 7dtr in next st*, rep from * to * 2x & * to ** 1x, 3dtr in same st as first sts, join with ss to 4th ch of stch. {14 sts on each side; 4 7-st cnrs}

R10: dc in same st as ss, *dc in next 2 sts, htr in next st, tr in next st, htr in next st, dc in next 3 sts, 2x [dc2tog over next 2 sts], dc in next 3 sts, htr in next st, tr in next st, htr in next st, dc in next 2 sts**, (dc, ch2, dc) in next st*, rep from * to * 2x & * to ** 1x, dc in same st as first st, ch2, join with ss to first st. Fasten off. {20 sts on each side; 4 2-ch cnr sps}

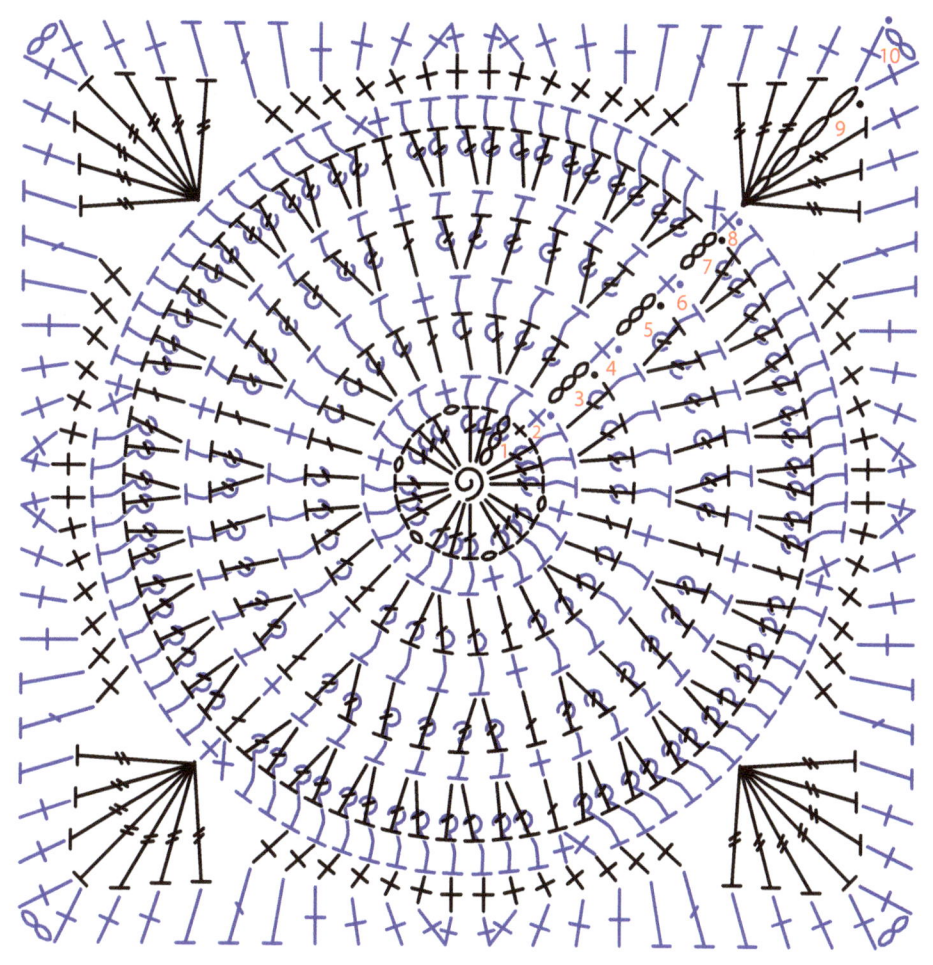

Kim

SMALL PATTERNS • 37

Ipheion

An Ipheion is a six-petalled, star-shaped flower.

 34 m / 37 yd

Begin with mc.

R1: ch3 (stch), 2tr, *ch1, 3tr*, rep from * to * 4x, join with dc to 3rd ch of stch. {18 sts, 6 1-ch sps}

R2: dc over joining dc, *ch2, tr3tog over next 3 sts, ch2**, dc in 1-ch sp*, rep from * to * 4x & * to ** 1x, join with ss to first st. {12 sts, 12 2-ch sps}

R3: ch3 (stch), *ch2, skip 2-ch sp, dc in next st, ch2, skip 2-ch sp**, (tr, ch2, tr) in next st*, rep from * to * 4x & * to ** 1x, tr in same st as first st, ch1, join with dc to 3rd ch of stch. {18 sts, 18 2-ch sps}

R4: dc over joining dc, *2x [dc in next st, 2dc in 2-ch sp], dc in next st**, dc in 2-ch sp*, rep from * to * 4x & * to ** 1x, join with ss to first st. {48 sts}

R5: turn, ch2 (stch), htr in next 47 sts, join with ss to 2nd ch of stch. {48 sts}

R6: turn, dc in next 48 sts, join with ss to first st. {48 sts}

R7: ch3 (stch), tr in next 2 sts, *ch2, skip 1 st, tr in next 3 sts*, rep from * to * 10x, ch1, join with dc to 3rd ch of stch. {36 sts, 12 2-ch sps}

R8: 2dc over joining dc, *dc in next 3 sts**, 3dc in 2-ch sp*, rep from * to * 10x & * to ** 1x, dc in same sp as first sts, join with ss to first st. {72 sts}

R9: ch3 (stch), tr in same st as ss, *tr in next st, htr next 2 sts, dc in next 11 sts, htr in next 2 sts, tr in next st**, (2tr, ch2, 2tr) in next st*, rep from * to * 2x & * to ** 1x, 2tr in same st as first sts, ch1, join with dc to 3rd ch of stch. {21 sts on each side; 4 2-ch cnr sps}

R10: dc over joining dc, *dc in next 21 sts**, (dc, ch2, dc) in 2-ch sp*, rep from * to * 2x & * to ** 1x, dc in same sp as first st, ch2, join with ss to first st. Fasten off. {23 sts on each side; 4 2-ch cnr sps}

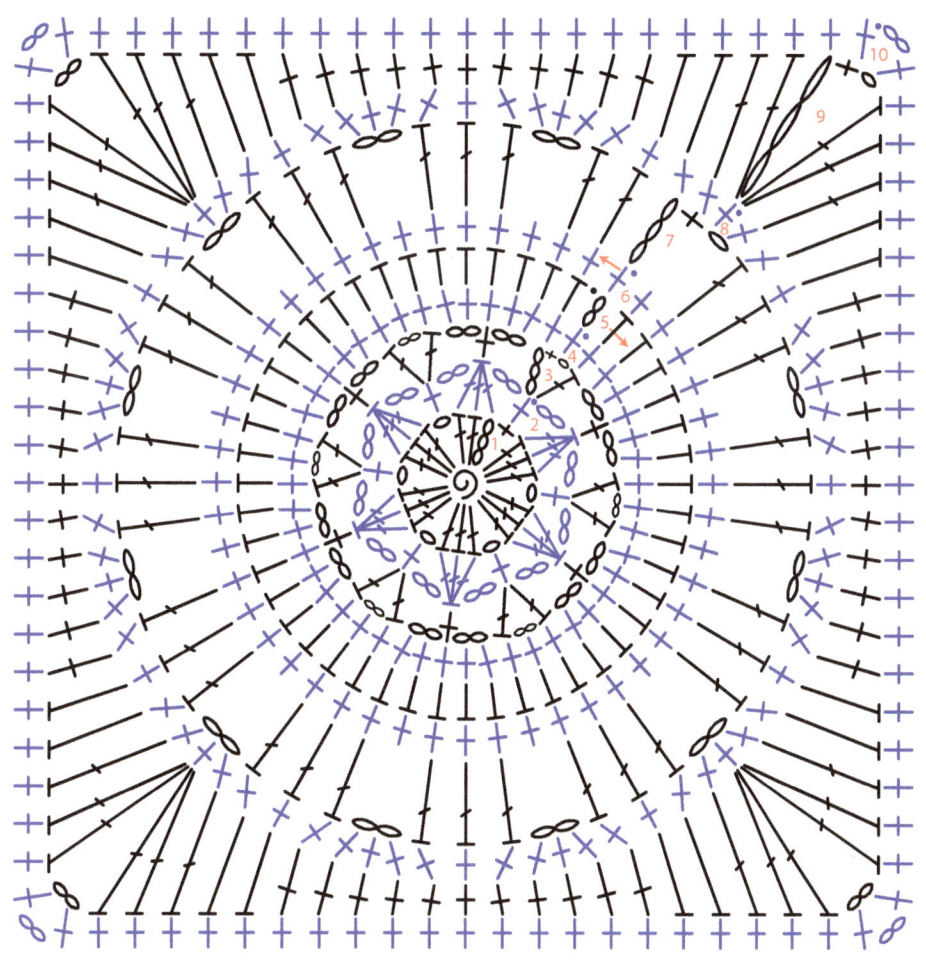

Kim *Kym*

SMALL PATTERNS • 39

Octad

Octad is a group of eight and as we have an eight-part shape in our circle, Octad it is.

 32 m / 35 yd

Begin with mc.

R1: ch3 (stch), 2tr, *ch2, dc, ch2**, 3tr*, rep from * to * 2x & * to ** 1x, join with ss to 3rd ch of stch. {1 st, 2 2-ch sps on each side; 4 3-st cnrs}

R2: dc in same st as ss, dc in next 2 sts, *ch2, skip 2-ch sp, 3trcl in next st, ch2, skip 2-ch sp**, dc in next 3 sts*, rep from * to * 2x & * to ** 1x, join with ss to first st. {1 st, 2 2-ch sps on each side; 4 3-st cnrs}

R3: dc in same st as ss, dc in next 2 sts, *2dc in 2-ch sp, fpdc around next st, 2dc in 2-ch sp**, dc in next 3 sts*, rep from * to * 2x & * to ** 1x, join with ss to first st. {32 sts}

R4: ch3 (stch), tr2tog over next 2 sts, *ch2, dc in next 2 sts, ch2, 3tr in next st, ch2, dc in next 2 sts, ch2**, tr3tog over next 3 sts*, rep from * to * 2x & * to ** 1x, join with ss to tr2tog. {32 sts, 16 2-ch sps}

R5: dc in same st as ss, *ch4, skip (2-ch sp & 2 sts), dc in 2-ch sp, dc in next 3 sts, dc in 2-ch sp, ch4, skip (2 sts & 2-ch sp)**, dc in next st*, rep from * to * 2x & * to ** 1x, join with ss to first st. {24 sts, 8 4-ch sps}

R6: ch3 (stch), *5tr in 4-ch sp, tr in next 5 sts, 5tr in 4-ch sp**, tr in next st*, rep from * to * 2x & * to ** 1x, join with ss to 3rd ch of stch. {64 sts}

R7: dc in same st as ss, dc in next 63 sts, join with ss to first st. {64 sts}

R8: ch4 (stch), dtr in same st as ss, *tr in next 2 sts, htr in next 2 sts, dc in next 7 sts, htr in next 2 sts, tr in next 2 sts**, (2dtr, ch2, 2dtr) in next st*, rep from * to * 2x & * to ** 1x, 2dtr in same st as first sts, ch1, join with dc to 4th ch of stch. {19 sts on each side; 4 2-ch cnr sps}

R9: dc over joining dc, *dc in next 19 sts**, (dc, ch2, dc) in 2-ch cnr sp*, rep from * to * 2x & * to ** 1x, dc in same sp as first st, ch2, join with ss to first st. Fasten off. {21 sts on each side; 4 2-ch cnr sps}

Kim

SMALL PATTERNS • 41

Stelliform

Stelliform quite literally means "star shaped".

 34 m / 37 yd

Begin with mc.

R1: ch3 (stch), *htr, dc, ch2, dc, htr, tr**, ch2, tr*, rep from * to * 2x & * to ** 1x, ch1, join with dc to 3rd ch of stch. {6 sts, 1 2-ch sp on each side; 4 2-ch cnr sps}

R2: dc over joining dc, *ch2, skip 3 sts, 3tr in 2-ch sp, ch2, skip 3 sts**, dc in 2-ch cnr sp*, rep from * to * 2x & * to ** 1x, join with ss to first st. {16 sts, 8 2-ch sps}

R3: dc in same st as ss, *3dc in 2-ch sp, dc in next 3 sts, 3dc in 2-ch sp**, dc in next st*, rep from * to * 2x & * to ** 1x, join with ss to first st. {40 sts}

R4: NOTE: intentional not to skip 1 after tr4tog

ch3 (stch), tr in same st as ss, *ch2, skip 1 st, dc in next st, ch2, skip 1 st, tr4tog over next 4 sts, ch2, dc in next st, ch2, skip 1 st**, 3tr in next st*, rep from * to * 2x & * to ** 1x, tr in same st as first sts, join with ss to 3rd ch of stch. {24 sts, 16 2-ch sps}

R5: dc in same st as ss, dc in next st, *ch2, skip 2-ch sp, fptr around next st, ch2, skip 2-ch sp, dc in next st, ch2, skip 2-ch sp, fptr around next st, ch2, skip 2-ch sp**, dc in next 3 sts*, rep from * to * 2x & * to ** 1x, dc in next st, join with ss to first st. {24 sts, 16 2-ch sps}

R6: dc in same st as ss, dc in next st, *3dc in 2-ch sp, skip 1 st, 3dc in 2-ch sp, dc in next st, 3dc in 2-ch sp, skip 1 st, 3dc in 2-ch sp**, dc in next 3 sts*, rep from * to * 2x & * to ** 1x, dc in next st, join with ss to first st. {64 sts}

R7: ch4 (stch), 2dtr in same st as ss, *skip 2 sts, dc in next 11 sts, skip 2 sts**, 5dtr in next st*, rep from * to * 2x & * to ** 1x, 2dtr in same st as first sts, join with ss to 4th ch of stch. {11 sts on each side; 4 5-st cnrs}

R8: dc in same st as ss, *2dc in next 2 sts, dc in blo of next 11 sts, 2dc in next 2 sts**, (dc, ch2, dc) in next st*, rep from * to * 2x & * to ** 1x, dc in same st as first st, ch1, join with dc to first st. {21 sts on each side; 4 2-ch cnr sps}

R9: ch3 (stch), *tr in next 21 sts**, (tr, ch2, tr) in 2-ch cnr sp*, rep from * to * 2x & * to ** 1x, tr in same sp as first st, ch2, join with ss to 3rd ch of stch. Fasten off. {23 sts on each side; 4 2-ch cnr sps}

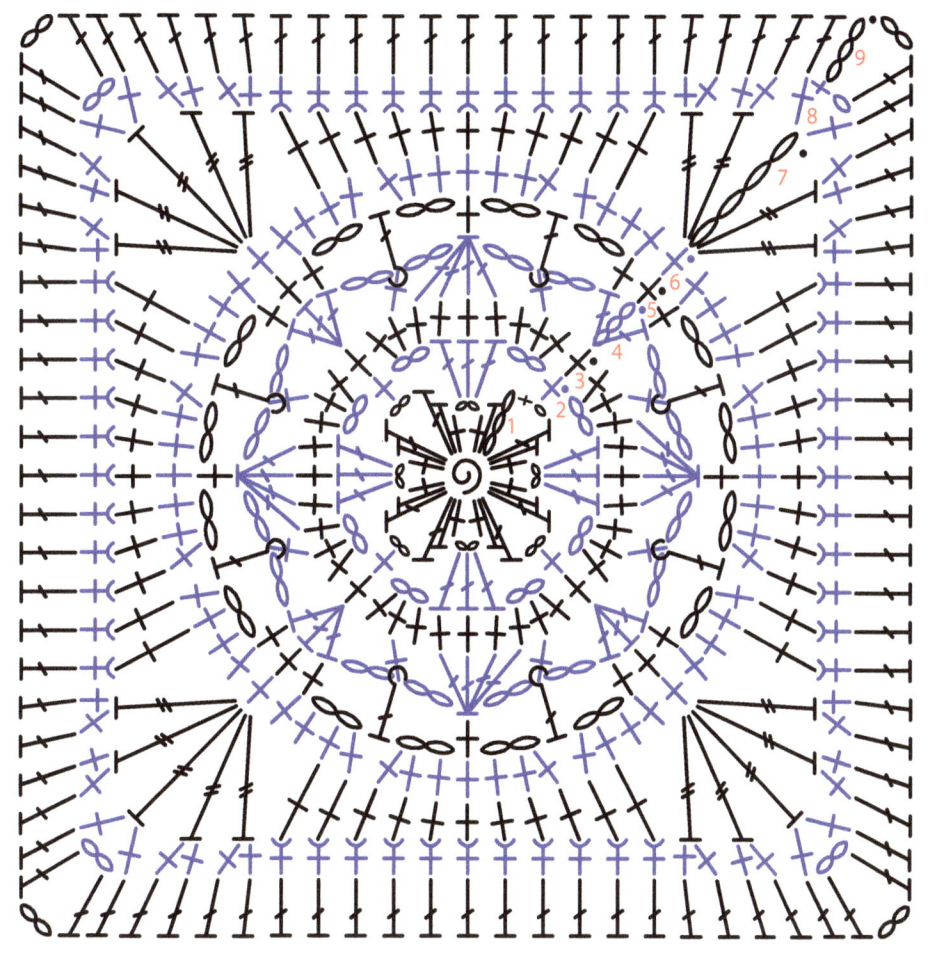

Kim

SMALL PATTERNS • 43

Betwixt

Between and betwixt. A lot of stitches are made betwixt others. A literal name.

 32 m / 35 yd

Begin with mc.

R1: ch4 (stch), 15dtr, join with ss to 4th ch of stch. {16 sts}

R2: dc in same st as ss, *dc between last and next st**, dc in next st*, rep from * to * 14x & * to ** 1x, join with ss to first st. {32 sts}

R3: ch4 (stch), dtr in same st as ss, *dtr in next st**, 2dtr in next st*, rep from * to * 14x & * to ** 1x, join with ss to 4th ch of stch. {48 sts}

R4: dc in same st as ss, dc in next 47 sts, join with ss to first st. {48 sts}

R5: ch4 (stch), hdtr in same st as ss, *tr in next 2 sts, htr in next 2 sts, dc in next 3 sts, htr in next 2 sts, tr in next 2 sts**, (hdtr, dtr, hdtr) in next st*, rep from * to * 2x & * to ** 1x, hdtr in same st as first sts, join with ss to 4th ch of stch. {11 sts on each side; 4 3-st cnrs}

R6: ch4 (stch), *dtr in next 13 sts**, (dtr, ch2, dtr) in next st*, rep from * to * 2x & * to ** 1x, dtr in same st as first st, ch1, join with dc to 4th ch of stch. {15 sts on each side; 4 2-ch cnr sps}

R7: dc over joining dc, *dc in next st, dc between last and next st, 13x [dc between next 2 sts], dc in next st**, (dc, ch2, dc) in 2-ch cnr sp*, rep from * to * 2x & * to ** 1x, dc in same sp as first st, ch2, join with ss to first st. Fasten off. {18 sts on each side; 4 2-ch cnr sps}

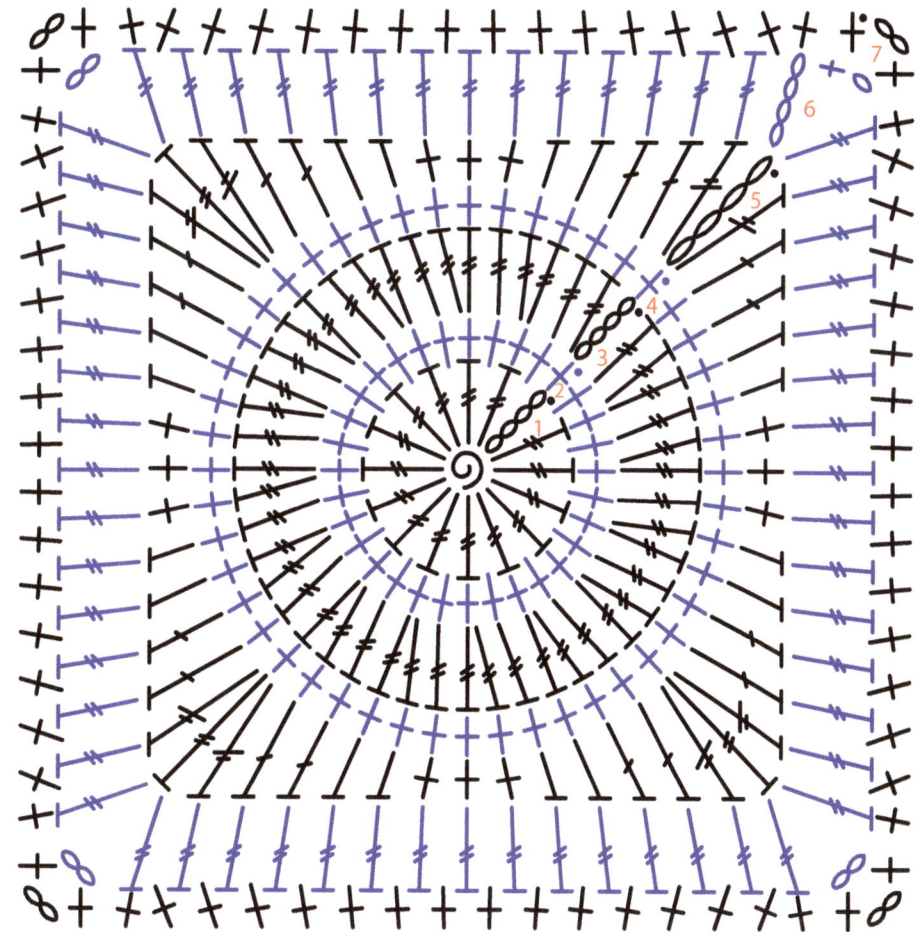

Kim

SMALL PATTERNS • 45

Covey

Covey is a word for a group of things, usually birds. This pattern has many clusters and groups of stitches, imagine them as birds if you will.

 42 m / 46 yd

Begin with mc.

R1: ch3 (stch), tr4tog, *ch2, 2tr, ch2**, tr5tog*, rep from * to * 2x & * to ** 1x, join with ss to top of tr4tog. {12 sts, 8 2-ch sps}

R2: *2dc in 2-ch sp, 2tr in next st, ch2, 2tr in next st, 2dc in 2-ch sp, skip 1 st*, rep from * to * 3x, join with ss to first st. {32 sts, 4 2-ch sps}

R3: fptr around R1 cluster below, tr in same st as ss, tr in next st, *dc in next 2 sts, dc in 2-ch sp, dc in next 2 sts, tr in next 2 sts**, fptr around R1 cluster below, tr in next 2 sts*, rep from * to * 2x & * to ** 1x, join with ss to first st. {40 sts}

R4: ch3 (stch), 2tr in same st as ss, *skip 2 sts, dc in next 5 sts, skip 2 sts**, 5tr in next st*, rep from * to * 2x & * to ** 1x, 2tr in same st as first sts, join with ss to 3rd ch of stch. {5 sts on each side; 4 5-st cnrs}

R5: dc in same st as ss, *dc in next 2 sts, dc between last and next st, dc in next 5 sts, dc between last and next st, dc in next 2 sts**, (dc, ch2, dc) in next st*, rep from * to * 2x & * to ** 1x, dc in same st as first st, ch1, join with dc to first st. {13 sts on each side; 4 2-ch cnr sps}

R6: ch3 (stch), *ch2, tr5tog over 2-ch cnr sp and next 4 sts, ch4, tr5tog over next 5 sts, ch4, tr5tog over next 4 sts and 2-ch cnr sp, ch2**, (tr, ch2, tr) in 2-ch cnr sp*, rep from * to * 2x & * to ** 1x, tr in same sp as first st, ch1, join with dc to 3rd ch of stch. {5 sts, 2 2-ch sps, 2 4-ch sps on each side; 4 2-ch cnr sps}

R7: ch3 (stch), tr over joining dc, *tr in next st, 2tr in 2-ch sp, 2x [tr in next st, 4tr in 4-ch sp], tr in next st, 2tr in 2-ch sp, tr in next st**, 3tr in 2-ch cnr sp*, rep from * to * 2x & * to ** 1x, tr in same sp as first sts, join with ss to 3rd ch of stch. {17 sts on each side; 4 3-st cnrs}

R8: ch2 (stch), *9x [fptr around next st, htr in next st], fptr around next st**, (htr, ch2, htr) in next st*, rep from * to * 2x & * to ** 1x, htr in same st as first st, ch1, join with dc to 2nd ch of stch. {21 sts on each side; 4 2-ch cnr sps}

R9: dc over joining dc, *dc in next 21 sts**, (dc, ch2, dc) in 2-ch cnr sp*, rep from * to * 2x & * to ** 1x, dc in same sp as first st, ch2, join with ss to first st. Fasten off. {23 sts on each side; 4 2-ch cnr sps}

Kim

SMALL PATTERNS • 47

Esker

Esker is a geographical term referring to a long ridge of gravel or sand deposited by glacial melt-water.

 42 m / 46 yd

Begin with mc.

R1: ch3 (stch), 15tr, join with ss to 3rd ch of stch. {16 sts}

R2: dc in same st as ss, *dc in flo of next 3 sts**, dc in next st*, rep from * to * 2x & * to ** 1x, join with ss to first st. {16 sts}

R3: ch3 (stch), *2tr in blo of next R1 st, tr in blo of next R1 st, 2tr in blo of next R1 st, skip 3 sts**, 2tr in next st*, rep from * to * 2x & * to ** 1x, tr in same st as first st, join with ss to 3rd ch of stch. {28 sts}

R4: dc in same st as ss, *dc in flo of next 5 sts**, dc in next 2 sts*, rep from * to * 2x & * to ** 1x, dc in next st, join with ss to first st. {28 sts}

R5: ch3 (stch), tr in same st as ss, *2tr in blo of next R3 st, tr in blo of next 3 R3 sts, 2tr in blo of next R3 st, skip 5 sts**, 2tr in next 2 sts*, rep from * to * 2x & * to ** 1x, 2tr in next st, join with ss to 3rd ch of stch. {44 sts}

R6: dc in same st as ss, *dc in flo of next 9 sts**, dc in next 2 sts*, rep from * to * 2x & * to ** 1x, dc in next st, join with ss to first st. {44 sts}

R7: ch3 (stch), tr in same st as ss, *2tr in blo of next R5 st, tr in blo of next 7 R5 sts, 2tr in blo of next R5 st, skip 9 sts**, 2tr in next 2 sts*, rep from * to * 2x & * to ** 1x, 2tr in next st, join with ss to 3rd ch of stch. {60 sts}

R8: dc in same st as ss, *dc in flo of next 13 sts**, dc in next 2 sts*, rep from * to * 2x & * to ** 1x, dc in next st, join with ss to first st. {60 sts}

R9: ch3 (stch), tr in same st as ss, *2tr in blo of next R7 st, tr in blo of next 12 R7 sts, skip 13 sts, 2tr in next st**, ch2, 2tr in next st*, rep from * to * 2x & * to ** 1x, ch1, join with dc to 3rd ch of stch. {18 sts on each side; 4 2-ch cnr sps}

R10: dc over joining dc, *dc in flo of next 18 sts**, (dc, ch2, dc) in 2-ch cnr sp*, rep from * to * 2x & * to ** 1x, dc in same sp as first st, ch1, join with dc to first st. {20 sts on each side; 4 2-ch cnr sps}

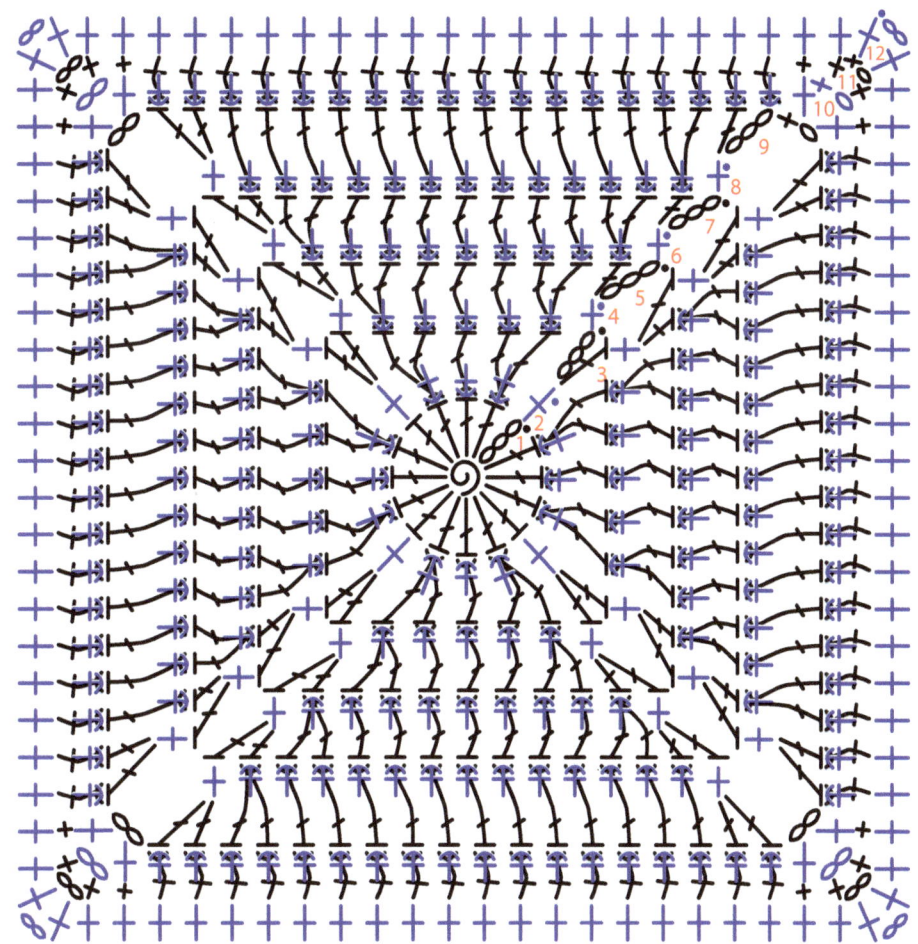

R11: dc over joining dc, *dc in next st, dc in blo of next 18 R9 sts, skip 18 sts, dc in next st**, (dc, ch2, dc) in 2-ch cnr sp*, rep from * to * 2x & * to ** 1x, dc in same sp as first st, ch1, join with dc to first st. {22 sts on each side; 4 2-ch cnr sps}

R12: dc over joining dc, *dc in next 22 sts**, (dc, ch2, dc) in 2-ch cnr sp*, rep from * to * 2x & * to ** 1x, dc in same sp as first st, ch2, join with ss to first st. Fasten off. {24 sts on each side; 4 2-ch cnr sps}

Kim

Little Avens

Bluet and Avens are the names of flowers. Bluets have 4 petals while Avens sometimes have 8. There is a large version of this pattern on page 88.

 37 m / 40 yd

Begin with mc.

R1: ch4 (stch), *ch2**, 3dtr*, rep from * to * 6x & * to ** 1x, 2dtr, join with ss to 4th ch of stch. {24 sts, 8 2-ch sps}

R2: *dc in 2-ch sp, dc in next 3 sts*, rep from * to * 7x, join with ss to first st. {32 sts}

R3: ch3 (stch), tr in next st, *ch2, skip 1 st**, tr in next 3 sts*, rep from * to * 6x & * to ** 1x, tr in next st, join with ss to 3rd ch of stch. {24 sts, 8 2-ch sps}

R4: NOTE: do not work false st. ch3 (stch), 2tr in next st, *ch3, dc in skipped st of R2 below in front of 2-ch sp, ch3, skip 2-ch sp**, 2tr in next 3 sts*, rep from * to * 6x & * to ** 1x, 2tr in next st, tr in same st as first st, join with inv join to first true st. {56 sts, 16 3-ch sps}

R5: Attach with a stdg bpdc to 4th st of any 6-st group, bpdc around next 2 sts, *ch2, skip (3-ch sp, 1 st & 3-ch sp)**, bpdc around next 6 sts*, rep from * to * 6x & * to ** 1x, bpdc around next 3 sts, join with ss to first st. {48 sts, 8 2-ch sps}

R6: ch4 (stch), 3hdtr in same st as ss, *skip 2 sts, htr in 2-ch sp, htr in next 6 sts, htr in 2-ch sp, skip 2 sts, (3hdtr, dtr) in next st**, (dtr, 3hdtr) in next st*, rep from * to * 2x & * to ** 1x, join with ss to 4th ch of stch. {8 sts on each side; 4 8-st cnrs}

R7: ch2 (stch), htr in same st as ss, *htr in lbv of next 14 sts, 2htr in next st**, ch2, 2htr in next st*, rep from * to * 2x & * to ** 1x, ch1, join with dc to 2nd ch of stch. {18 sts on each side; 4 2-ch cnr sps}

R8: ch2 (stch), *htr in next 18 sts**, (htr, ch2, htr) in 2-ch cnr sp*, rep from * to * 2x & * to ** 1x, htr in same sp as first st, ch2, join with ss to 2nd ch of stch. Fasten off. {20 sts on each side; 4 2-ch cnr sps}

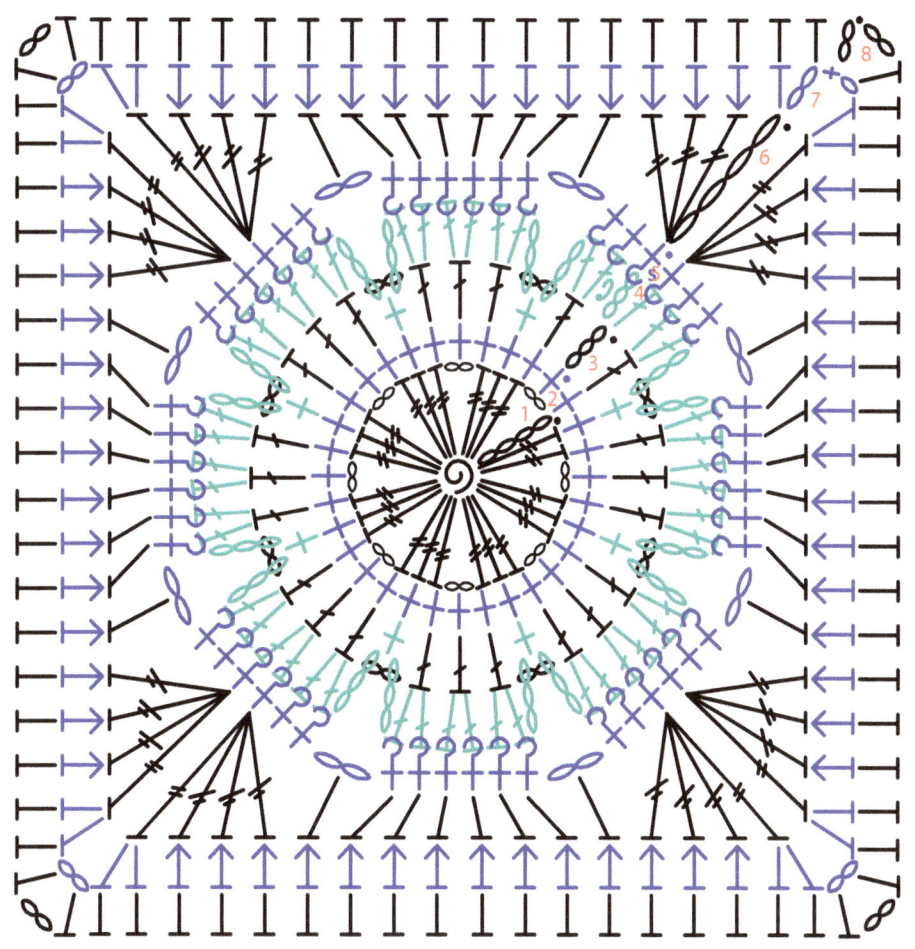

Kim

Kym

SMALL PATTERNS • 51

Little Bluet

Bluet and Avens are the names of flowers. Bluets have 4 petals while Avens sometimes have 8. There is a large version of this pattern on page 92.

 36 m / 40 yd

Begin with mc.

R1: ch4 (stch), *ch2**, 3dtr*, rep from * to * 6x & * to ** 1x, 2dtr, join with ss to 4th ch of stch. {24 sts, 8 2-ch sps}

R2: *dc in 2-ch sp, dc in next 3 sts*, rep from * to * 7x, join with ss to first st. {32 sts}

R3: ch3 (stch), tr in next st, *ch2, skip 1 st**, tr in next 3 sts*, rep from * to * 6x & * to ** 1x, tr in next st, join with ss to 3rd ch of stch. {24 sts, 8 2-ch sps}

R4: ch3 (stch), 2tr in next st, *ch3, dc in skipped st of R2 below in front of 2-ch sp, ch3, skip 2-ch sp**, 2tr in next 3 sts*, rep from * to * 6x & * to ** 1x, 2tr in next st, tr in same st as first st, join with ss to 3rd ch of stch. {56 sts, 16 3-ch sps}

R5: dc in same st as ss, dc in next 2 sts, *ch2, skip (3-ch sp, 1 st & 3-ch sp), bpdc around next 6 sts, ch2, skip (3-ch sp, 1 st & 3-ch sp)**, dc in next 6 sts*, rep from * to * 2x & * to ** 1x, dc in next 3 sts, join with ss to first st. {48 sts, 8 2-ch sps}

R6: ch4 (stch), 3hdtr in same st as ss, *skip 2 sts, htr in 2-ch sp, htr in next 6 sts, htr in 2-ch sp, skip 2 sts, (3hdtr, dtr) in next st**, (dtr, 3hdtr) in next st*, rep from * to * 2x & * to ** 1x, join with ss to 4th ch of stch. {8 sts on each side; 4 8-st cnrs}

R7: ch2 (stch), htr in same st as ss, *htr in lbv of next 14 sts, 2htr in next st**, ch2, 2htr in next st*, rep from * to * 2x & * to ** 1x, ch1, join with dc to 2nd ch of stch. {18 sts on each side; 4 2-ch cnr sps}

R8: ch2 (stch), *htr in next 18 sts**, (htr, ch2, htr) in 2-ch cnr sp*, rep from * to * 2x & * to ** 1x, htr in same sp as first st, ch2, join with ss to 2nd ch of stch. Fasten off. {20 sts on each side; 4 2-ch cnr sps}

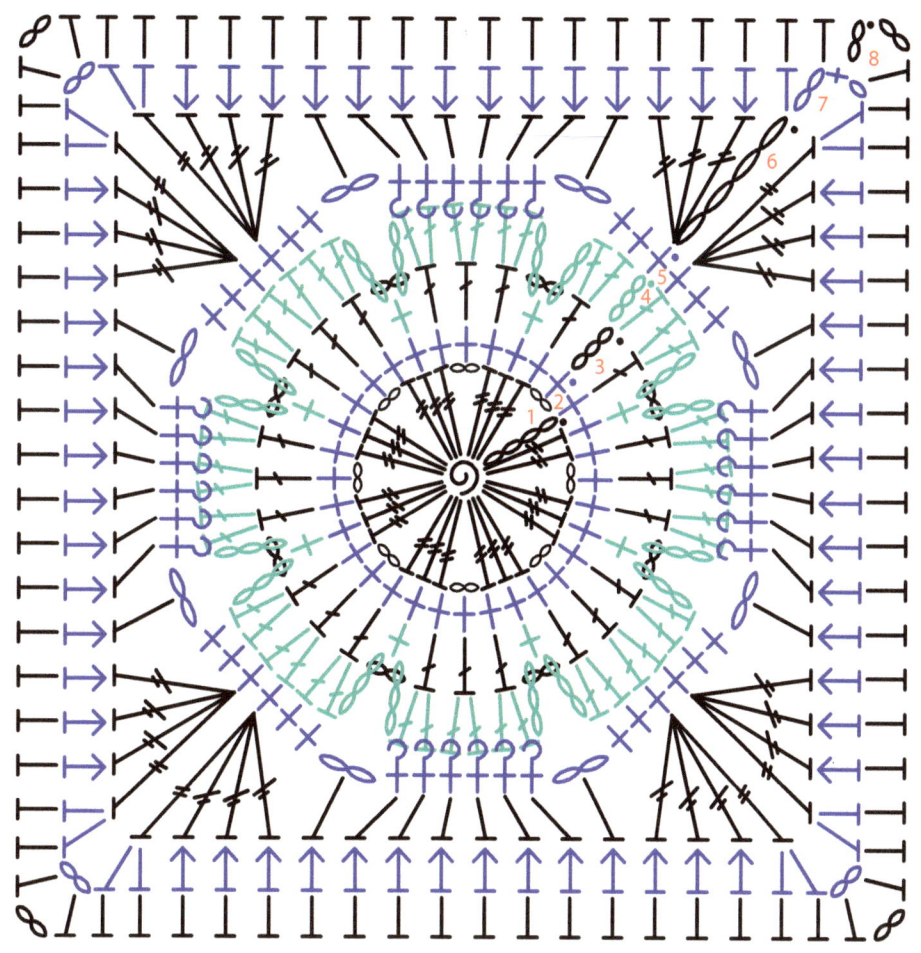

Kim Kym

SMALL PATTERNS • 53

Passionflower

Have you ever studied a passionfruit flower? They have some interesting circle shapes with lines. A bit of an abstract reference to our pattern.

 45 m / 49 yd

Begin with mc.

R1: ch4 (stch), 2dtr, *ch2, 3dtr*, rep from * to * 6x, ch1, join with dc to 4th ch of stch. {24 sts, 8 2-ch sps}

R2: dc over joining dc, *skip 1 st, (tr, 3dtr, tr) in next st, skip 1 st**, dc in 2-ch sp*, rep from * to * 6x & * to ** 1x, join with ss to first st. {48 sts}

R3: dc in same st as ss, *ch4, skip 5 sts**, dc in next st*, rep from * to * 6x & * to ** 1x, join with ss to first st. {8 sts, 8 4-ch sps}

R4: ch3 (stch), *5tr in 4-ch sp**, tr in next st*, rep from * to * 6x & * to ** 1x, join with ss to 3rd ch of stch. {48 sts}

R5: dc in same st as ss, *fpdtr around 1st of 3 R1 sts below, fpss around next 5 sts, fpdtr around 3rd of 3 R1 sts below**, dc in next st*, rep from * to * 6x & * to ** 1x, join with ss to first st. {64 sts}

R6: dc in same st as ss, dc in next st, *htr in next 5 sts of R4, skip 5 sts**, dc in next 3 sts*, rep from * to * 6x & * to ** 1x, dc in next st, join with ss to first st. {64 sts}

R7: ch1, dc in next 63 sts, join with inv join to first true st. {64 sts}

R8: join with stdg tr to blo of any stitch above the middle of the 2 fp sts, tr in blo of next 63 sts, join with ss to first st. {64 sts}

R9: ch4 (stch), 2hdtr in same st as ss, *tr in next 2 sts, htr in next 2 sts, dc in next 7 sts, htr in next 2 sts, tr in next 2 sts**, (2hdtr, dtr, 2hdtr) in next st*, rep from * to * 2x & * to ** 1x, 2hdtr in same st as first sts, join with ss to 4th ch of stch. {15 sts on each side; 4 5-st cnrs}

R10: dc in same st as ss, *dc in next 19 sts**, (dc, ch2, dc) in next st*, rep from * to * 2x & * to ** 1x, dc in same st as first st, ch2, join with ss to first st. Fasten off. {21 sts on each side; 4 2-ch cnr sps}

Kim

Kym

SMALL PATTERNS • 55

Petite Lavallière

A Lavallière is an ornamental pendant, usually jewelled, worn on a chain around the neck. It is a French word and as this is the smallest of the three similar patterns, petite it is.

 41 m / 45 yd

Begin with mc.

R1: ch3 (stch), 15tr, join with ss to 3rd ch of stch. {16 sts}

R2: dc in same st as ss, *(dc, ch6, dc) in next st**, dc in next st*, rep from * to * 6x & * to ** 1x, join with ss to first st. {24 sts, 8 6-ch sps}

R3: ch3 (stch), tr in same st as ss, *tr2tog over next 2 sts pulling 6-ch sp to front**, 3tr in next st*, rep from * to * 6x & * to ** 1x, tr in same st as first sts, join with ss to 3rd ch of stch. {32 sts}

R4: dc in same st as ss, dc in next st, *dc in 6-ch sp of R2 and next st at the same time**, dc in next 3 sts*, rep from * to * 6x & * to ** 1x, dc in next st, join with ss to first st. {32 sts}

R5: (dc, ch6, dc) in same st as ss, *dc in next st**, (dc, ch6, dc) in next st*, rep from * to * 14x & * to ** 1x, join with ss to first st. {48 sts, 16 6-ch sps}

R6: tr2tog over same st as ss and next st pulling 6-ch sp to front, *3tr in next st**, tr2tog over next 2 sts pulling 6-ch sp to front*, rep from * to * 14x & * to ** 1x, join with ss to first st. {64 sts}

R7: dc in 6-ch sp of R5 and same st as ss at the same time, *dc in next 3 sts**, dc in 6-ch sp of R5 and next st at the same time*, rep from * to * 14x & * to ** 1x, join with ss to first st. {64 sts}

R8: ch4 (stch), hdtr in same st as ss, *tr in next 2 sts, htr in next 2 sts, dc in next 7 sts, htr in next 2 sts, tr in next 2 sts**, (hdtr, dtr, hdtr) in next st*, rep from * to * 2x & * to ** 1x, hdtr in same st as first sts, join with ss to 4th ch of stch. {15 sts on each side; 4 3-st cnrs}

R9: ch2 (stch), *htr in next 17 sts**, (htr, ch2, htr) in next st**, rep from * to * 2x & * to ** 1x, htr in same st as first st, ch1, join with dc to 2nd ch of stch. {19 sts on each side; 4 2-ch cnr sps}

R10: dc over joining dc, *dc in next 19 sts**, (dc, ch2, dc) in 2-ch cnr sp*, rep from * to * 2x & * to ** 1x, dc in same sp as first st, ch2, join with ss to first st. Fasten off. {21 sts on each side; 4 2-ch cnr sps}

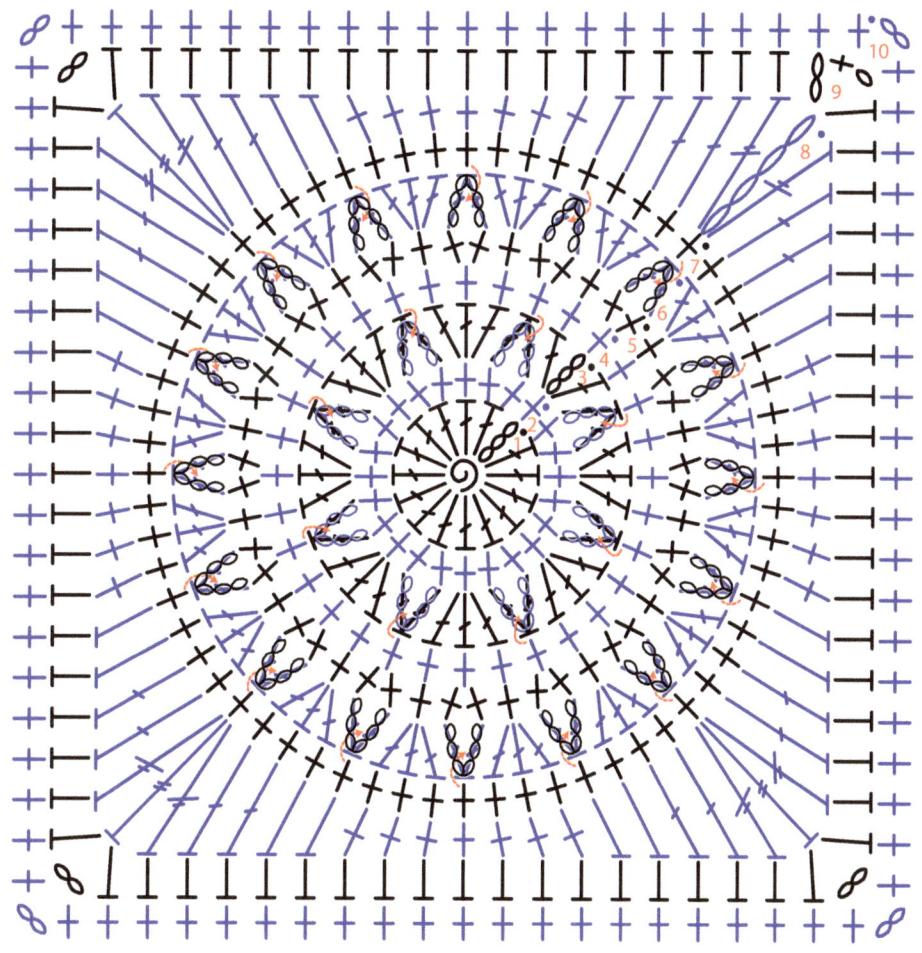

Kim

Kim

Kim

Kym

SMALL PATTERNS • 57

Spiderweb

I really don't think you need me to explain this one.

 41 m / 44 yd

Begin with mc.

R1: ch1, *dc, ch3*, rep from * to * 7x, join with ss to first st. {8 sts, 8 3-ch sps}

R2: fptr around same st as ss, *ch2, skip 3-ch sp**, fptr around next st*, rep from * to * 6x & * to ** 1x, join with ss to first st. {8 sts, 8 2-ch sps}

R3: fptr around same st as ss, *2tr in 3-ch sp of R1 behind 2-ch sp, skip 2-ch sp**, fptr around next st*, rep from * to * 6x & * to ** 1x, join with ss to first st. {24 sts}

R4: fptr around same st as ss, *ch3, skip 2 sts**, fptr around next st*, rep from * to * 6x & * to ** 1x, join with ss to first st. {8 sts, 8 3-ch sps}

R5: fptr around same st as ss, *2tr in next st of R3 behind 3-ch sp, tr in next st of R3 behind 3-ch sp, skip 3-ch sp**, fptr around next st*, rep from * to * 6x & * to ** 1x, join with ss to first st. {32 sts}

R6: fptr around same st as ss, *ch4, skip 3 sts**, fptr around next st*, rep from * to * 6x & * to ** 1x, join with ss to first st. {8 sts, 8 4-ch sps}

R7: fptr around same st as ss, *2tr in next st of R5 behind 4-ch sp, tr in next st of R5 behind 4-ch sp, 2tr in next st of R5 behind 4-ch sp, skip 4-ch sp**, fptr around next st*, rep from * to * 6x & * to ** 1x, join with ss to first st. {48 sts}

R8: fptr around same st as ss, *dc in next 5 sts**, fptr around next st*, rep from * to * 6x & * to ** 1x, join with ss to first st. {48 sts}

R9: ch4 (stch), 2hdtr in same st as ss, *tr in next 2 sts, htr in next 2 sts, dc in next 3 sts, htr in next 2 sts, tr in next 2 sts**, (2hdtr, dtr, 2hdtr) in next st*, rep from * to * 2x & * to ** 1x, 2hdtr in same st as first sts, join with ss to 4th ch of stch. {11 sts on each side; 4 5-st cnrs}

R10: ch3 (stch), tr in same st as ss, *7x [tr in next st, ch1, skip 1 st], tr in next st**, (tr, hdtr, tr) in next st*, rep from * to * 2x & * to ** 1x, tr in same st as first sts, join with ss to 3rd ch of stch. {8 sts, 7 1-ch sps on each side; 4 3-st cnrs}

58 • SMALL PATTERNS

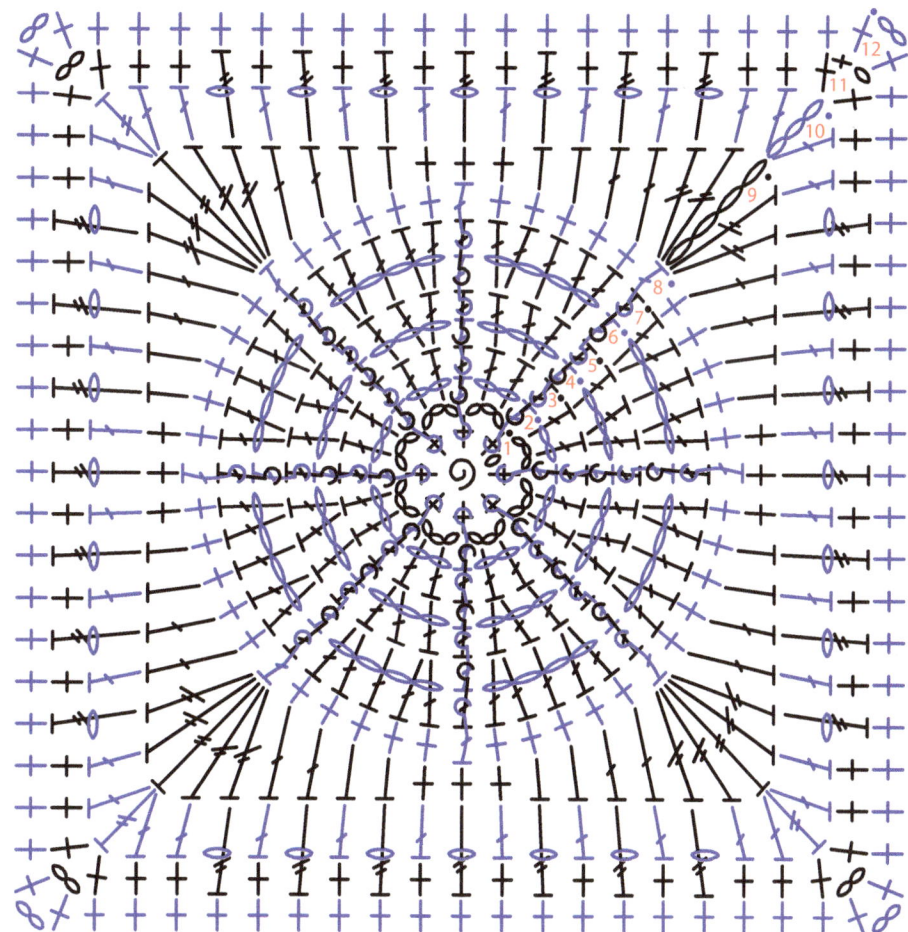

R11: dc in same st as ss, *dc in next 2 sts, 7x [hdtr in skipped st of R9 behind 1-ch sp, skip 1-ch sp, dc in next st], dc in next st**, (dc, ch2, dc) in next st*, rep from * to * 2x & * to ** 1x, dc in same st as first st, ch1, join with dc to first st. {19 sts on each side; 4 2-ch cnr sps}

R12: dc over joining dc, *dc in next 19 sts**, (dc, ch2, dc) in 2-ch cnr sp*, rep from * to * 2x & * to ** 1x, dc in same sp as first st, ch2, join with ss to first st. Fasten off. {21 sts on each side; 4 2-ch cnr sps}

Kim

SMALL PATTERNS

Wee Octamerous

Octamerous means a thing in eight sections as our pattern is defined by the eight spokes. Wee as there is a large pattern with a similar effect called Big Octamerous on page 134.

 41 m / 44 yd

Begin with mc.

R1: ch3 (stch), *ch2**, tr*, rep from * to * 6x & * to ** 1x, join with ss to 3rd ch of stch. {8 sts, 8 2-ch sps}

R2: ch3 (stch), tr in same st as ss, *ch2, dc in 2-ch sp, ch2**, 3tr in next st*, rep from * to * 6x & * to ** 1x, tr in same st as first sts, join with ss to 3rd ch of stch. {32 sts, 16 2-ch sps}

R3: fpdtr around R1 st below, skip same st as ss, *dc in next st, ch2, skip (2-ch sp, 1 st & 2-ch sp), dc in next st**, fpdtr around R1 st below, skip 1 st*, rep from * to * 6x & * to ** 1x, join with ss to first st. {24 sts, 8 2-ch sps}

R4: ch3 (stch), tr in next st, *3tr in 2-ch sp**, tr in next 3 sts*, rep from * to * 6x & * to ** 1x, tr in next st, join with ss to 3rd ch of stch. {48 sts}

R5: dc in same st as ss, *fpdtr around R3 st below**, dc in next 6 sts*, rep from * to * 6x & * to ** 1x, dc in next 5 sts, join with ss to first st. {56 sts}

R6: dc in blo of next 56 sts, join with ss to first st. {56 sts}

R7: ch4 (stch), 2hdtr in same st as ss, *tr in next 2 sts, htr in next 2 sts, dc in next 5 sts, htr in next 2 sts, tr in next 2 sts**, (2hdtr, dtr, 2hdtr) in next st*, rep from * to * 2x & * to ** 1x, 2hdtr in same st as first sts, join with ss to 4th ch of stch. {13 sts on each side; 4 5-st cnrs}

R8: fpdtr around R5 st below, skip same st as ss, *dc in next 17 sts**, fpdtr around R5 st below, skip 1 st*, rep from * to * 2x & * to ** 1x, join with ss to first st. {17 sts on each side; 4 1-st cnrs}

R9: ch3 (stch), tr in same st as ss, *htr in next 17 sts**, (2tr, ch2, 2tr) in next st*, rep from * to * 2x & * to ** 1x, 2tr in same st as first sts, ch1, join with dc to 3rd ch of stch. {21 sts on each side; 4 2-ch cnr sps}

R10: dc over joining dc, *dc in next 21 sts**, (dc, ch2, dc) in 2-ch cnr sp*, rep from * to * 2x & * to ** 1x, dc in same sp as first st, ch2, join with ss to first st. Fasten off. {23 sts on each side; 4 2-ch cnr sps}

Kim

Kym

SMALL PATTERNS

Stellate

Stellate describes anything star shaped. Look for the large version of this pattern on page 154.

 54 m / 59 yd

Begin with mc.

R1: ch3 (stch), 15tr, join with ss to 3rd ch of stch. {16 sts}

R2: dc between same st as ss and next st, *ch1**, dc between next 2 sts*, rep from * to * 14x & * to ** 1x, join with ss to first st. {16 sts, 16 1-ch sps}

R3: ch3 (stch), tr2tog over (1-ch sp & next st), *ch2, dc in 1-ch sp, ch2**, tr3tog over (next st, 1-ch sp & next st)*, rep from * to * 6x & * to ** 1x, join with ss to top of tr2tog. {16 sts, 16 2-ch sps}

R4: dc in same st as ss, *ch5, skip (2-ch sp, 1 st & 2-ch sp)**, dc in next st*, rep from * to * 6x & * to ** 1x, join with ss to first st. {8 sts, 8 5-ch sps}

R5: ch3 (stch), *5tr in R3 st behind 5-ch sp, skip 5-ch sp**, tr in next st*, rep from * to * 6x & * to ** 1x, join with ss to 3rd ch of stch. {48 sts}

R6: dc in same st as ss, *ch3, pull 5-ch sp of R4 to the back through the st the 5tr are worked into, dc in that 5-ch sp, ch3, skip 5 sts**, dc in next st*, rep from * to * 6x & * to ** 1x, join with ss to first st. {16 sts, 16 3-ch sps}

R7: dc in same st as ss, *3dc in 3-ch sp**, dc in next st*, rep from * to * 14x & * to ** 1x, join with ss to first st. {64 sts}

R8: *fptr around R5 st below, 2tr in next 5 sts of R5*, rep from * to * 7x, join with ss to first st. (skip all R7 sts) {88 sts}

R9: dc in same st as ss, *tr in next 7 sts of R7 behind the 5tr of R5, skip 10 sts**, dc in next st*, rep from * to * 6x & * to ** 1x, join with ss to first st. {64 sts}

R10: skip same st as ss, *fptr around R8 fp st below, htr in next 3 sts, dc between middle 10 sts of R8 and next st at the same time, htr in next 3 sts**, skip 1 st*, rep from * to * 6x & * to ** 1x, join with ss to first st. {64 sts}

R11: dc in same st as ss, dc in next 63 sts, join with ss to first st. {64 sts}

R12: ch4 (stch), 3dtr in same st as ss, *ch2, fpdc around R10 st in middle of 10 R8 sts, ch5, fpdc around fp st of R10, ch5, fpdc around R10 st in middle of 10 R8 sts, ch2, skip 15 sts**, 7dtr in next st, rep from * to * 2x & * to ** 1x, 3dtr in same st as ss, join with ss to 4th ch of stch. {3 sts, 2 2-ch sps & 2 5-ch sps on each side; 4 7-st cnrs}

R13: dc in same st as ss, *dc in next 3 sts, skip (2-ch sp, 1 st & 3 sts of R11), htr in next 4 sts of R11, skip 5-ch sp, htr in next st and next st of R11 at the same time, htr in next 4 sts of R11, skip (5-ch sp, 1 st & 2-ch sp), dc in next 3 sts**, (dc, ch2, dc) in next st*, rep from * to * 2x & * to ** 1x, dc in same st as first st, ch1, join with dc to first st. {17 sts on each side; 4 2-ch cnr sps}

R14: dc over joining dc, *dc in next 4 sts, 2dc in next st, dc in next 7 sts, 2dc in next st, dc in next 4 sts**, (dc, ch2, dc) in 2-ch cnr sp*, rep from * to * 2x & * to ** 1x, dc in same sp as first st, ch2, join with ss to first st. Fasten off. {21 sts on each side; 4 2-ch cnr sps}

Kim

SMALL PATTERNS • 63

Wellspring

This one reminds me of a bird's-eye view of an ornate fountain. Wellspring is another name for fountain-head, so that's the link.

 42 m / 46 yd

Begin with mc.

R1: ch3 (stch), 4tr, *ch1, 5tr*, rep from * to * 4x, join with dc to 3rd ch of stch. Pull mc until 1 cm hole remains. {30 sts, 6 1-ch sps}

R2: dc over joining dc, *dc in both 1-ch sps either side of next 5 sts at the same time**, dc in 1-ch sp*, rep from * to * 4x & * to ** 1x, join with ss to first st. Pull mc as tight as you can and secure the end. {12 sts}

R3: ch3 (stch), tr in same st as ss, 2tr in next 11 sts, join with ss to 3rd ch of stch. {24 sts}

R4: ch3 (stch), tr in same st as ss, *fptr around next st**, 2tr in next st*, rep from * to * 10x & * to ** 1x. Do not join. {36 sts}

R5: dc in blo of false st or 3rd ch of stch of R4, dc in blo of next 35 sts. Do not join. {36 sts}

R6: *dc in blo of next 3 sts, fptr around R4 fp st below*, rep from * to * 11x, join with ss to first st. {48 sts}

R7: ch3 (stch), tr2tog over next 2 sts, *ch1, (fptr around, tr in, fptr around) next st, ch1**, tr3tog over next 3 sts*, rep from * to * 10x & * to ** 1x, join with ss to top of tr2tog. {48 sts, 24 1-ch sps}

R8: dc in same st as ss, *dc in 1-ch sp, dc in next 3 sts, dc in 1-ch sp**, dc in next st*, rep from * to * 10x & * to ** 1x, join with ss to first st. {72 sts}

R9: ch4 (stch), 2dtrcl in same st as ss, *skip 3 sts, htr in next 2 sts, dc in next 7 sts, htr in next 2 sts, skip 3 sts**, (3dtrcl, ch4, 3dtrcl) in next st*, rep from * to * 2x & * to ** 1x, 3dtrcl in same st as first sts, ch2, join with tr to top of 2dtrcl. {13 sts on each side; 4 4-ch cnr sps}

R10: trtr in same st as R9 clusters between them, 2htr over joining tr, *htr in blo of next 13 sts, 2htr in 4-ch sp**, trtr in same st as R9 clusters between them, 2htr in 4-ch sp*, rep from * to * 2x & * to ** 1x, join with ss to first st. {17 sts on each side; 4 1-st cnrs}

R11: ch3 (stch), *htr in next 4 sts, dc in next 9 sts, htr in next 4 sts**, (tr, ch2, tr) in next st*, rep from * to * 2x & * to ** 1x, tr in same st as first st, ch2, join with ss to 3rd ch of stch. Fasten off. {19 sts on each side; 4 2-ch cnr sps}

Kim   *Kym*

SMALL PATTERNS • 65

Medium

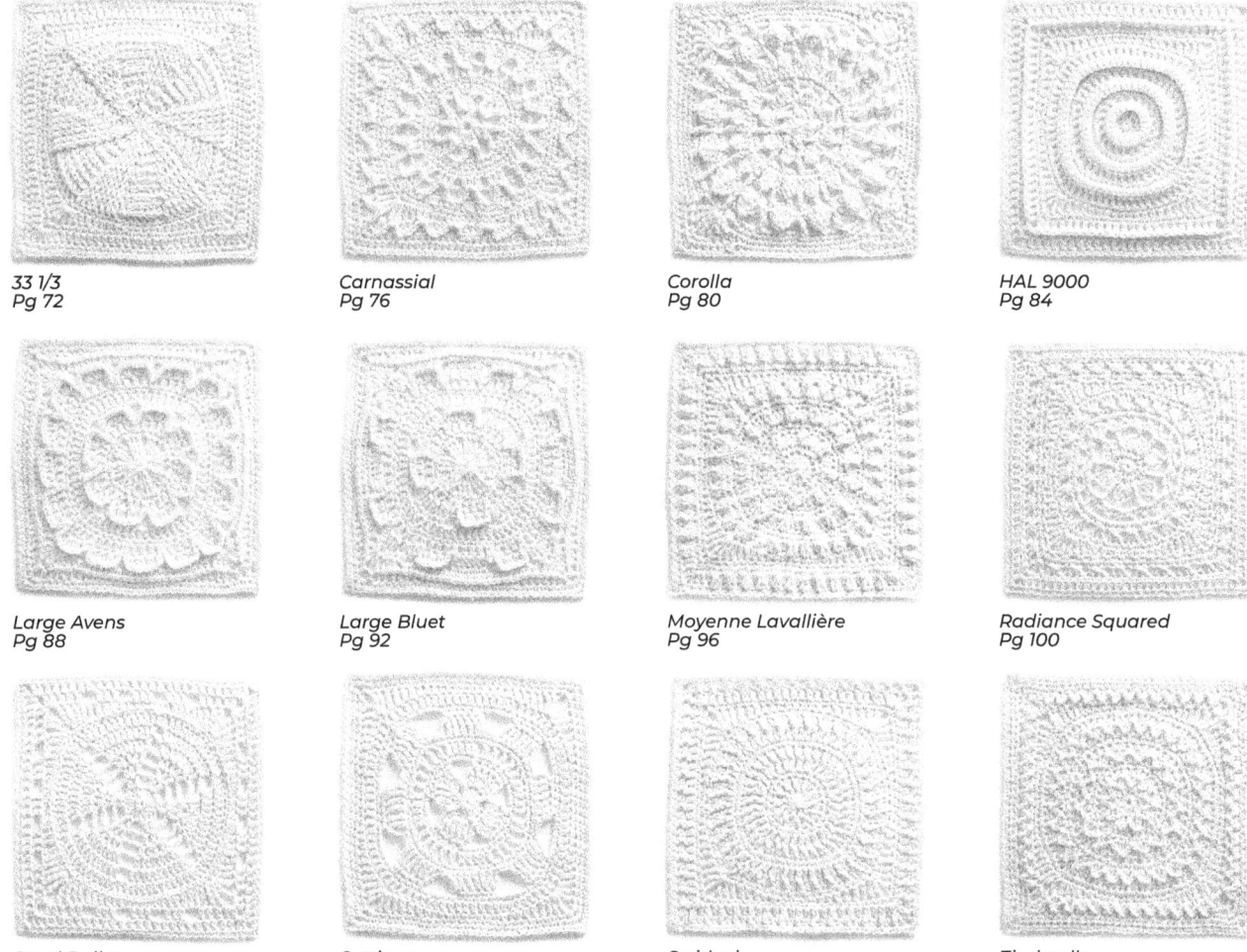

33 1/3
Pg 72

Carnassial
Pg 76

Corolla
Pg 80

HAL 9000
Pg 84

Large Avens
Pg 88

Large Bluet
Pg 92

Moyenne Lavallière
Pg 96

Radiance Squared
Pg 100

Sand Dollar
Pg 104

Settings
Pg 68

Swirlygig
Pg 108

Zinderella
Pg 112

Here's a guide to the expected finished size of the squares made with different yarn weights and hook sizes. The amount of yarn listed on each pattern page is based on using the medium weight yarn and corresponding hook size. The amount of yarn needed for the other yarn weights is listed on page 200.

Hook	3.5 mm hook	4.5 mm hook	5.5 mm hook
Yarn	4 ply/sock/fingering	8 ply/DK/light worsted	10 ply/aran/worsted
Size	7.5"	9"	10.5"

MEDIUM PATTERNS

Settings

Is it time to check your phone settings? I see the settings icon when I look at this granny square.

 70 m / 77 yd

Begin with mc.

R1: ch3 (stch), 15tr, join with ss to 3rd ch of stch. {16 sts}

R2: ch4 (stch), dtr in same st as ss, *dtr in next st, ch3, fpdc around next st, ch3, dtr in next st**, 3dtr in next st*, rep from * to * 2x & * to ** 1x, dtr in same st as first sts, join with ss to 4th ch of stch. {1 st, 2 3-ch sps on each side; 4 5-st cnrs}

R3: dc in same st as ss, dc in next 2 sts, *ch5, skip (3-ch sp, 1 st & 3-ch sp)**, dc in next 5 sts*, rep from * to * 2x & * to ** 1x, dc in next 2 sts, join with ss to first st. {20 sts, 4 5-ch sps} (may be a little cupped)

R4: dc in same st as ss, dc in next 2 sts, *5dc in 5-ch sp**, dc in next 5 sts*, rep from * to * 2x & * to ** 1x, dc in next 2 sts, join with ss to first st. {40 sts}

R5: ch3 (stch), 2x [ch1, tr in next st], *ch1, tr in next 5 sts**, 5x [ch1, tr in next st]*, rep from * to * 2x & * to ** 1x, ch1, 2x [tr in next st, ch1], join with ss to 3rd ch of stch. {40 sts, 24 1-ch sps}

R6: dc in same st as ss, 2x [dc in 1-ch sp, dc in next st], *dc in 1-ch sp, dc in next 5 sts**, 5x [dc in 1-ch sp, dc in next st]*, rep from * to * 2x & * to ** 1x, 2x [dc in 1-ch sp, dc in next st], dc in 1-ch sp, join with ss to first st. {64 sts}

R7: ch4 (stch), dtr in next 2 sts, *ch3, dc in next 3 sts, ch3**, dtr in next 5 sts*, rep from * to * 6x & * to ** 1x, dtr in next 2 sts, join with ss to 4th ch of stch. {64 sts, 16 3-ch sps}

R8: dc in same st as ss, dc in next 2 sts, *ch6, skip (3-ch sp, 3 sts & 3-ch sp)**, dc in next 5 sts*, rep from * to * 6x & * to ** 1x, dc in next 2 sts, join with ss to first st. {40 sts, 8 6-ch sps} (may be cupped)

R9: dc in same st as ss, dc in next 2 sts, *6dc in 6-ch sp**, dc in next 5 sts*, rep from * to * 6x & * to ** 1x, dc in next 2 sts, join with ss to first st. {88 sts}

R10: ch3 (stch), tr in next 87 sts, join with ss to 3rd ch of stch. {88 sts}

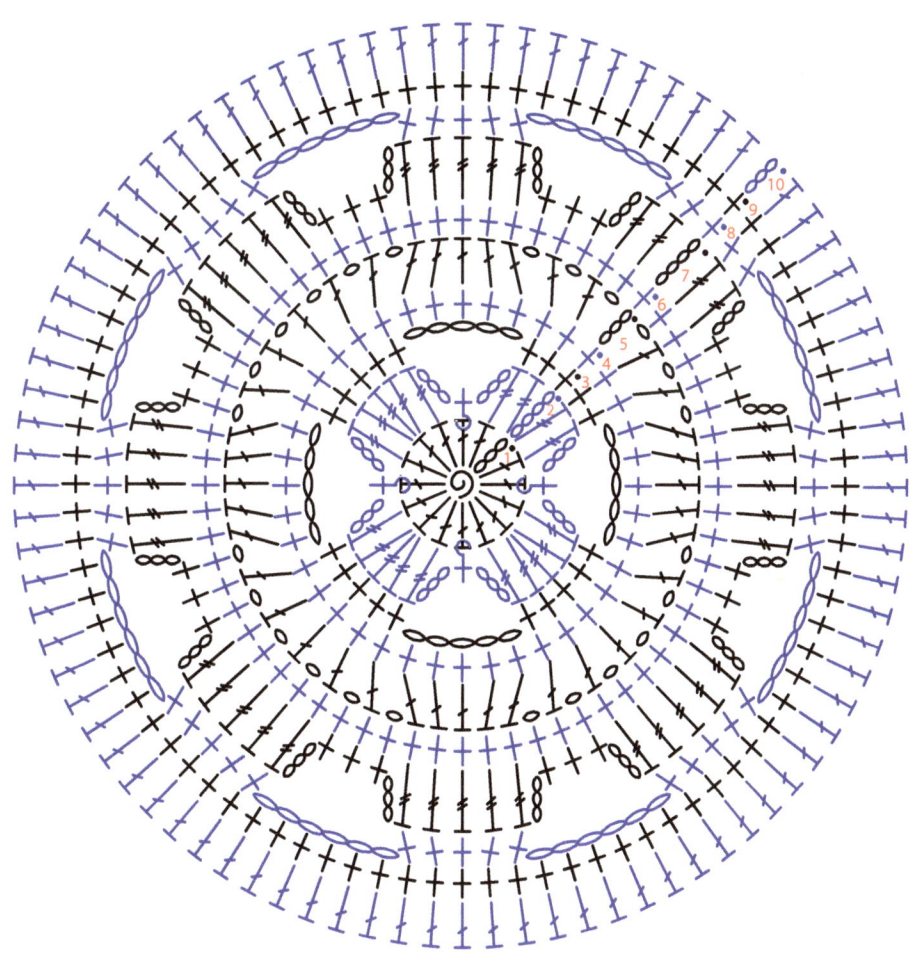

MEDIUM PATTERNS • 69

R11: ch4 (stch), dtr in same st as ss, *hdtr in next 2 sts, tr in next 2 sts, htr in next 3 sts, dc in next 7 sts, htr in next 3 sts, tr in next 2 sts, hdtr in next 2 sts**, (2dtr, ch2, 2dtr) in next st*, rep from * to * 2x & * to ** 1x, 2dtr in same st as first sts, ch1, join with dc to 4th ch of stch. **{25 sts on each side; 4 2-ch cnr sps}**

R12: dc over joining dc, *dc in next 25 sts**, (dc, ch2, dc) in 2-ch cnr sp*, rep from * to * 2x & * to ** 1x, dc in same sp as first st, ch1, join with dc to first st. **{27 sts on each side; 4 2-ch cnr sps}**

R13: dc over joining dc, *dc in next 27 sts**, (dc, ch2, dc) in 2-ch cnr sp*, rep from * to * 2x & * to ** 1x, dc in same sp as first st, ch1, join with dc to first st. **{29 sts on each side; 4 2-ch cnr sps}**

R14: dc over joining dc, *dc in next 29 sts**, (dc, ch2, dc) in 2-ch cnr sp*, rep from * to * 2x & * to ** 1x, dc in same sp as first st, ch2, join with ss to first st. Fasten off. **{31 sts on each side; 4 2-ch cnr sps}**

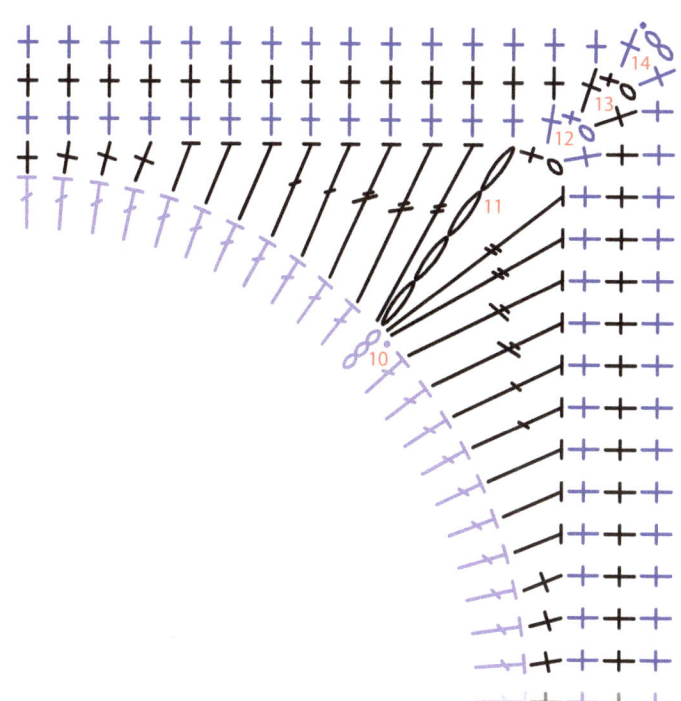

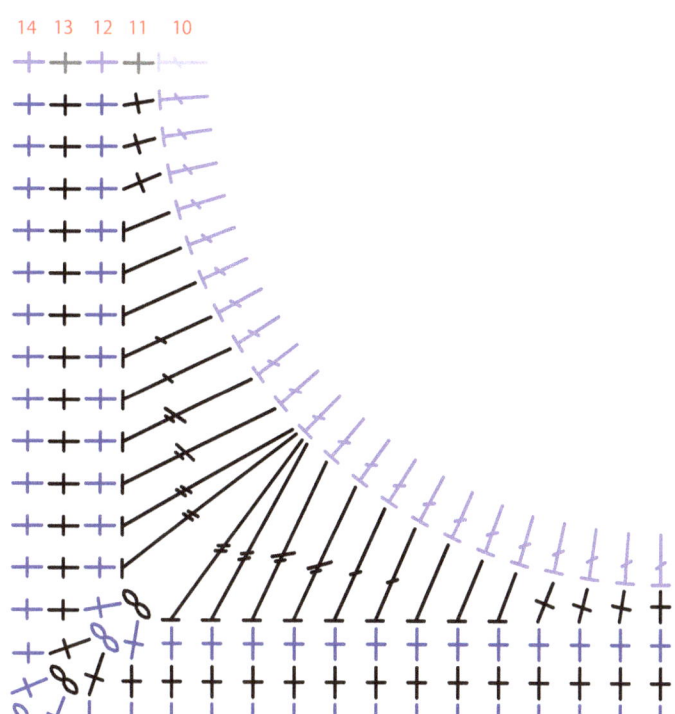

Kim

Kym

MEDIUM PATTERNS • 71

33 ⅓

What was your favourite vinyl long playing record?

 102 m / 112 yd

Begin with mc.

R1: ch3 (stch), 11tr, join with ss to 3rd ch of stch. {12 sts}

R2: ch3 (stch), fptr around same st as ss, *(tr in, bptr around) next st**, (tr in, fptr around) next st*, rep from * to * 4x & * to ** 1x, join with ss to 3rd ch of stch. {24 sts}

R3: ch3 (stch), fptr around same st as ss, fptr around next st, *(tr in, bptr around) next st, bptr around next st**, (tr in, fptr around) next st, fptr around next st*, rep from * to * 4x & * to ** 1x, join with ss to 3rd ch of stch. {36 sts}

R4: ch3 (stch), fptr around same st as ss, fptr around next 2 sts, *(tr in, bptr around) next st, bptr around next 2 sts**, (tr in, fptr around) next st, fptr around next 2 sts*, rep from * to * 4x & * to ** 1x, join with ss to 3rd ch of stch. {48 sts}

R5: ch3 (stch), fptr around same st as ss, fptr around next 3 sts, *(tr in, bptr around) next st, bptr around next 3 sts**, (tr in, fptr around) next st, fptr around next 3 sts*, rep from * to * 4x & * to ** 1x, join with ss to 3rd ch of stch. {60 sts}

R6: fptr around same st as ss, fptr around next 4 sts, *bptr around next 5 sts**, fptr around next 5 sts*, rep from * to * 4x & * to ** 1x, join with ss to first st. {60 sts}

R7: ch3 (stch), fptr around same st as ss, fptr around next 4 sts, *(tr in, bptr around) next st, bptr around next 4 sts**, (tr in, fptr around) next st, fptr around next 4 sts*, rep from * to * 4x & * to ** 1x, join with ss to 3rd ch of stch. {72 sts}

R8: fptr around same st as ss, fptr around next 5 sts, *bptr around next 6 sts**, fptr around next 6 sts*, rep from * to * 4x & * to ** 1x, join with ss to first st. {72 sts}

R9: ch3 (stch), fptr around same st as ss, fptr around next 5 sts, *(tr in, bptr around) next st, bptr around next 5 sts**, (tr in, fptr around) next st, fptr around next 5 sts*, rep from * to * 4x & * to ** 1x, join with ss to 3rd ch of stch. {84 sts}

MEDIUM PATTERNS

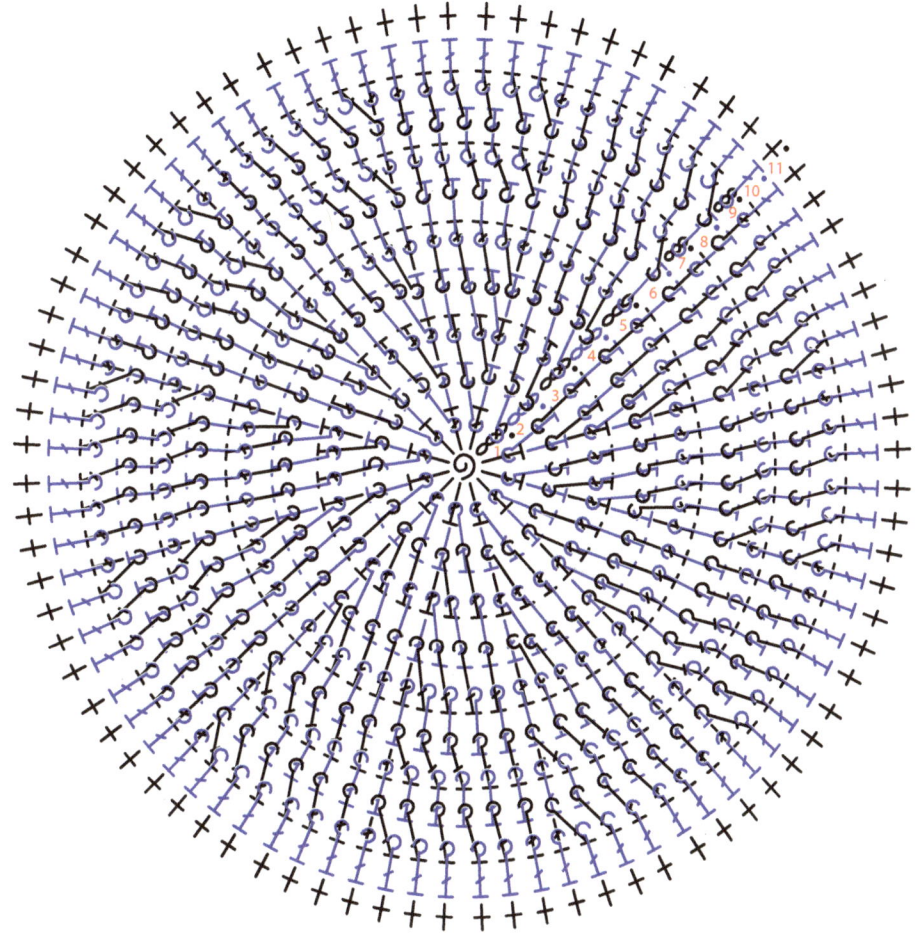

R10: fptr around same st as ss, fptr around next 6 sts, *bptr around next 7 sts**, fptr around next 7 sts*, rep from * to * 4x & * to ** 1x, join with ss to first st. {84 sts}

R11: dc in same st as ss, dc in next 83 sts, join with ss to first st. {84 sts}

R12: ch4 (stch), 2hdtr in same st as ss, *tr in next 3 sts, htr in next 4 sts, dc in next 6 sts, htr in next 4 sts, tr in next 3 sts**, (2hdtr, dtr, 2hdtr) in next st*, rep from * to * 2x & * to ** 1x, 2hdtr in same st as first sts, join with ss to 4th ch of stch. {20 sts on each side; 4 5-st cnrs}

R13: dc in same st as ss, *dc in next 24 sts**, (dc, ch2, dc) in next st*, rep from * to * 2x & * to ** 1x, dc in same st as first st, ch1, join with dc to first st. {26 sts on each side; 4 2-ch cnr sps}

R14: ch3 (stch), 2tr over joining dc, *tr in next 26 sts**, (2tr, hdtr, 2tr) in 2-ch cnr sp*, rep from * to * 2x & * to ** 1x, 2tr in same sp as first sts, join with ss to 3rd ch of stch. {26 sts on each side; 4 5-st cnrs}

R15: dc in same st as ss, *dc in next 30 sts**, (dc, ch2, dc) in next st*, rep from * to * 2x & * to ** 1x, dc in same st as first st, ch1, join with dc to first st. {32 sts on each side; 4 2-ch cnr sps}

R16: dc over joining dc, *dc in next 32 sts**, (dc, ch2, dc) in 2-ch cnr sp*, rep from * to * 2x & * to ** 1x, dc in same sp as first st, ch2, join with ss to first st. Fasten off. {34 sts on each side; 4 2-ch cnr sps}

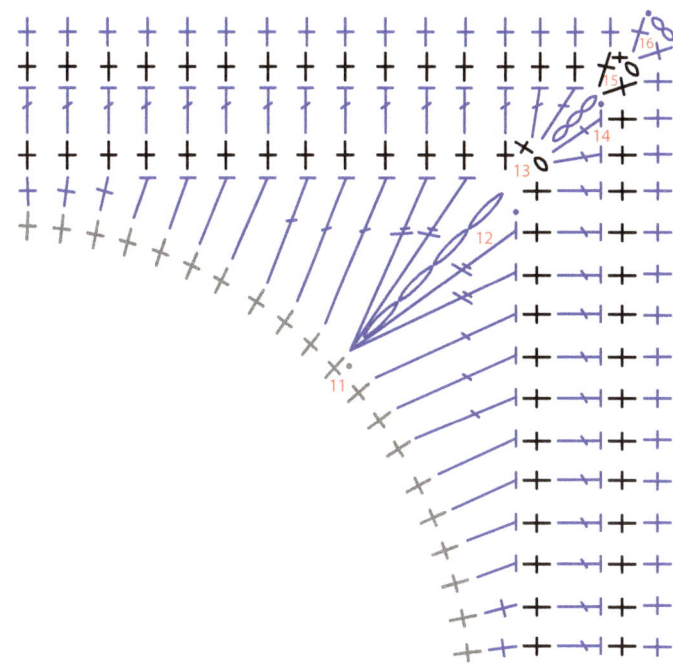
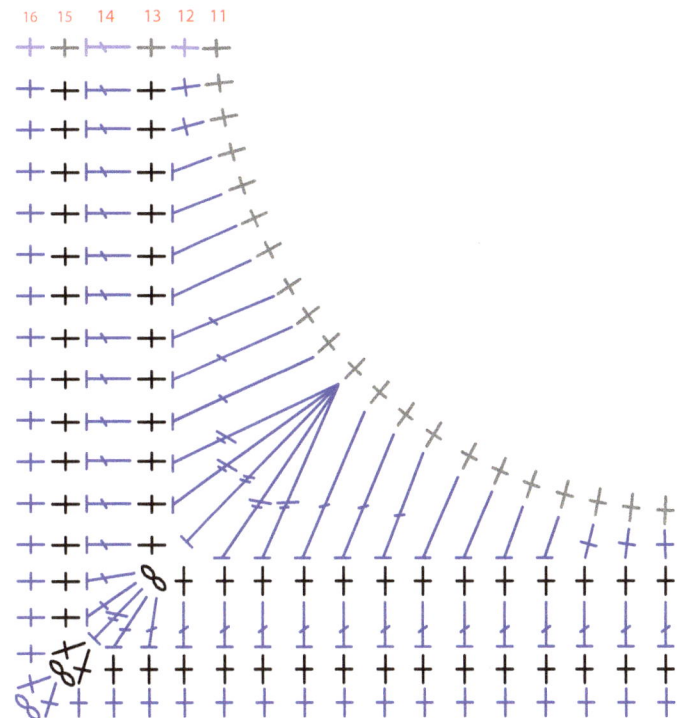

Kim

Kym

MEDIUM PATTERNS • 75

Carnassial

Toothsome! Carnassial teeth are large upper and lower teeth of carnivores, adapted for shearing flesh.

 94 m / 103 yd

Begin with mc.

R1: ch3 (stch), 2tr, *ch2, dc, ch2**, 3tr* rep from * to * 4x & * to ** 1x, join with ss to 3rd ch of stch. {24 sts, 12 2-ch sps}

R2: ch3 (stch), tr in next 2 sts, *ch2, skip (2-ch sp, 1 st & 2-ch sp)**, tr in next 3 sts*, rep from * to * 4x & * to ** 1x, join with ss to 3rd ch of stch. {18 sts, 6 2-ch sps}

R3: *ch3, fpdc around next 3 R1 sts, ch3, skip 3 sts, 3dc in 2-ch sp*, rep from * to * 5x, do not join. {36 sts, 12 3-ch sps}

R4: *tr in next st of R2, 2tr in next st of R2, tr in next st of R2, skip (3-ch sp, 3 sts & 3-ch sp), dc in next 3 sts*, rep from * to * 5x, join with ss to first st. {42 sts}

R5: dc in same st as ss, dc in next 41 sts, join with ss to first st. {42 sts}

R6: ch3 (stch), tr in next 2 sts, *ch2**, tr in next 3 sts*, rep from * to * 12x & * to ** 1x, join with ss to 3rd ch of stch. {42 sts, 14 2-ch sps}

R7: ch3 (stch), 2tr in next st, tr in next st, *ch2, skip 2-ch sp**, tr in next st, 2tr in next st, tr in next st*, rep from * to * 12x & * to ** 1x, join with ss to 3rd ch of stch. {56 sts, 14 2-ch sps}

R8: *ch3, fpdc around next 3 R6 sts, ch3, skip 4 sts, 3dc in 2-ch sp*, rep from * to * 13x, do not join. {84 sts, 28 3-ch sps}

R9: *tr in next st of R7, tr2tog over next 2 sts of R7, tr in next st of R7, skip (3-ch sp, 3 sts & 3-ch sp), dc in next 3 sts*, rep from * to * 13x, join with ss first st. {84 sts}

R10: dc in same st as ss, dc in next 83 sts, join with ss to first st. {84 sts}

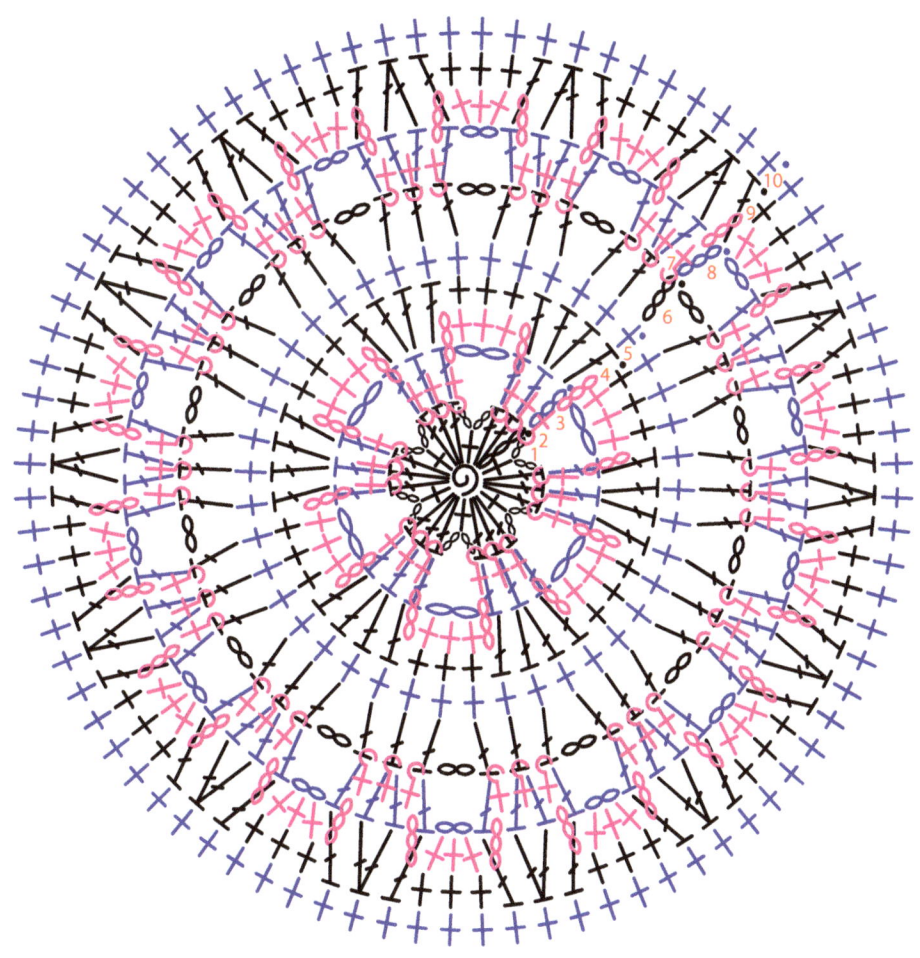

R11: ch4 (stch), dtr in same st as ss, *hdtr in next 2 sts, tr in next 2 sts, htr in next 2 sts, dc in next 8 sts, htr in next 2 sts, tr in next 2 sts, hdtr in next 2 sts**, (2dtr, ch2, 2dtr) in next st*, rep from * to * 2x & * to ** 1x, 2dtr in same st as first sts, ch1, join with dc to 4th ch of stch. {24 sts on each side; 4 2-ch cnr sps}

R12: ch3 (stch), tr over joining dc, *tr in next 24 sts**, (tr, hdtr, tr) in 2-ch cnr sp*, rep from * to * 2x & * to ** 1x, tr in same sp as first sts, join with ss to 3rd ch of stch. {24 sts on each side; 4 3-st cnrs}

R13: dc in same st as ss, *ch3, fpdc around first 2 sts of R11, ch3, skip 3 sts, dc in next st, ch3, skip 2 sts of R11, fpdc around next 2 sts of R11, ch3, skip 4 sts, dc in next st, ch2, skip 2 sts of R11, fpdc around next 3 sts of R11, ch2, skip 3 sts, dc in next 2 sts, ch2, skip 2 sts of R11, fpdc around next 3 sts of R11, ch2, skip 3 sts, dc in next st, ch3, skip 2 sts of R11, fpdc around next 2 sts of R11, ch3, skip 4 sts, dc in next st, ch3, skip 2 sts of R11, fpdc around next 2 sts of R11, ch3, skip 3 sts**, (dc, ch2, dc) in next st*, rep from * to * 2x & * to ** 1x, dc in same st as first st, ch1, join with dc to first st. {22 sts, 8 3-ch sps and 4 2-ch sps on each side; 4 2-ch cnr sps}

R14: dc over joining dc, *dc in next st, htr in next 3 sts of R12, skip (3-ch sp, 2 sts & 3-ch sp), dc in next st, htr in next 4 sts of R12, skip (3-ch sp, 2 sts & 3-ch sp), dc in next st, htr in next 3 sts of R12, skip (2-ch sp, 3 sts & 2-ch sp), dc in next 2 sts, htr in next 3 sts of R12, skip (2-ch sp, 3 sts & 2-ch sp), dc in next st, htr in next 4 sts of R12, skip (3-ch sp, 2 sts & 3-ch sp), dc in next st, htr in next 3 sts of R12, skip (3-ch sp, 2 sts & 3-ch sp), dc in next st**, (dc, ch2, dc) in 2-ch cnr sp*, rep from * to * 2x & * to ** 1x, dc in same sp as first st, ch1, join with dc to first st. {30 sts on each side; 4 2-ch cnr sps}

R15: ch2 (stch), *htr in next 30 sts**, (htr, ch2, htr) in 2-ch cnr sp*, rep from * to * 2x & * to ** 1x, htr in same sp as first st, ch1, join with dc to 2nd ch of stch. {32 sts on each side; 4 2-ch cnr sps}

R16: dc over joining dc, *dc in next 32 sts**, (dc, ch2, dc) in 2-ch cnr sp*, rep from * to * 2x & * to ** 1x, dc in same sp as first st, ch2, join with ss to first st. Fasten off. {34 sts on each side; 4 2-ch cnr sps}

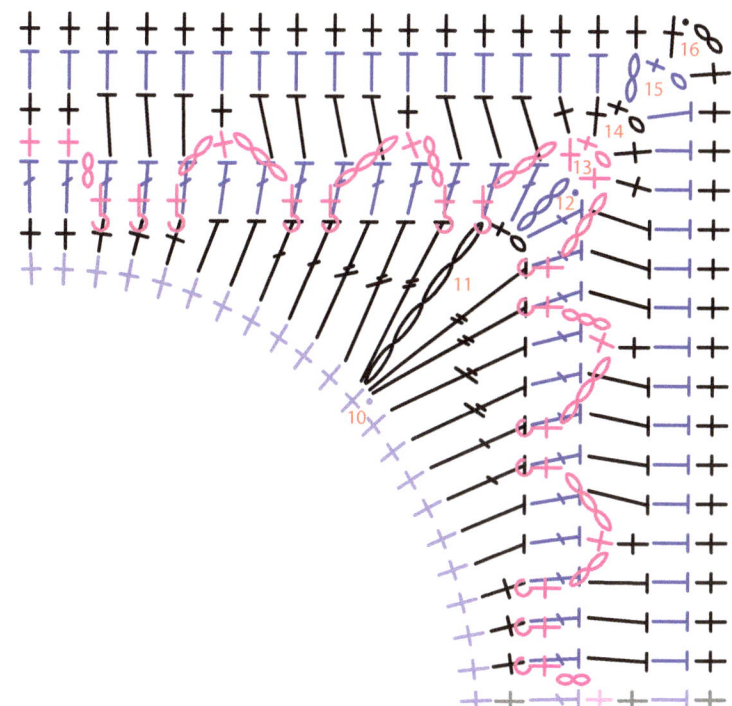

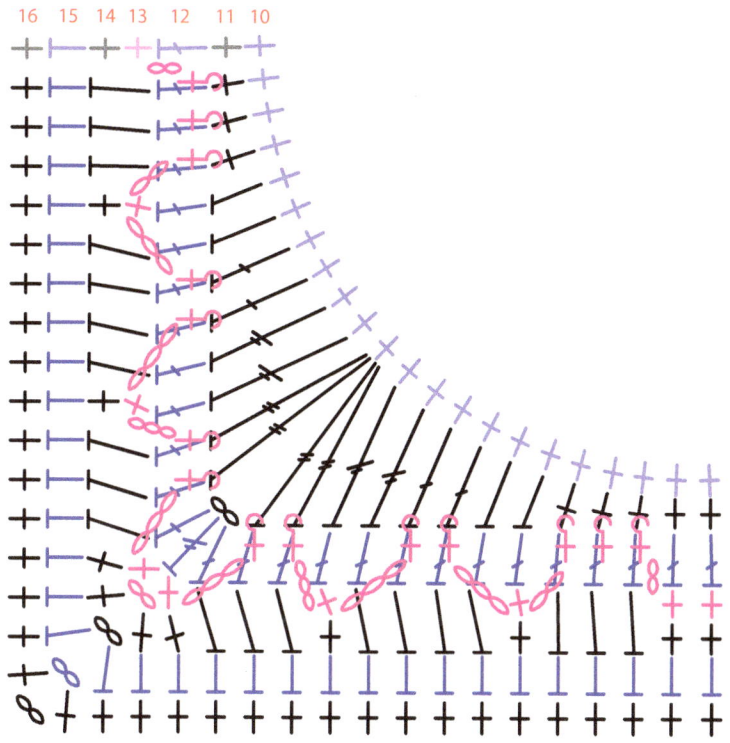

Kim

Kym

MEDIUM PATTERNS • 79

Corolla

No, this one does not remind me of a car. Corolla describes the petals of a flower.

 92 m / 101 yd

Begin with mc.

R1: ch1, *dc, ch2, tr3tog, ch2*, rep from * to * 3x, join with ss to first st. {8 sts, 8 2-ch sps}

R2: fptr around same st as ss, *ch2, skip 2-ch sp, fpdc around next st, ch2, skip 2-ch sp**, fptr around next st*, rep from * to * 2x & * to ** 1x, join with ss to first st. {8 sts, 8 2-ch sps}

R3: fpdc around same st as ss, *2dc in 2-ch sp**, fpdc around next st*, rep from * to * 6x & * to ** 1x, join with ss to first st. {24 sts}

R4: dc in same st as ss, *ch2, tr4tog over next 2 sts with 2 sts begun in each st, ch2**, dc in next st*, rep from * to * 6x & * to ** 1x, join with ss to first st. {16 sts, 16 2-ch sps}

R5: fptr around same st as ss, *ch2, skip 2-ch sp, fpdc around next st, ch2, skip 2-ch sp**, fptr around next st*, rep from * to * 6x & * to ** 1x, join with ss to first st. {16 sts, 16 2-ch sps}

R6: fpdc around same st as ss, *3dc in 2-ch sp**, fpdc around next st*, rep from * to * 14x & * to ** 1x, join with ss to first st. {64 sts}

R7: dc in same st as ss, *ch3, dtr3tog over next 3 sts, ch3**, dc in next st*, rep from * to * 14x & * to ** 1x, join with ss to first st. {32 sts, 32 3-ch sps}

R8: ch1, fpdtr around same st as ss, *ch2, skip 3-ch sp, fpdc around next st, ch2, skip 3-ch sp**, fpdtr around next st*, rep from * to * 14x & * to ** 1x, join with ss to first st. {32 sts, 32 2-ch sps}

R9: fpdc around same st as ss, *2dc in 2-ch sp**, fpdc around next st*, rep from * to * 30x & * to ** 1x, join with ss to first st. {96 sts}

R10: dc in same st as ss, *ch3, dtr5tog over next 5 sts, ch3**, dc in next st*, rep from * to * 14x & * to ** 1x, join with ss to first st. {32 sts, 32 3-ch sps}

R11: ch1, fpdtr around same st as ss, *ch2, skip 3-ch sp, fpdc around next st, ch2, skip 3-ch sp**, fpdtr around next st*, rep from * to * 14x & * to ** 1x, join with ss to first st. {32 sts, 32 2-ch sps} (may be a little cupped)

R12: fpdc around same st as ss, *3dc in 2-ch sp**, fpdc around next st*, rep from * to * 30x & * to ** 1x, join with ss to first st. {128 sts}

R13: ch5 (stch), 3trtr in same st as ss, *skip 4 sts, dc in next 23 sts, skip 4 sts**, 7trtr in next st*, rep from * to * 2x & * to ** 1x, 3trtr in same st as first sts, join with ss to 5th ch of stch.
{23 sts on each side; 4 7-st cnrs}

R14: dc in same st as ss, *dc in next st, htr in next 2 sts, tr in next st, htr in next st, dc in next 19 sts, htr in next st, tr in next st, htr in next 2 sts, dc in next st**, (dc, ch2, dc) in next st*, rep from * to * 2x & * to ** 1x, dc in same st as first st, ch1, join with dc to first st.
{31 sts on each side; 4 2-ch cnr sps}

R15: ch3 (stch), htr over joining dc, *htr in next 4 sts, tr2tog over next 2 sts, htr in next st, dc in next 17 sts, htr in next st, tr2tog over next 2 sts, htr in next 4 sts**, (htr, tr, htr) in 2-ch cnr sp*, rep from * to * 2x & * to ** 1x, htr in same sp as first sts, join with ss to 3rd ch of stch.
{31 sts on each side; 4 3-st cnrs}

R16: dc in same st as ss, *dc in next 31 sts**, (dc, ch2, dc) in next st*, rep from * to * 2x & * to ** 1x, dc in same st as first st, ch2, join with ss to first st. Fasten off.
{33 sts on each side; 4 2-ch cnr sps}

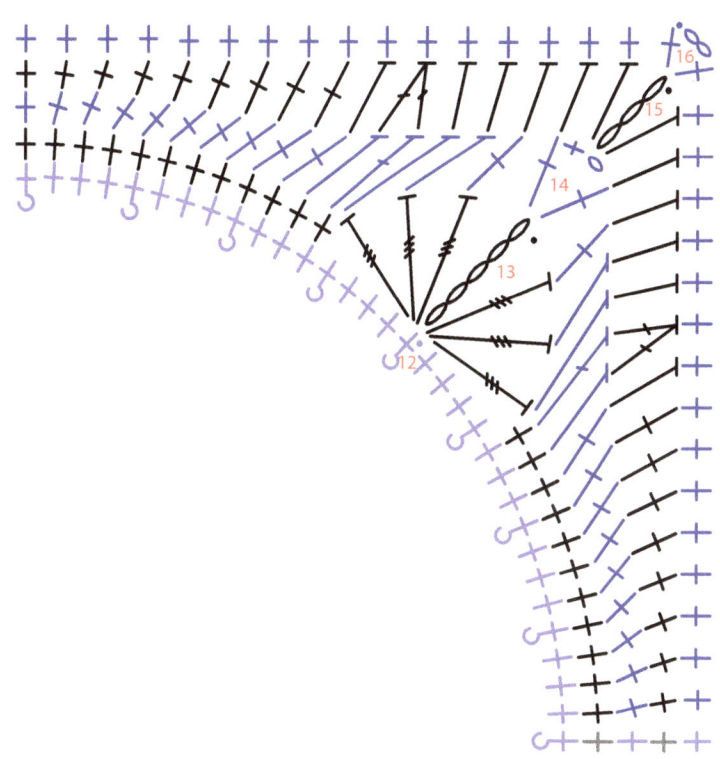
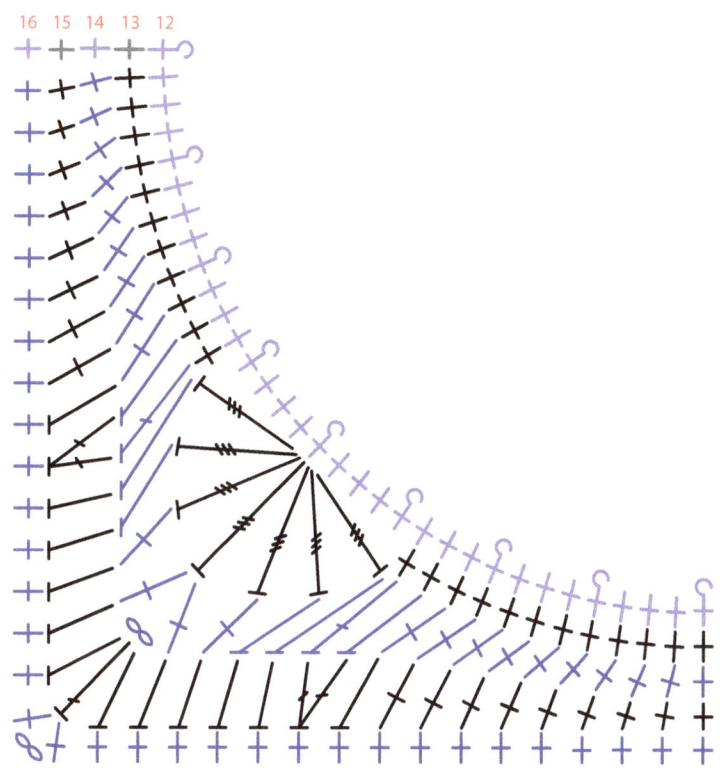

Kim

Kym

Kym

MEDIUM PATTERNS

HAL 9000

What are you doing Dave? If you have never seen 2001: A Space Odyssey, this won't mean anything to you.

 92 m / 101 yd

Begin with mc.

NOTE: Rounds 3, 7 & 11 are intentionally cupped.

R1: ch1, 10dc, join with ss to first st. {10 sts}

R2: ch3 (stch), tr in same st as ss, 2tr in next 9 sts, join with ss to 3rd ch of stch. {20 sts}

R3: ch1 (stch), dc in next 19 sts, join with inv join to first true st. {20 sts}

R4: Attach with stdg bptr around any R2 st, bptr around next 19 sts of R2, join with ss to first st. {20 sts}

R5: dc in same st as ss, *dc between last and next st**, dc in next st*, rep from * to * 18x & * to ** 1x, join with ss to first st. {40 sts}

R6: ch3 (stch), tr in same st as ss, *tr in next 9 sts**, 2tr in next st*, rep from * to * 2x & * to ** 1x, join with ss to 3rd ch of stch. {44 sts}

R7: ch1 (stch), dc in next 43 sts, join with inv join to first true st. {44 sts}

R8: Attach with stdg bptr around any R6 st, bptr around next 43 sts of R6, join with ss to first st. {44 sts}

R9: dc in same st as ss, *dc between last and next st, skip 1 st, dc between last and next st**, dc in next st*, rep from * to * 20x & * to ** 1x, join with ss to first st. {66 sts}

R10: ch3 (stch), tr in same st as ss, *tr in next 32 sts*, 2tr in next st, rep from * to * 1x, join with ss to 3rd ch of stch. {68 sts}

R11: ch1 (stch), dc in next 67 sts, join with inv join to first true st. {68 sts}

R12: Attach with stdg bptr around any R10 st, bptr around next 67 sts of R10, join with ss to first st. {68 sts}

R13: dc between same st as ss and next st, 67x [dc between next 2 sts], join with ss to first st. {68 sts}

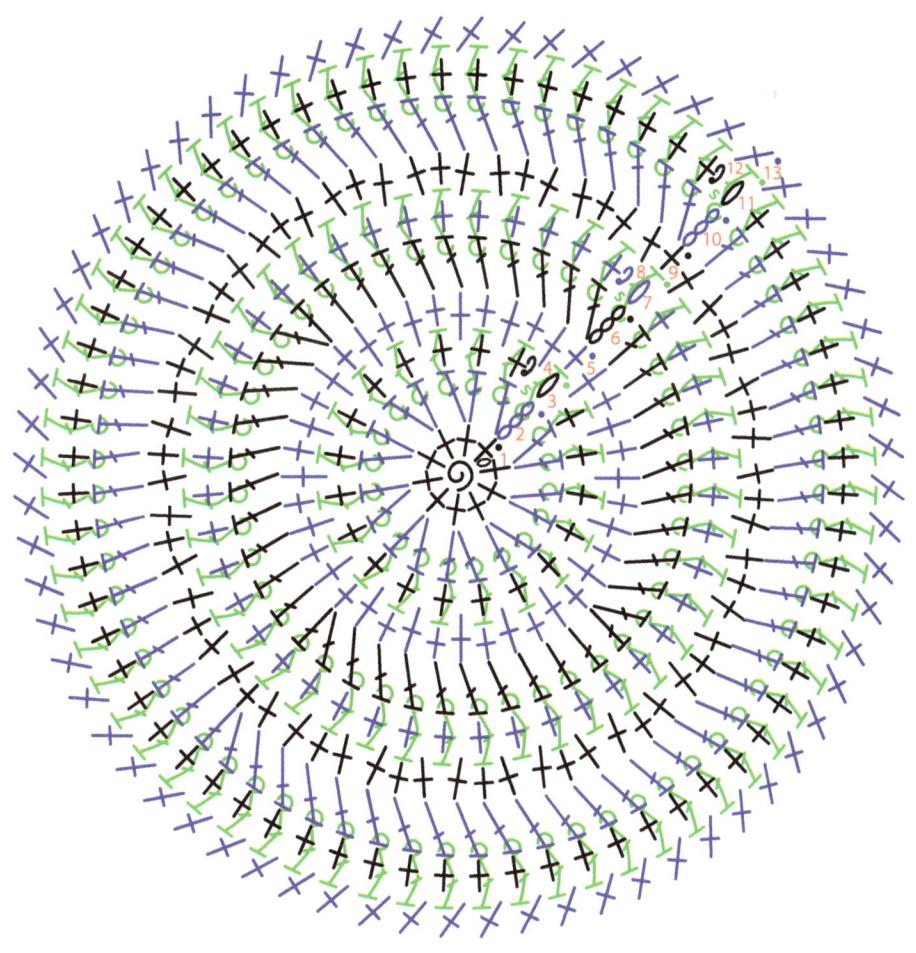

MEDIUM PATTERNS • 85

R14: ch4 (stch), dtr in same st as ss, *tr in next 3 sts, htr in next 3 sts, dc in next 4 sts, htr in next 3 sts, tr in next 3 sts**, (2dtr, ch2, 2dtr) in next st*, rep from * to * 2x & * to ** 1x, 2dtr in same st as first sts, ch1, join with dc to 4th ch of stch. {20 sts on each side; 4 2-ch cnr sps}

R15: dc over joining dc, *7x [dc between next 2 sts], skip 1 st, dc in next 4 sts, dc between last and next st, 7x [dc between next 2 sts], skip 1 st**, (dc, ch2, dc) in 2-ch cnr sp*, rep from * to * 2x & * to ** 1x, dc in same sp as first st, ch1, join with dc to first st. {21 sts on each side; 4 2-ch cnr sps}

R16: ch3 (stch), *tr in next 21 sts**, (tr, ch2, tr) in 2-ch cnr sp*, rep from * to * 2x & * to ** 1x, tr in same sp as first st, ch1, join with dc to 3rd ch of stch. {23 sts on each side; 4 2-ch cnr sps}

R17: ch2 (stch), *bptr around next 23 sts**, (htr, ch2, htr) in 2-ch cnr sp*, rep from * to * 2x & * to ** 1x, htr in same sp as first st, ch1, join with dc to 2nd ch of stch. {25 sts on each side; 4 2-ch cnr sps}

R18: ch3 (stch), *tr in next 25 sts**, (tr, ch2, tr) in 2-ch cnr sp*, rep from * to * 2x & * to ** 1x, tr in same sp as first st, ch1, join with dc to 3rd ch of stch. {27 sts on each side; 4 2-ch cnr sps}

R19: dc over joining dc, *dc in next 27 sts**, (dc, ch2, dc) in 2-ch cnr sp*, rep from * to * 2x & * to ** 1x, dc in same sp as first st, ch2, join with ss to first st. Fasten off. {29 sts on each side; 4 2-ch cnr sps}

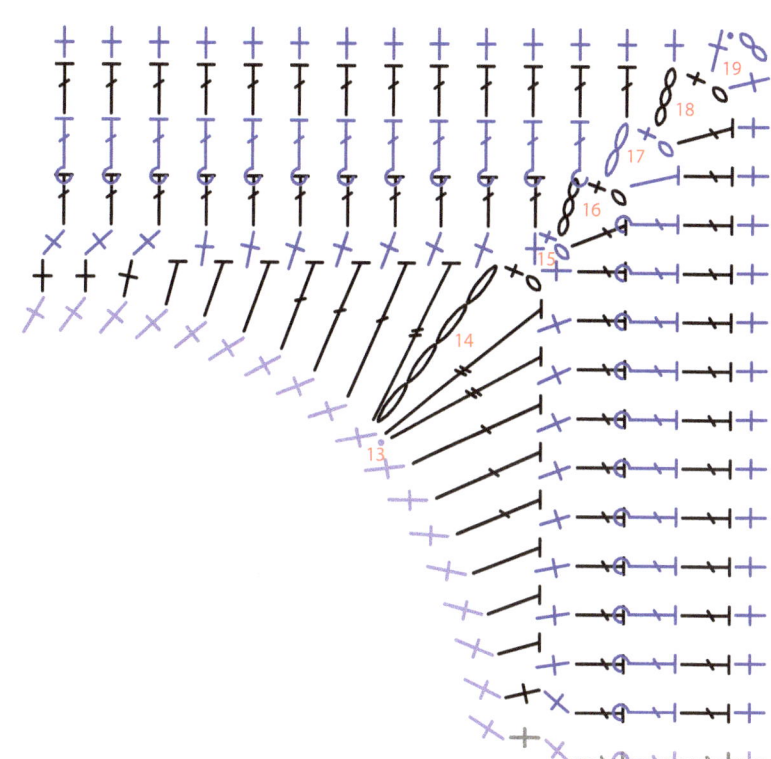

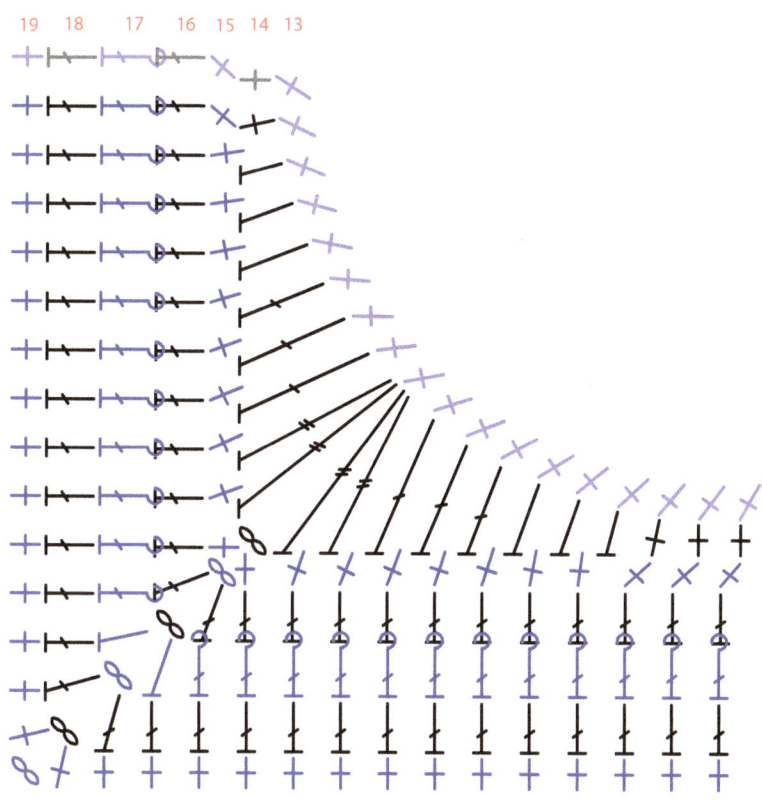

Kim

Kym

MEDIUM PATTERNS • 87

Large Avens

Bluet and Avens are the names of flowers. Bluets have 4 petals while Avens sometimes have 8. There is a small version of this pattern on page 50.

 84 m / 91 yd

Begin with mc.

R1: ch4 (stch), *ch2**, 3dtr*, rep from * to * 6x & * to ** 1x, 2dtr, join with ss to 4th ch of stch. {24 sts, 8 2-ch sps}

R2: *dc in 2-ch sp, dc in next 3 sts*, rep from * to * 7x, join with ss to first st. {32 sts}

R3: ch3 (stch), tr in next st, *ch2, skip 1 st**, tr in next 3 sts*, rep from * to * 6x & * to ** 1x, tr in next st, join with ss to 3rd ch of stch. {24 sts, 8 2-ch sps}

R4: NOTE: do not work false st. ch3 (stch), 2tr in next st, *ch3, dc in skipped st of R2 below in front of 2-ch sp, ch3, skip 2-ch sp**, 2tr in next 3 sts*, rep from * to * 6x & * to ** 1x, 2tr in next st, tr in same st as first st, join with inv join to first true st. {56 sts, 24 3-ch sps}

R5: Attach with a stdg bpdc to 4th st of any 6-st group, bpdc around next 2 sts, *ch2, skip (3-ch sp, 1 st & 3-ch sp)**, bpdc around next 6 sts*, rep from * to * 6x & * to ** 1x, bpdc around next 3 sts, join with ss to first st. {48 sts, 8 2-ch sps}

R6: ch3 (stch), tr in next 2 sts, *2tr in 2-ch sp**, tr in next 6 sts*, rep from * to * 6x & * to ** 1x, tr in next 3 sts, join with ss to 3rd ch of stch. {64 sts}

R7: dc in same st as ss, dc in next 63 sts, join with ss to first st. {64 sts}

R8: ch3 (stch), tr in next st, *ch2, skip 1 st**, tr in next 3 sts*, rep from * to *14x & * to ** 1x, tr in next st, join with ss to 3rd ch of stch. {48 sts, 16 2-ch sps}

R9: NOTE: do not work false st. ch3 (stch), 2tr in next st, *ch3, dc in skipped st of R7 below in front of 2-ch sp, ch3, skip 2-ch sp**, 2tr in next 3 sts*, rep from * to *14x & * to ** 1x, 2tr in next st, tr in same st as first st, join with inv join to first true st. {112 sts, 32 3-ch sps}

R10: Attach with a stdg bpdc to 4th st of any 6-st group, bpdc around next 2 sts, *ch2, skip (3-ch sp, 1 st & 3-ch sp)**, bpdc around next 6 sts*, rep from * to *14x & * to ** 1x, bpdc around next 3 sts, join with ss to first st. {96 sts, 16 2-ch sps}

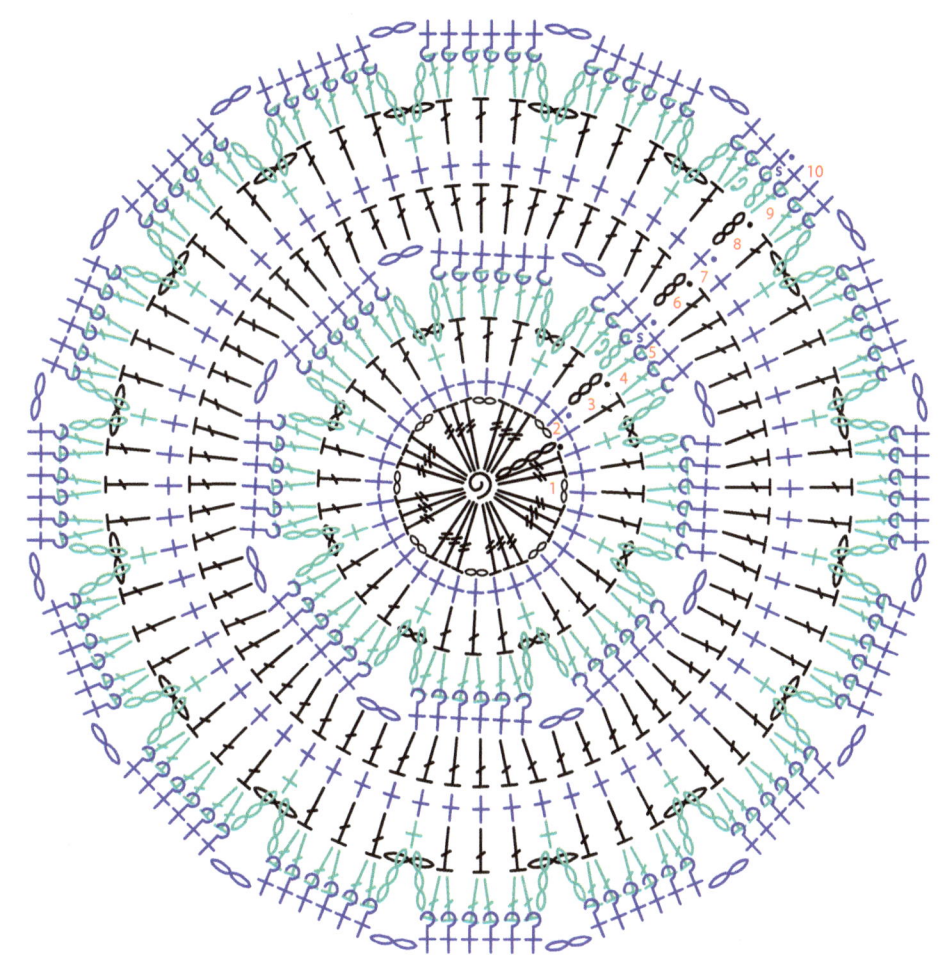

R11: ch4 (stch), 3hdtr in same st as ss, *skip 2 sts, 3x [htr in 2-ch sp, htr in next 6 sts], htr in 2-ch sp, skip 2 sts, (3hdtr, dtr) in next st**, (dtr, 3hdtr) in next st*, rep from * to * 2x & * to ** 1x, join with ss to 4th ch of stch. {22 sts on each side; 4 8-st cnrs}

R12: ch2 (stch), *htr in lbv of next 2 sts, tr in lbv of next 2 sts, htr in lbv of next 2 sts, dc in lbv of next 16 sts, htr in lbv of next 2 sts, tr in lbv of next 2 sts, htr in lbv of next 2 sts, htr in next st**, ch2, htr in next st*, rep from * to * 2x & * to ** 1x, ch1, join with dc to 2nd ch of stch. {30 sts on each side; 4 2-ch cnr sps}

R13: dc over joining dc, *dc in next 30 sts**, (dc, ch2, dc) in 2-ch sp*, rep from * to * 2x & * to ** 1x, dc in same sp as first st, ch1, join with dc to first st. {32 sts on each side; 4 2-ch cnr sps}

R14: dc over joining dc, *dc in next 32 sts**, (dc, ch2, dc) in 2-ch sp*, rep from * to * 2x & * to ** 1x, dc in same sp as first st, ch2, join with ss to first st. Fasten off. {34 sts on each side; 4 2-ch cnr sps}

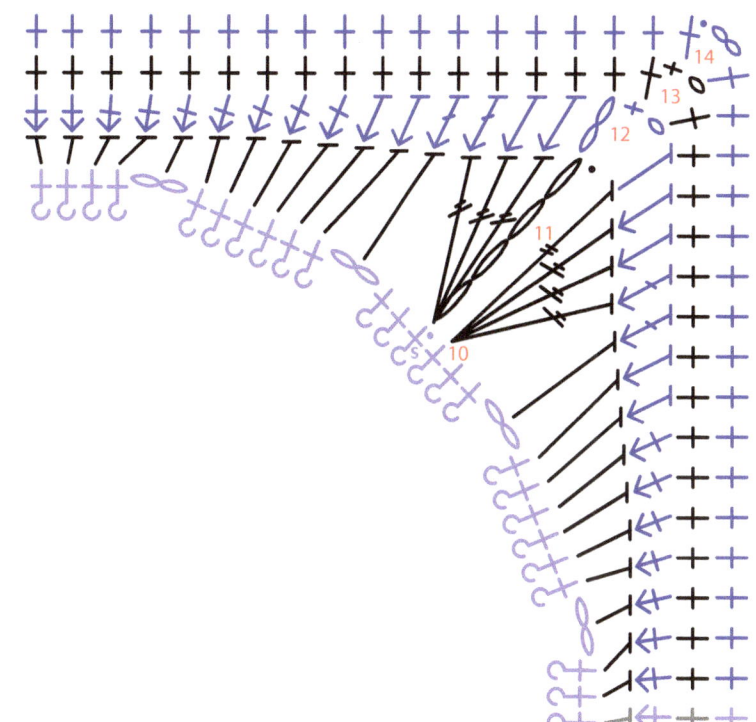

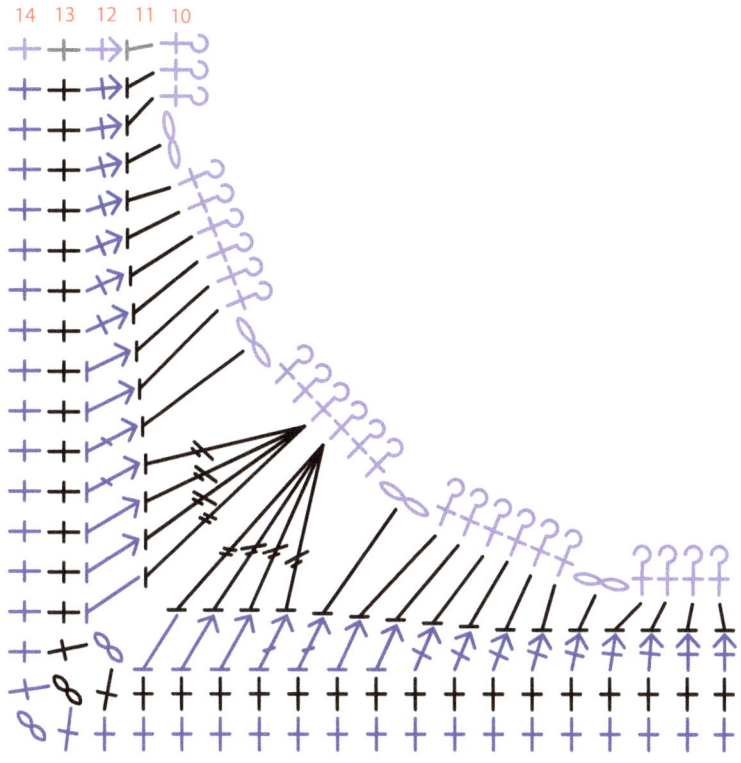

Kim

Kym

MEDIUM PATTERNS • 91

Large Bluet

Bluet and Avens are the names of flowers. Bluets have 4 petals while Avens sometimes have 8. There is a small version of this pattern on page 52.

 84 m / 92 yd

Begin with mc.

R1: ch4 (stch), *ch2**, 3dtr*, rep from * to * 6x & * to ** 1x, 2dtr, join with ss to 4th ch of stch. {24 sts, 8 2-ch sps}

R2: *dc in 2-ch sp, dc in next 3 sts*, rep from * to * 7x, join with ss to first st. {32 sts}

R3: ch3 (stch), tr in next st, *ch2, skip 1 st**, tr in next 3 sts*, rep from * to * 6x & * to ** 1x, tr in next st, join with ss to 3rd ch of stch. {24 sts, 8 2-ch sps}

R4: ch3 (stch), 2tr in next st, *ch3, dc in skipped st of R2 below in front of 2-ch sp, ch3, skip 2-ch sp**, 2tr in next 3 sts*, rep from * to * 6x & * to ** 1x, 2tr in next st, tr in same st as first st, join with ss to 3rd ch of stch. {56 sts, 16 3-ch sps}

R5: dc in same st as ss, dc in next 2 sts, *ch2, skip (3-ch sp, 1 st & 3-ch sp), bpdc around next 6 sts, ch2, skip (3-ch sp, 1 st & 3-ch sp)**, dc in next 6 sts*, rep from * to * 2x & * to ** 1x, dc in next 3 sts, join with ss to first st. {48 sts, 8 2-ch sps}

R6: ch3 (stch), tr in next 2 sts, *2tr in 2-ch sp**, tr in next 6 sts*, rep from * to * 6x & * to ** 1x, tr in next 3 sts, join with ss to 3rd ch of stch. {64 sts}

R7: dc in same st as ss, dc in next 63 sts, join with ss to first st. {64 sts}

R8: ch3 (stch), tr in next st, *ch2, skip 1 st**, tr in next 3 sts*, rep from * to * 14x & * to ** 1x, tr in next st, join with ss to 3rd ch of stch. {48 sts, 16 2-ch sps}

R9: ch3 (stch), 2tr in next st, *ch3, dc in skipped st of R7 below in front of 2-ch sp, ch3, skip 2-ch sp**, 2tr in next 3 sts*, rep from * to * 14x & * to ** 1x, 2tr in next st, tr in same st as first st, join with ss to 3rd ch of stch. {112 sts, 32 3-ch sps}

R10: dc in same st as ss, dc in next 2 sts, *ch2, skip (3-ch sp, 1 st & 3-ch sp), bpdc around next 6 sts, ch2, skip (3-ch sp, 1 st & 3-ch sp)**, dc in next 6 sts*, rep from * to * 6x & * to ** 1x, dc in next 3 sts, join with ss to first st. {96 sts, 16 2-ch sps}

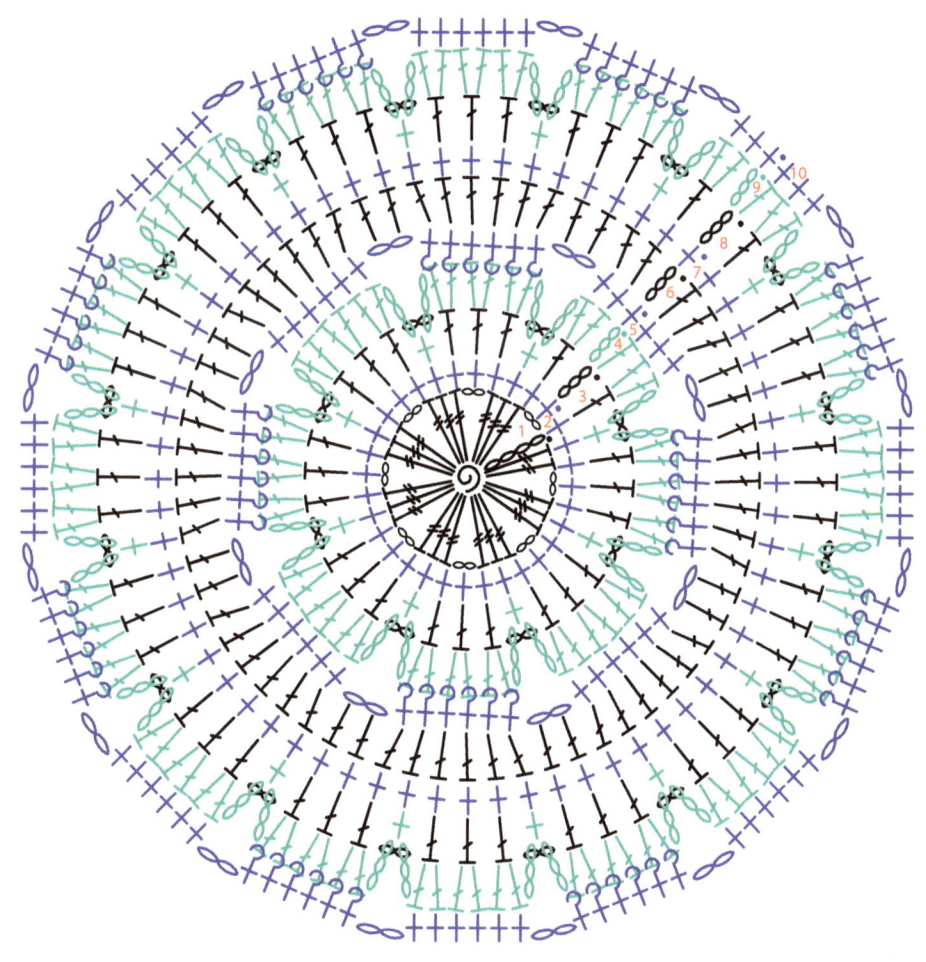

MEDIUM PATTERNS • 93

R11: ch4 (stch), 3hdtr in same st as ss, *skip 2 sts, 3x [htr in 2-ch sp, htr in next 6 sts], htr in 2-ch sp, skip 2 sts, (3hdtr, dtr) in next st**, (dtr, 3hdtr) in next st*, rep from * to * 2x & * to ** 1x, join with ss to 4th ch of stch. {22 sts on each side; 4 8-st cnrs}

R12: ch2 (stch), *htr in lbv of next 2 sts, tr in lbv of next 2 sts, htr in lbv of next 2 sts, dc in lbv of next 16 sts, htr in lbv of next 2 sts, tr in lbv of next 2 sts, htr in lbv of next 2 sts, htr in next st**, ch2, htr in next st*, rep from * to * 2x & * to ** 1x, ch1, join with dc to 2nd ch of stch. {30 sts on each side; 4 2-ch cnr sps}

R13: dc over joining dc, *dc in next 30 sts**, (dc, ch2, dc) in 2-ch sp*, rep from * to * 2x & * to ** 1x, dc in same sp as first st, ch1, join with dc to first st. {32 sts on each side; 4 2-ch cnr sps}

R14: dc over joining dc, *dc in next 32 sts**, (dc, ch2, dc) in 2-ch sp*, rep from * to * 2x & * to ** 1x, dc in same sp as first st, ch2, join with ss to first st. Fasten off. {34 sts on each side; 4 2-ch cnr sps}

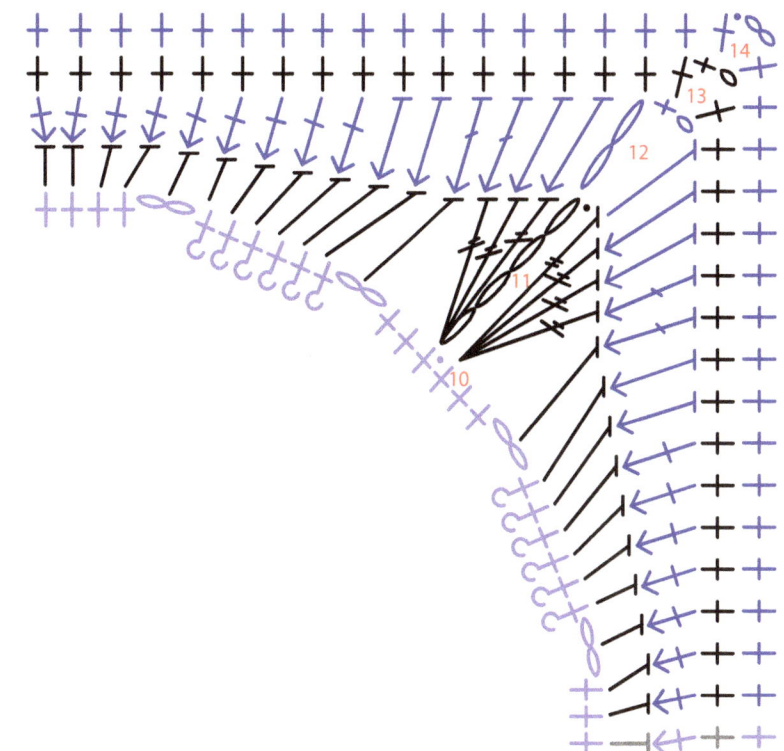

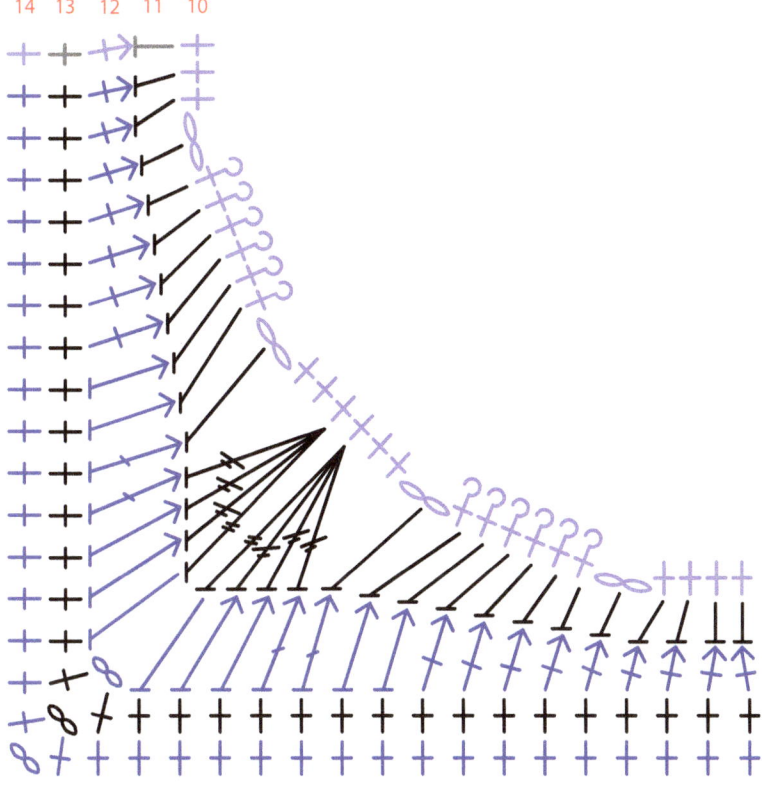

Kim

Kym

MEDIUM PATTERNS • 95

Moyenne Lavallière

A Lavallière is an ornamental pendant, usually jewelled, worn on a chain around the neck. It is a French word and as this is the middle sized of the three similar patterns, moyenne means medium in French.

 107 m / 117 yd

Begin with mc.

R1: ch3 (stch), 15tr, join with ss to 3rd ch of stch. {16 sts}

R2: dc in same st as ss, *(dc, ch6, dc) in next st**, dc in next st*, rep from * to * 6x & * to ** 1x, join with ss to first st. {24 sts, 8 6-ch sps}

R3: ch3 (stch), tr in same st as ss, *tr2tog over next 2 sts pulling 6-ch sp to front**, 3tr in next st*, rep from * to * 6x & * to ** 1x, tr same st as first sts, join with ss to 3rd ch of stch. {32 sts}

R4: dc in same st as ss, dc in next st, *dc in 6-ch sp of R2 and next st at the same time**, dc in next 3 sts*, rep from * to * 6x & * to ** 1x, dc in next st, join with ss to first st. {32 sts}

R5: (dc, ch6, dc) in same st as ss, *dc in next st**, (dc, ch6, dc) in next st*, rep from * to * 14x & * to ** 1x, join with ss to first st. {48 sts, 16 6-ch sps}

R6: tr2tog over same st as ss and next st pulling 6-ch sp to front, *3tr in next st**, tr2tog over next 2 sts pulling 6-ch sp to front*, rep from * to * 14x & * to ** 1x, join with ss to first st. {64 sts}

R7: dc in 6-ch sp of R5 and same st as ss at the same time, *dc in next 3 sts**, dc in 6-ch sp of R5 and next st at the same time*, rep from * to * 14x & * to ** 1x, join with ss to first st. {64 sts}

R8: (dc, ch6, dc) in same st as ss, *dc in next st**, (dc, ch6, dc) in next st*, rep from * to * 30x & * to ** 1x, join with ss to first st. {96 sts, 32 6-ch sps}

R9: tr2tog over same st as ss and next st pulling 6-ch sp to front, *tr in next st**, tr2tog over next 2 sts pulling 6-ch sp to front*, rep from * to * 30x & * to ** 1x, join with ss to first st. {64 sts}

R10: dc in 6-ch sp of R8 and same st as ss at the same time, *2dc in next st, dc in 6-ch sp of R8 and next st at the same time, dc in next st**, dc in 6-ch sp of R8 and next st at the same time*, rep from * to * 14x & * to ** 1x, join with ss to first st. {80 sts}

MEDIUM PATTERNS • 97

R11: ch5 (stch), 2dtr in same st as ss, *hdtr in next 2 sts, tr in next 2 sts, htr in next 2 sts, dc in next 7 sts, htr in next 2 sts, tr in next 2 sts, hdtr in next 2 sts**, (2dtr, trtr, 2dtr) in next st*, rep from * to * 2x & * to ** 1x, 2dtr in same st as first sts, join with ss to 5th ch of stch. {19 sts on each side, 4 5-st cnrs}

R12: dc in same st as ss, *dc in next 23 sts**, (dc, ch2, dc) in next st*, rep from * to * 2x & * to ** 1x, dc in same st as first st, ch1, join with dc to first st. {25 sts on each side; 4 2-ch cnr sps}

R13: dc over joining dc, *12x [dc in next st, (dc, ch6, dc) in next st], dc in next st**, (dc, ch2, dc) in 2-ch cnr sp*, rep from * to * 2x & * to ** 1x, dc in same sp as first st, ch1, join with dc to first st. {39 sts, 12 6-ch sps on each side; 4 2-ch cnr sps}

R14: ch3 (stch), tr over joining dc, *tr in next 2 sts, 12x [tr2tog over next 2 sts pulling 6-ch sp to front, tr in next st], tr in next st**, (tr, hdtr, tr) in 2-ch cnr sp*, rep from * to * 2x & * to ** 1x, tr in same sp as first sts, join with ss to 3rd ch of stch. {27 sts on each side; 4 3-st cnrs}

R15: dc in same st as ss, *dc in next 3 sts, 12x [dc in 6-ch sp of R13 and next st at the same time, dc in next st], dc in next 2 sts**, (dc, ch2, dc) in next st*, rep from * to * 2x & * to ** 1x, dc in same st as first st, ch1, join with dc to first st. {31 sts on each side; 4 2-ch cnr sps}

R16: dc over joining dc, *dc in next 31 sts**, (dc, ch2, dc) in 2-ch cnr sp*, rep from * to * 2x & * to ** 1x, dc in same sp as first st, ch2, join with ss to first st. Fasten off. {33 sts on each side; 4 2-ch cnr sps}

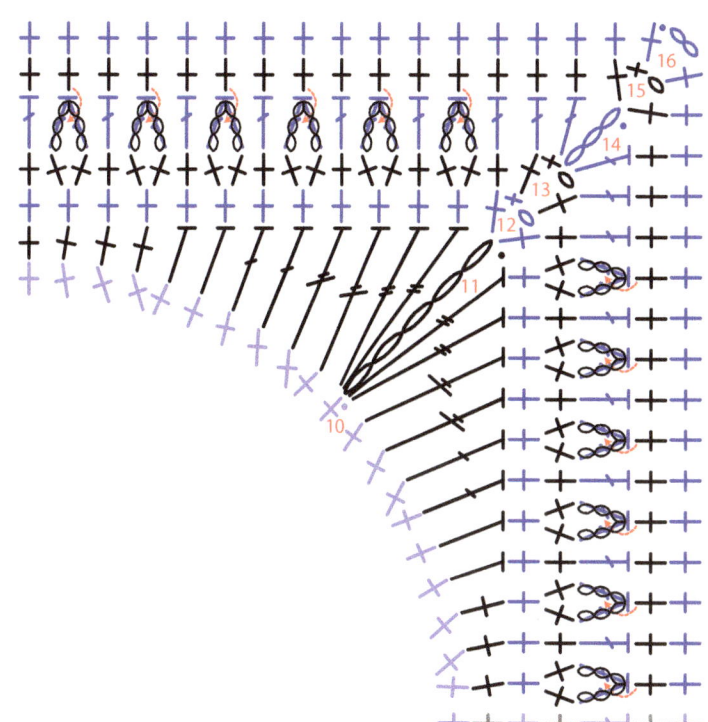

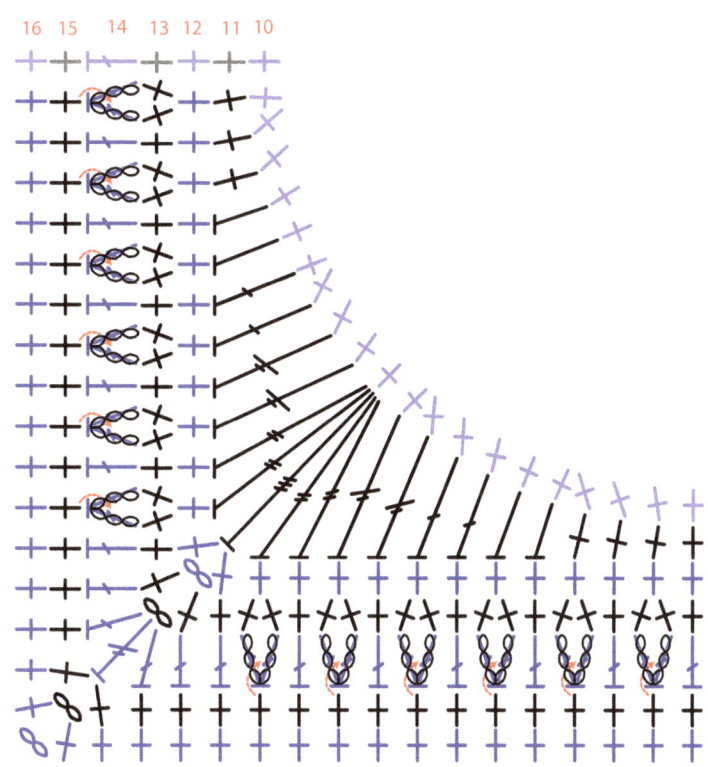

Kim

Kim

Kym

MEDIUM PATTERNS • 99

Radiance Squared

The round section is from a floor rug I designed called Radiance.

 77 m / 84 yd

Begin with mc.

R1: ch1, 12dc, join with ss to first st. {12 sts}

R2: dc in same st as ss, *ch1**, dc in next st*, rep from * to * 10x & * to ** 1x, join with ss to first st. {12 sts, 12 1-ch sps}

R3: ch3 (stch), 2tr in same st as ss, *skip 1-ch sp, dc in next st, skip 1-ch sp**, 5tr in next st*, rep from * to * 4x & * to ** 1x, 2tr in same st as first sts, join with ss to 3rd ch of stch. {36 sts}

R4: dc in same st as ss, *ch3, skip 2 sts, fpdtr around R2 st below, ch3, skip 3 sts**, dc in next st*, rep from * to * 4x & * to ** 1x, join with ss to first st. {12 sts, 12 3-ch sps}

R5: ss to 3-ch sp, 3dc in same 3-ch sp, *bpdc around next st**, 3dc in 3-ch sp*, rep from * to * 10x & * to ** 1x, join with ss to first st. {48 sts}

R6: dc in same st as ss, *ch2, skip 1 st**, dc in next st*, rep from * to * 22x & * to ** 1x, join with ss to first st. {24 sts, 24 2-ch sps}

R7: dc in same st as ss, *2dc in 2-ch sp**, dc in next st*, rep from * to * 22x & * to ** 1x, join with ss to first st. {72 sts}

R8: ch3 (stch), tr in next st, tr in last st of R7, *skip 1 st, tr in next 2 sts, tr in skipped st*, rep from * to * 22x, join with ss to 3rd ch of stch. {72 sts}

R9: dc in next 72 sts, join with ss to first st. {72 sts}

MEDIUM PATTERNS • 101

R10: ch4 (stch), 2dtr in same st as ss, *hdtr in next 2 sts, tr in next 2 sts, htr in next 2 sts, dc in next 5 sts, htr in next 2 sts, tr in next 2 sts, hdtr in next 2 sts**, 5dtr in next st*, rep from * to * 2x & * to ** 1x, 2dtr in same st as first sts, join with ss to 4th ch of stch. {17 sts on each side; 4 5-st cnrs}

R11: dc in same st as ss, *10x [ch1, skip 1 st, dc in next st], ch1, skip 1 st**, (dc, ch2, dc) in next st*, rep from * to * 2x & * to ** 1x, dc in same st as first st, ch1, join with dc to first st. {12 sts, 11 1-ch sps on each side; 4 2-ch cnr sps}

R12: dc over joining dc, *11x [dc in next st, dc in 1-ch sp], dc in next st**, (dc, ch2, dc) in 2-ch cnr sp*, rep from * to * 2x & * to ** 1x, dc in same sp as first st, ch1, join with dc to first st. {25 sts on each side; 4 2-ch cnr sps}

R13: ch3 (stch), tr over joining dc, *skip 1 st, 8x [skip 1 st, tr in next 2 sts, tr in skipped st]**, (tr, hdtr, tr) in 2-ch cnr sp*, rep from * to * 2x & * to ** 1x, tr in same sp as first sts, join with ss to 3rd ch of stch. {24 sts on each side; 4 3-st cnrs}

R14: dc in same st as ss, *dc in next 26 sts**, (dc, ch2, dc) in next st*, rep from * to * 2x & * to ** 1x, dc in same st as first st, ch1, join with dc to first st. {28 sts on each side; 4 2-ch cnr sps}

R15: ch2 (stch), *htr in blo of next 28 sts**, (htr, ch2, htr) in 2-ch cnr sp*, rep from * to * 2x & * to ** 1x, htr in same sp as first st, ch1, join with dc to 2nd ch of stch. {30 sts on each side; 4 2-ch cnr sps}

R16: dc over joining dc, *dc in blo of next 30 sts**, (dc, ch2, dc) in 2-ch cnr sp*, rep from * to * 2x & * to ** 1x, dc in same sp as first st, ch2, join with ss to first st. Fasten off. {32 sts on each side; 4 2-ch cnr sps}

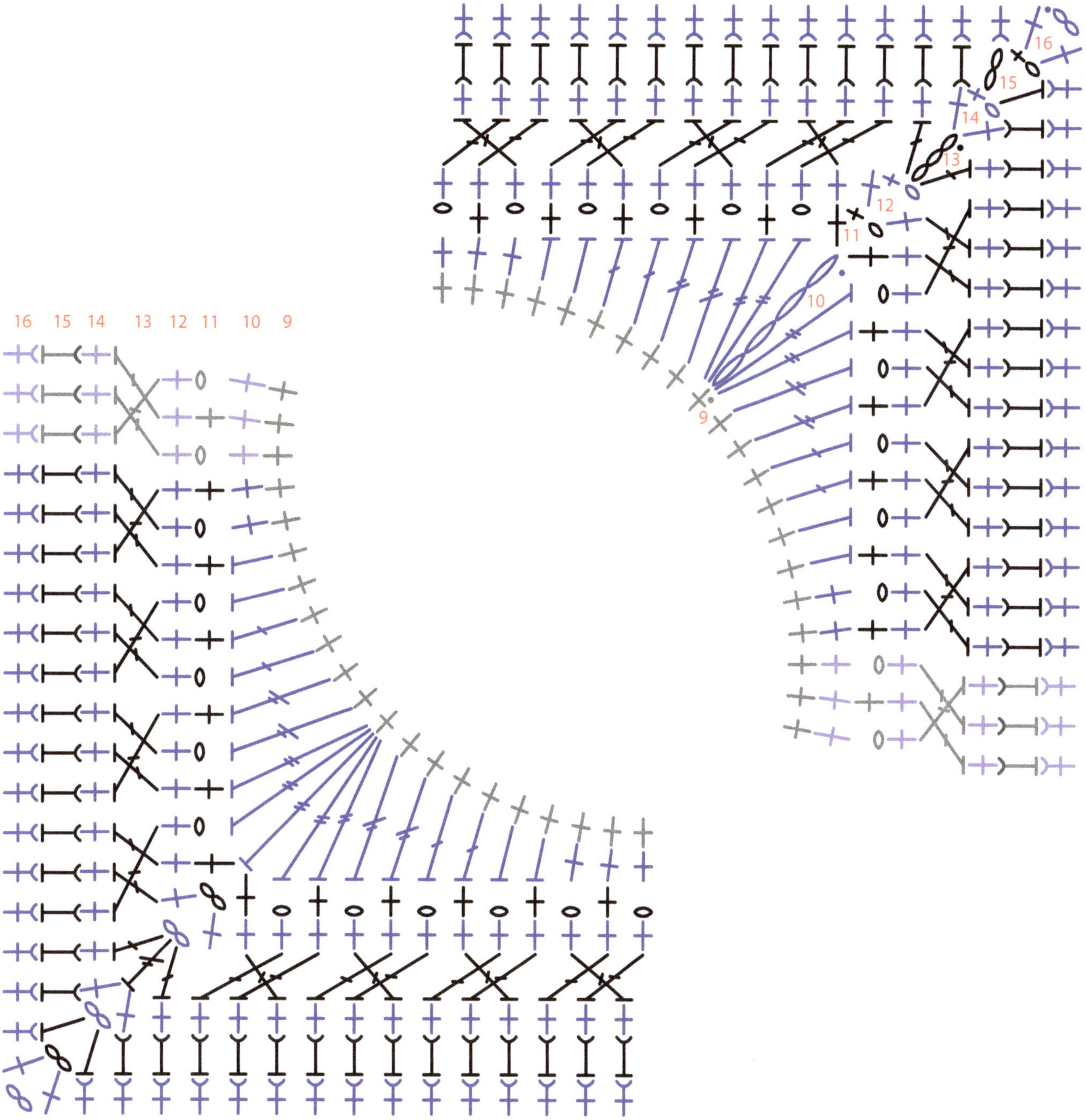

Kim

Kym

MEDIUM PATTERNS • 103

Sand Dollar

Reminiscent of sand dollars found on the beach.

 70 m / 77 yd

Begin with mc.

R1: ch3 (stch), 17tr, join with ss to 3rd ch of stch. {18 sts}

R2: ch3 (stch), tr in next st, *ch3, skip 1 st**, tr in next 2 sts*, rep from * to * 4x & * to ** 1x, join with ss to 3rd ch of stch. {12 sts, 6 3-ch sps}

R3: ch3 (stch), tr between same st as ss and next st, tr in next st, *ch4, skip 3-ch sp**, tr in next st, tr between last and next st, tr in next st*, rep from * to * 4x & * to ** 1x, join with ss to 3rd ch of stch. {18 sts, 6 4-ch sps}

R4: ch3 (stch), *2x [tr between last and next st, tr in next st], ch3, skip 4-ch sp**, tr in next st*, rep from * to * 4x & * to ** 1x, join with ss to 3rd ch of stch. {30 sts, 6 3-ch sps}

R5: ch3 (stch), *4x [tr between last and next st, tr in next st], ch3, skip 3-ch sp**, tr in next st*, rep from * to * 4x & * to ** 1x, join with ss to 3rd ch of stch. {54 sts, 6 3-ch sps}

R6: ch3 (stch), tr in same st as ss, *tr in next 7 sts, 2tr in next st, ch2, skip 3-ch sp**, 2tr in next st*, rep from * to * 4x & * to ** 1x, join with ss to 3rd ch of stch. {66 sts, 6 2-ch sps}

R7: ch3 (stch), tr in same st as ss, *tr in next 9 sts, 2tr in next st, tr in 2-ch sp**, 2tr in next st*, rep from * to * 4x & * to ** 1x, join with ss to 3rd ch of stch. {84 sts}

R8: ch1 (stch), dc in next 83 sts, join with inv join to first true st. {84 sts}

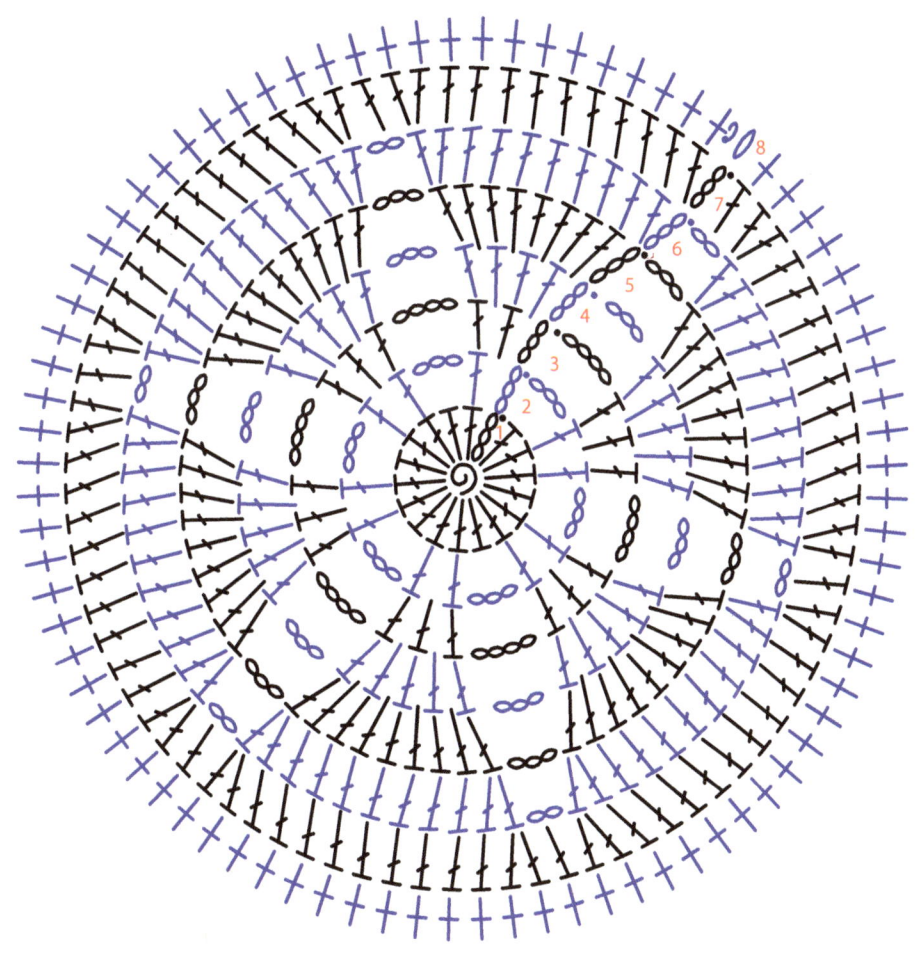

MEDIUM PATTERNS • 105

R9: attach with stdg trtr to blo of any st above chain sps, trtr in same blo, *dtr in blo of next 2 sts, hdtr in blo of next 2 sts, tr in blo of next 2 sts, htr in blo of next 2 sts, dc in blo of next 4 sts, htr in blo of next 2 sts, tr in blo of next 2 sts, hdtr in blo of next 2 sts, dtr in blo of next 2 sts**, (2trtr, ch2, 2trtr) in blo of next st*, rep from * to * 2x & * to ** 1x, 2trtr in same blo as first sts, ch1, join with dc to first st. {24 sts on each side; 4 2-ch cnr sps}

R10: ch3 (stch), tr over joining dc, *skip 1 st, 4x [tr in next 3 sts, ch2, skip 2 sts], tr in next 3 sts**, (2tr, ch2, 2tr) in 2-ch cnr sp*, rep from * to * 2x & * to ** 1x, 2tr in same sp as first sts, ch1, join with dc to 3rd ch of stch. {19 sts, 4 2-ch sps on each side; 4 2-ch cnr sps}

R11: ch3 (stch), tr over joining dc, *tr in next 5 sts, 3x [tr in 2-ch sp, tr in next 3 sts], tr in 2-ch sp, tr in next 5 sts**, (2tr, ch2, 2tr) in 2-ch cnr sp*, rep from * to * 2x & * to ** 1x, 2tr in same sp as first sts, ch1, join with dc to 3rd ch of stch. {27 sts on each side; 4 2-ch cnr sps}

R12: dc over joining dc, *dc in blo of next 27 sts**, (dc, ch2, dc) in 2-ch cnr sp*, rep from * to * 2x & * to ** 1x, dc in same sp as first st, ch2, join with ss to first st. Fasten off. {29 sts on each side; 4 2-ch cnr sps}

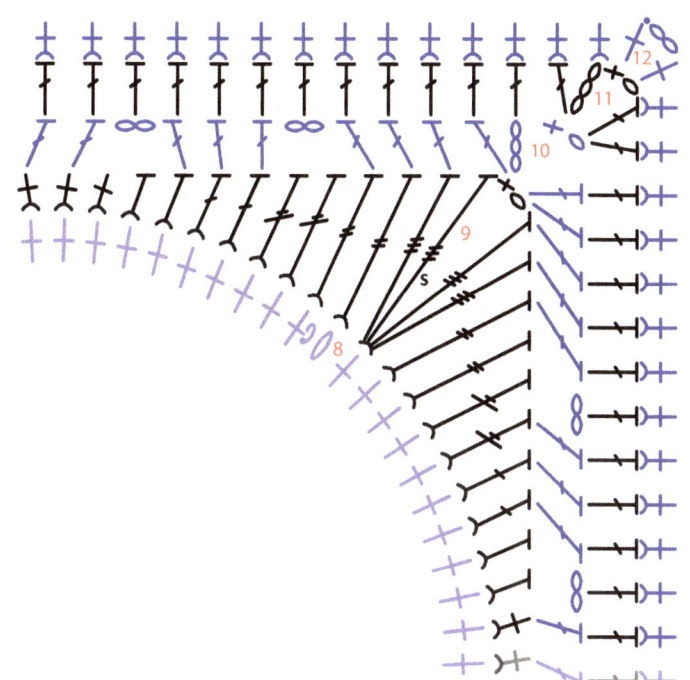

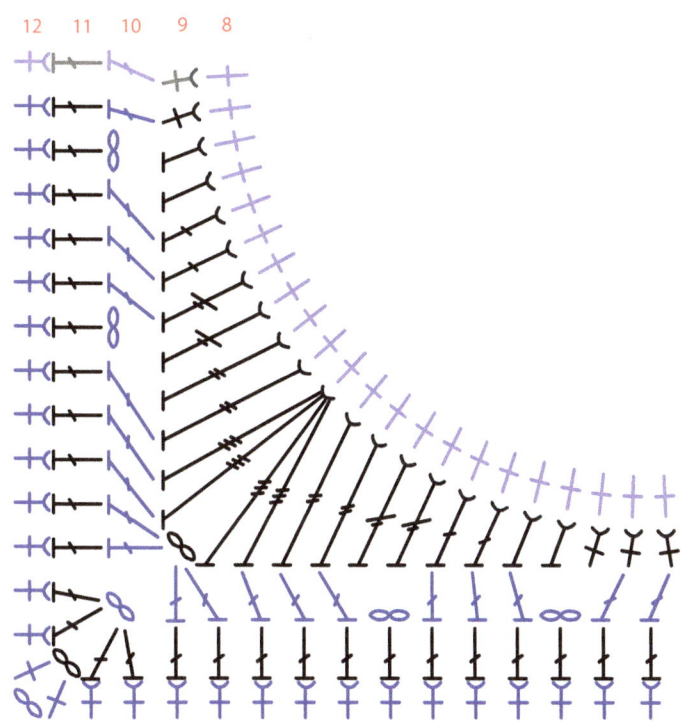

Kim

Kym

MEDIUM PATTERNS • 107

Swirlygig

Here we go round the... granny square. Dance as you twirl.

 83 m / 91 yd

Begin with mc.

R1: ch3 (stch), 11tr, join with ss to 3rd ch of stch. {12 sts}

R2: ch3 (stch), fptr around last st of R1, *tr in next st, fptr around previous st*, rep from * to * 10x, join with ss to 3rd ch of stch. {24 sts}

R3: dc in same st as ss, dc in next 23 sts, join with ss to first st. {24 sts}

R4: ch3 (stch), tr in same st as ss, *tr in next st**, 2tr in next st*, rep from * to * 10x & * to ** 1x, join with ss to 3rd ch of stch. {36 sts}

R5: ch3 (stch), fptr around last st of R4, *tr in next st, fptr around previous st*, rep from * to * 34x, join with ss to 3rd ch of stch. {72 sts}

R6: dc in same st as ss, dc in next 71 sts, join with ss to first st. {72 sts}

R7: ch3 (stch), tr in next 71 sts, join with ss to 3rd ch of stch. {72 sts}

R8: ch3 (stch), tr in next st, fptr around same st as ss, *tr in next 2 sts, fptr around same st as 1st of 2 sts just made*, rep from * to * 34x, join with ss to 3rd ch of stch. {108 sts} Will be ruffled.

R9: dc in same st as ss, *dc2tog over next 2 sts**, dc in next st*, rep from * to * 34x & * to ** 1x, join with ss to first st. {72 sts}

108 • MEDIUM PATTERNS

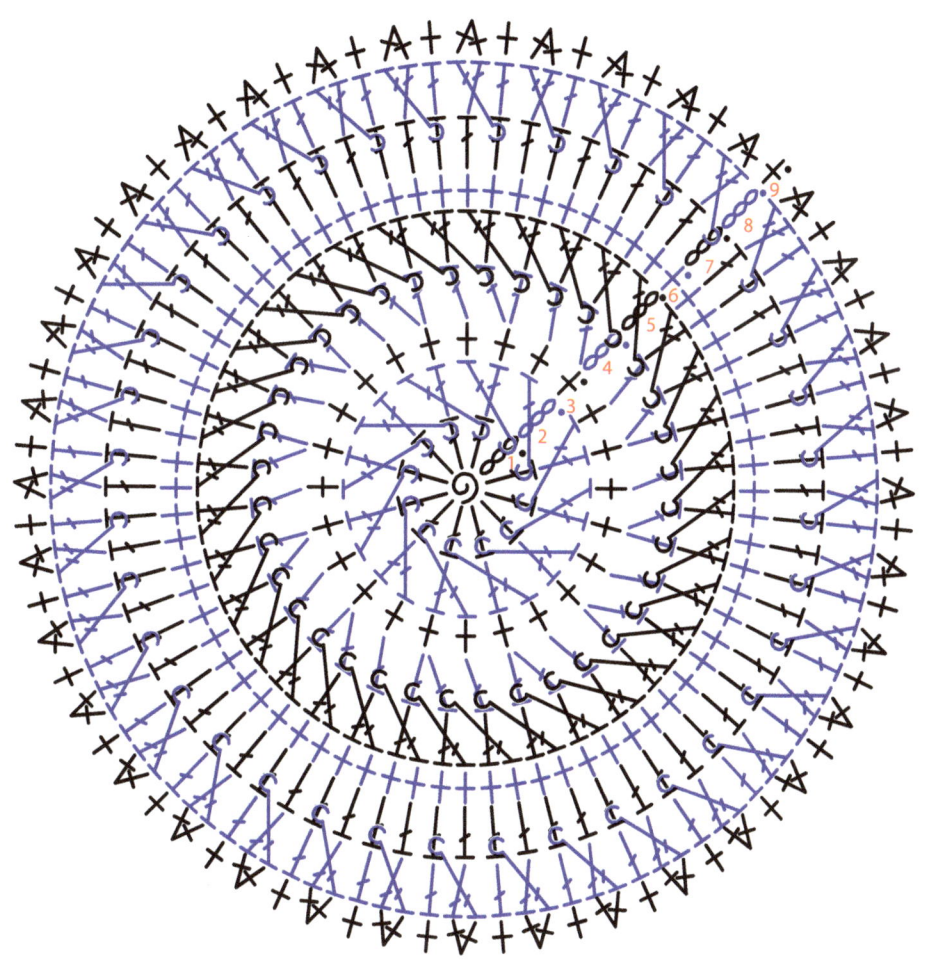

MEDIUM PATTERNS • 109

R10: ch4 (stch), dtr in same st as ss, *hdtr in next 2 sts, tr in next 2 sts, htr in next 2 sts, dc in next 5 sts, htr in next 2 sts, tr in next 2 sts, hdtr in next 2 sts**, (2dtr, ch2, 2dtr) in next st*, rep from * to * 2x & * to ** 1x, 2dtr in same st as first sts, ch1, join with dc to 4th ch of stch. {21 sts on each side; 4 2-ch cnr sps}

R11: dc over joining dc, *dc in next 21 sts**, (dc, ch2, dc) in 2-ch cnr sp*, rep from * to * 2x & * to ** 1x, dc in same st as first st, ch1, join with dc to first st. {23 sts on each side; 4 2-ch cnr sps}

R12: ch3 (stch), tr over joining dc, *tr in next 23 sts**, (2tr, ch2, 2tr) in 2-ch cnr sp*, rep from * to * 2x & * to ** 1x, 2tr in same sp as first sts, ch1, join with dc to 3rd ch of stch. {27 sts on each side; 4 2-ch cnr sps}

R13: ch2 (stch), *13x [fptr around next st, htr in next st], fptr around next st**, (htr, ch2, htr) in 2-ch cnr sp*, rep from * to * 2x & * to ** 1x, htr in same sp as first st, ch1, join with dc to 2nd ch of stch. {29 sts on each side; 4 2-ch cnr sps}

R14: dc over joining dc, *dc in next 29 sts**, (dc, ch2, dc) in 2-ch cnr sp*, rep from * to * 2x & * to ** 1x, dc in same sp as first st, ch2, join with ss to first st. Fasten off. {31 sts on each side; 4 2-ch cnr sps}

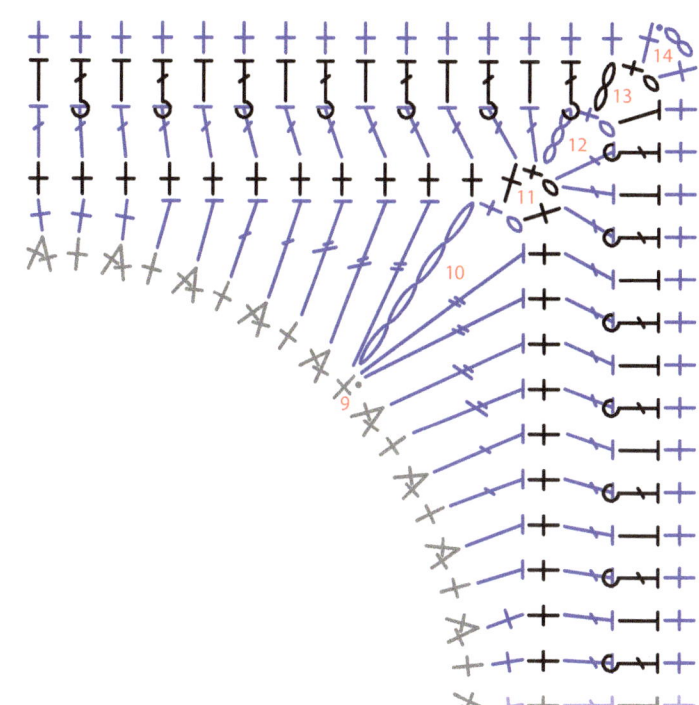

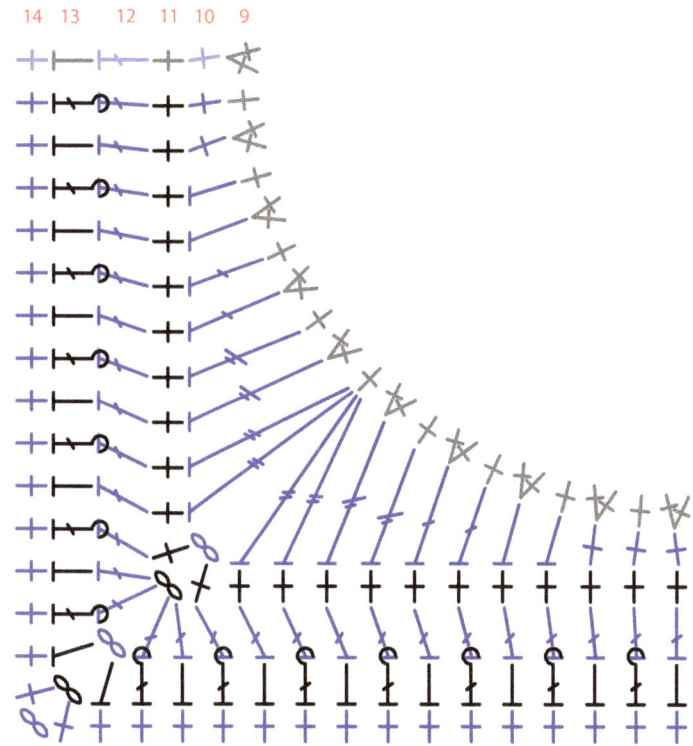

Kim

Kym

MEDIUM PATTERNS • 111

Zinderella

Zig Zags. Zinnia Flowers. Zinderella is a type of Zinnia flower.

 94 m / 102 yd

Begin with mc.

NOTE: if you find the zig zags are pulling your square in, chain 3 instead of 2.

- R1: ch1, 20dc, join with ss to first st. {20 sts}
- R2: ch3 (stch), *tr in blo of next st**, tr in next st*, rep from * to * 8x & * to ** 1x, join with ss to 3rd ch of stch. {20 sts}
- R3: dc in same st as ss, *ch2, ss in flo of next st of R1, ch2, skip 1 st**, dc in next st*, rep from * to * 8x & * to ** 1x, join with ss to first st. {20 sts, 20 2-ch sps}
- R4: bpdc around same st as ss, *2htr in next st of R2, skip (2-ch sp, 1 st & 2-ch sp)**, bpdc around next st*, rep from * to * 8x & * to ** 1x, join with ss to first st. {30 sts}
- R5: dc in same st as ss, dc in next 29 sts, join with ss to first st. {30sts}
- R6: ch3 (stch), *2tr in blo of next st**, tr in next st*, rep from * to * 13x & * to ** 1x, join with ss to 3rd ch of stch. {45 sts}
- R7: dc in same st as ss, *ch2, ss in flo of next st of R5, ch2, skip 2 sts**, dc in next st*, rep from * to * 13x & * to ** 1x, join with ss to first st. {30 sts, 30 2-ch sps}
- R8: bpdc around same st as ss, *htr in next 2 sts of R6, skip (2-ch sp, 1 st & 2-ch sp)**, bpdc around next st*, rep from * to * 13x & * to ** 1x, join with ss to first st. {45 sts}
- R9: 2dc in same st as ss, *dc in next 2 sts**, 2dc in next st*, rep from * to * 13x & * to ** 1x, join with ss to first st. {60 sts}
- R10: ch3 (stch), *tr in blo of next st**, tr in next st*, rep from * to * 28x & * to ** 1x, join with ss to 3rd ch of stch. {60 sts}
- R11: dc in same st as ss, *ch2, ss in flo of next st of R9, ch2, skip 1 st**, dc in next st*, rep from * to * 28x & * to ** 1x, join with ss to first st. {60 sts, 60 2-ch sps}

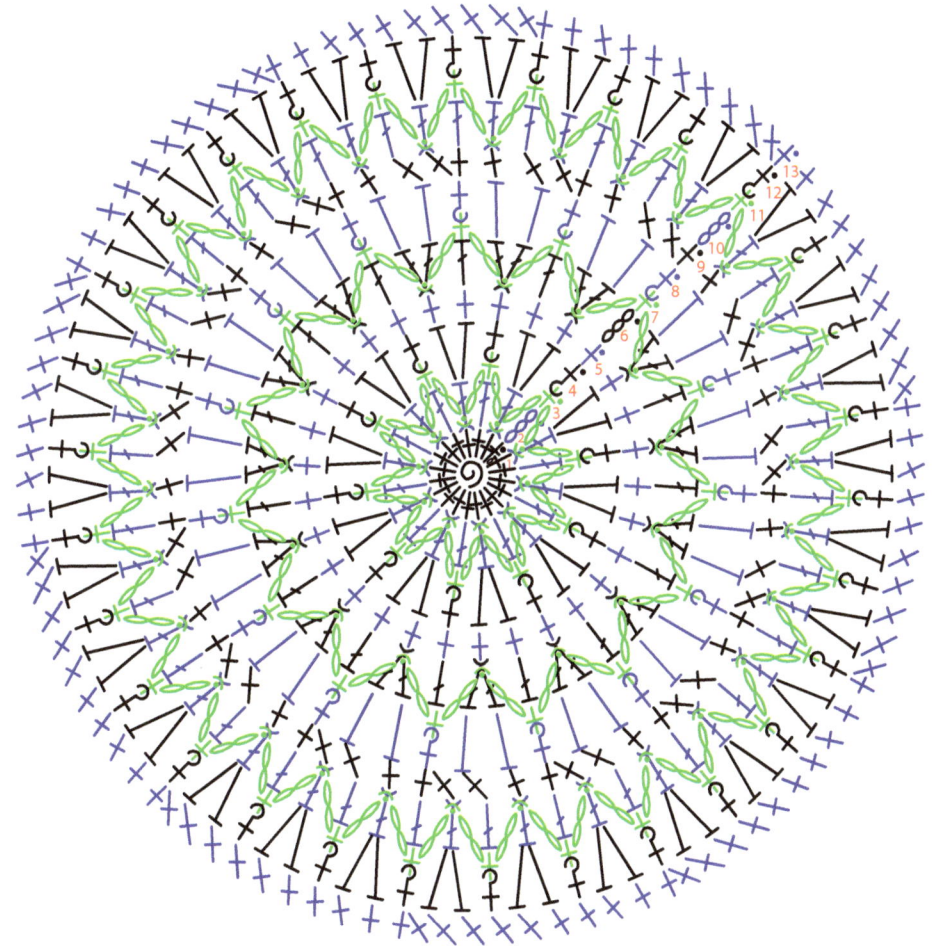

R12: bpdc around same st as ss, *2htr in next st of R10, skip (2-ch sp, 1 st & 2-ch sp)**, bpdc around next st*, rep from * to * 28x & * to ** 1x, join with ss to first st. {90 sts}

R13: 2dc in same st as ss, *dc in next 8 sts**, 2dc in next st*, rep from * to * 8x & * to ** 1x, join with ss to first st. {100 sts}

MEDIUM PATTERNS • 113

R14: ch4 (stch), *hdtr in next 2 sts, tr in next 2 sts, htr in next 2 sts, dc in next 5 sts, dc2tog over next 2 sts, dc in next 5 sts, htr in next 2 sts, tr in next 2 sts, hdtr in next 2 sts**, (dtr, ch2, dtr) in next st*, rep from * to * 2x & * to ** 1x, dtr in same st as first st, ch1, join with dc to 4th ch of stch. {25 sts on each side; 4 2-ch cnr sps}

R15: ch3 (stch), *tr in blo of next st, tr in next st, 3x [htr in blo of next st, htr in next st], 4x [dc in blo of next st, dc in next st], dc in blo of next st, 3x [htr in next st, htr in blo of next st], tr in next st, tr in blo of next st**, (tr, ch2, tr) in 2-ch cnr sp*, rep from * to * 2x & * to ** 1x, tr in same sp as first st, ch1, join with dc to 3rd ch of stch. {27 sts on each side; 4 2-ch cnr sps}

R16: dc over joining dc, *13x [dc in next st, ch2, ss in flo of next st of R14, ch2, skip 1 st], dc in next st**, (dc, ch2, dc) in 2-ch cnr sp*, rep from * to * 2x & * to ** 1x, dc in same sp as first st, ch1, join with dc to first st. {29 sts, 26 2-ch sps on each side; 4 2-ch cnr sps}

R17: dc over joining dc, *dc in next 2 sts, 12x [htr in next st of R15, skip (2-ch sp, 1 st & 2-ch sp), bpdc around next st], htr in next st of R15, skip (2-ch sp, 1 st & 2-ch sp), dc in next 2 sts**, (dc, ch2, dc) in 2-ch cnr sp*, rep from * to * 2x & * to ** 1x, dc in same sp as first st, ch1, join with dc to first st. {31 sts on each side; 4 2-ch cnr sps}

R18: turn, ch2 (stch), *htr in next 30 sts, skip 1 st**, (htr, ch2, htr) in 2-ch cnr sp*, rep from * to * 2x & * to ** 1x, htr in same sp as first st, ch1, join with dc to 2nd ch of stch. {32 sts on each side; 4 2-ch cnr sps}

R19: turn, dc over 1-ch, *dc in next 32 sts**, (dc, ch2, dc) in 2-ch cnr sp*, rep from * to * 2x & * to ** 1x, dc in same sp as first st, ch2, join with ss to first st. Fasten off. {34 sts on each side; 4 2-ch cnr sps}

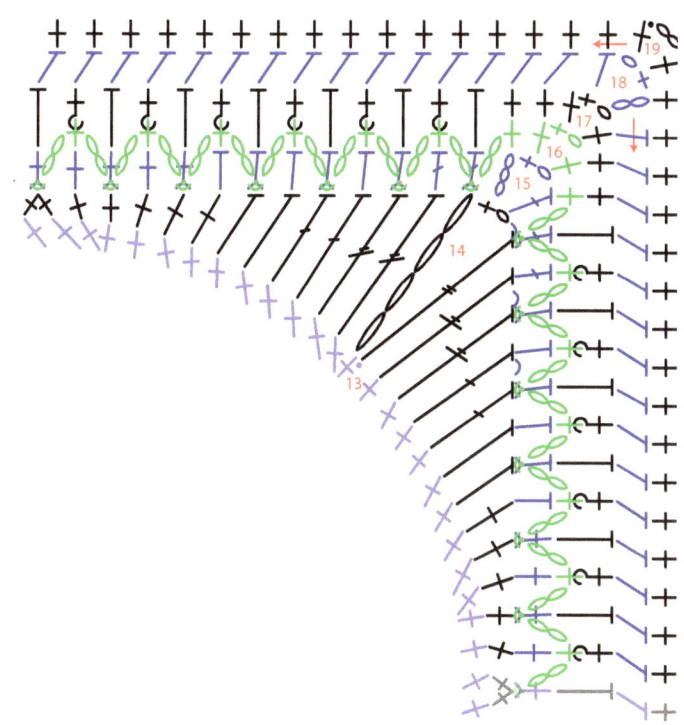

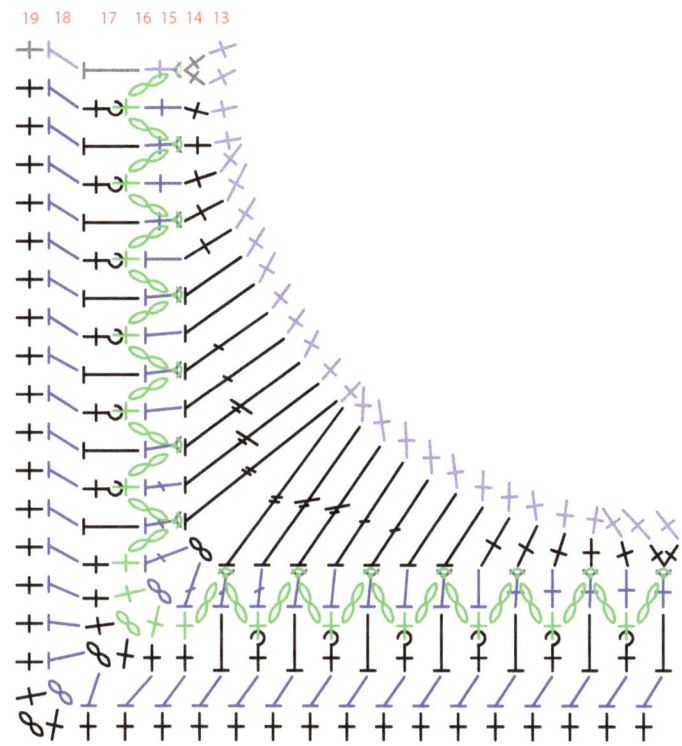

Kim

Kym

MEDIUM PATTERNS • 115

Large

78
Pg 118

Big Octamerous
Pg 134

Camarilla
Pg 150

Cambric
Pg 138

Empyreal
Pg 122

Grande Lavallière
Pg 142

Picquant
Pg 126

Serry
Pg 146

Stellate Stratified
Pg 154

Sunbeams
Pg 130

Here's a guide to the expected finished size of the squares made with different yarn weights and hook sizes. The amount of yarn listed on each pattern page is based on using the medium weight yarn and corresponding hook size. The amount of yarn needed for the other yarn weights is listed on page 200.

Hook	3.5 mm hook	4.5 mm hook	5.5 mm hook
Yarn	4 ply/sock/fingering	8 ply/DK/light worsted	10 ply/aran/worsted
Size	10"	12"	14"

LARGE PATTERNS

78

Before the days of 45s and 33⅓s came 78s with old timey tunes.

 193 m / 211 yd

Begin with mc.

R1: ch3 (stch), 11tr, join with ss to 3rd ch of stch. {12 sts}

R2: ch3 (stch), fptr around same st as ss, *(tr in, bptr around) next st**, (tr in, fptr around) next st*, rep from * to * 4x & * to ** 1x, join with ss to 3rd ch of stch. {24 sts}

R3: ch3 (stch), fptr around same st as ss, fptr around next st, *(tr in, bptr around) next st, bptr around next st**, (tr in, fptr around) next st, fptr around next st*, rep from * to * 4x & * to ** 1x, join with ss to 3rd ch of stch. {36 sts}

R4: ch3 (stch), fptr around same st as ss, fptr around next 2 sts, *(tr in, bptr around) next st, bptr around next 2 sts**, (tr in, fptr around) next st, fptr around next 2 sts*, rep from * to * 4x & * to ** 1x, join with ss to 3rd ch of stch. {48 sts}

R5: ch3 (stch), fptr around same st as ss, fptr around next 3 sts, *(tr in, bptr around) next st, bptr around next 3 sts**, (tr in, fptr around) next st, fptr around next 3 sts*, rep from * to * 4x & * to ** 1x, join with ss to 3rd ch of stch. {60 sts}

R6: fptr around same st as ss, fptr around next 4 sts, *bptr around next 5 sts**, fptr around next 5 sts*, rep from * to * 4x & * to ** 1x, join with ss to first st. {60 sts}

R7: ch3 (stch), fptr around same st as ss, fptr around next 4 sts, *(tr in, bptr around) next st, bptr around next 4 sts**, (tr in, fptr around) next st, fptr around next 4 sts*, rep from * to * 4x & * to ** 1x, join with ss to 3rd ch of stch. {72 sts}

R8: fptr around same st as ss, fptr around next 5 sts, *bptr around next 6 sts**, fptr around next 6 sts*, rep from * to * 4x & * to ** 1x, join with ss to first st. {72 sts}

R9: ch3 (stch), fptr around same st as ss, fptr around next 5 sts, *(tr in, bptr around) next st, bptr around next 5 sts**, (tr in, fptr around) next st, fptr around next 5 sts*, rep from * to * 4x & * to ** 1x, join with ss to 3rd ch of stch. {84 sts}

R10: fptr around same st as ss, fptr around next 6 sts, *bptr around next 7 sts**, fptr around next 7 sts*, rep from * to * 4x & * to ** 1x, join with ss to first st. {84 sts}

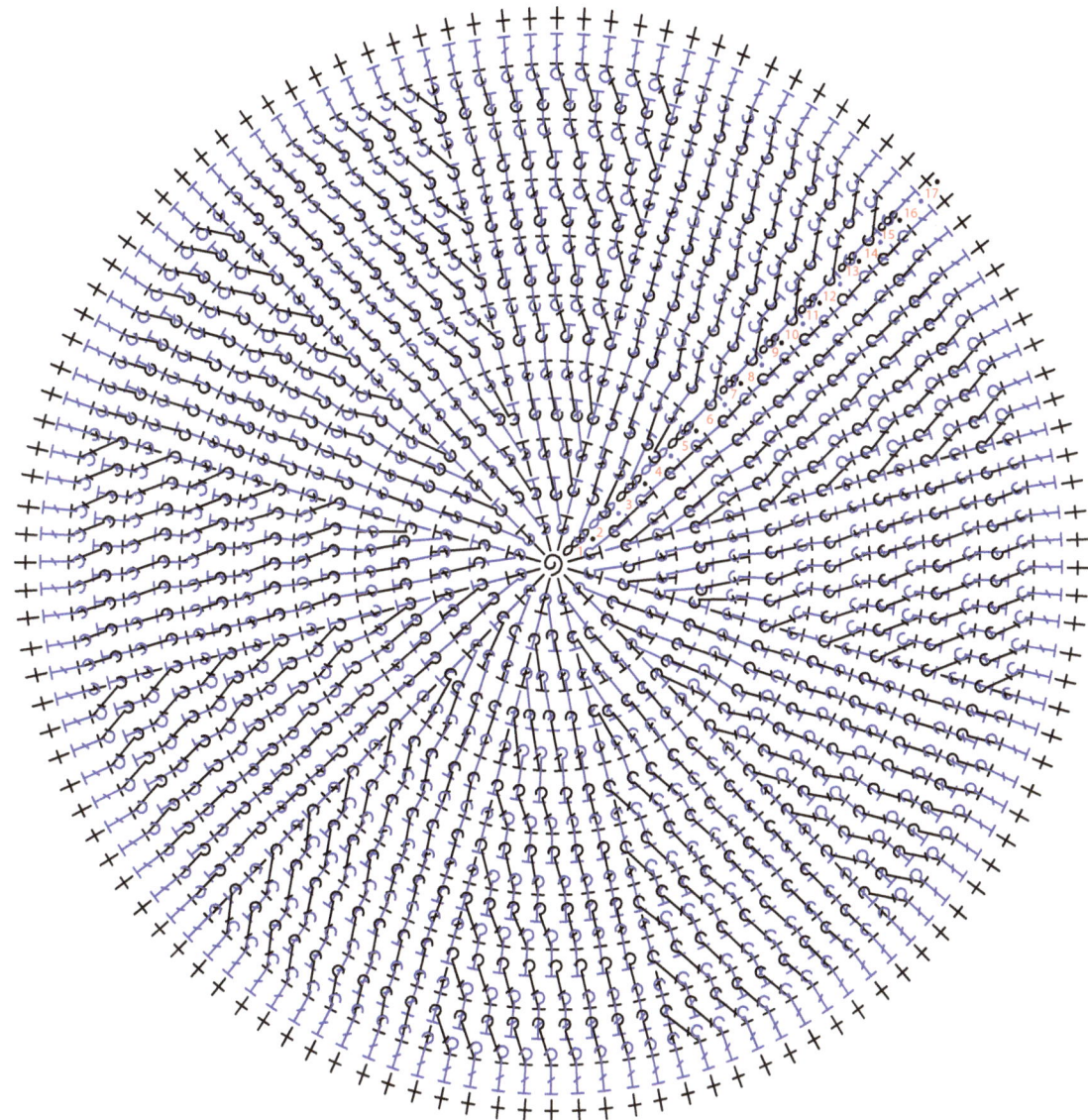

R11: ch3 (stch), fptr around same st as ss, fptr around next 6 sts, *(tr in, bptr around) next st, bptr around next 6 sts**, (tr in, fptr around) next st, fptr around next 6 sts*, rep from * to * 4x & * to ** 1x, join with ss to 3rd ch of stch. {96 sts}

R12: fptr around same st as ss, fptr around next 7 sts, *bptr around next 8 sts**, fptr around next 8 sts*, rep from * to * 4x & * to ** 1x, join with ss to first st. {96 sts}

R13: ch3 (stch), fptr around same st as ss, fptr around next 7 sts, *(tr in, bptr around) next st, bptr around next 7 sts**, (tr in, fptr around) next st, fptr around next 7 sts*, rep from * to * 4x & * to ** 1x, join with ss to 3rd ch of stch. {108 sts}

R14: fptr around same st as ss, fptr around next 8 sts, *bptr around next 9 sts**, fptr around next 9 sts*, rep from * to * 4x & * to ** 1x, join with ss to first st. {108 sts}

R15: ch3 (stch), fptr around same st as ss, fptr around next 8 sts, *(tr in, bptr around) next st, bptr around next 8 sts**, (tr in, fptr around) next st, fptr around next 8 sts*, rep from * to * 4x & * to ** 1x, join with ss to 3rd ch of stch. {120 sts}

R16: fptr around same st as ss, fptr around next 9 sts, *bptr around next 10 sts**, fptr around next 10 sts*, rep from * to * 4x & * to ** 1x, join with ss to first st. {120 sts}

LARGE PATTERNS

R17: dc in same st as ss, dc in next 119 sts, join with ss to first st. {120 sts}

R18: ch5 (stch), 2dtr in same st as ss, *hdtr in next 2 sts, tr in next 3 sts, htr in next 4 sts, dc in next 11 sts, htr in next 4 sts, tr in next 3 sts, hdtr in next 2 sts**, (2dtr, trtr, 2dtr) in next st*, rep from * to * 2x & * to ** 1x, 2dtr in same st as first sts, join with ss to 5th ch of stch. {29 sts on each side; 4 5-st cnrs}

R19: dc in same st as ss, *dc in next 33 sts**, (dc, ch2, dc) in next st*, rep from * to * 2x & * to ** 1x, dc in same st as first st, ch1, join with dc to first st. {35 sts on each side; 4 2-ch cnr sps}

R20: ch3 (stch), 2tr over joining dc, *tr in next 2 sts, htr in next 6 sts, dc in next 19 sts, htr in next 6 sts, tr in next 2 sts**, (2tr, hdtr, 2tr) in 2-ch cnr sp*, rep from * to * 2x & * to ** 1x, 2tr in same sp as first sts, join with ss to 3rd ch of stch. {35 sts on each side; 4 5-st cnrs}

R21: dc in same st as ss, *dc in next 39 sts**, (dc, ch2, dc) in next st*, rep from * to * 2x & * to ** 1x, dc in same st as first st, ch1, join with dc to first st. {41 sts on each side; 4 2-ch cnr sps}

R22: ch3 (stch), htr over joining dc, *htr in next 41 sts**, (htr, tr, htr) in 2-ch cnr sp*, rep from * to * 2x & * to ** 1x, htr in same sp as first sts, join with ss to 3rd ch of stch. {41 sts on each side; 4 3-st cnrs}

R23: dc in same st as ss, *dc in next 43 sts**, (dc, ch2, dc) in next st*, rep from * to * 2x & * to ** 1x, dc in same st as first st, ch2, join with ss to first st. Fasten off. {45 sts on each side; 4 2-ch cnr sps}

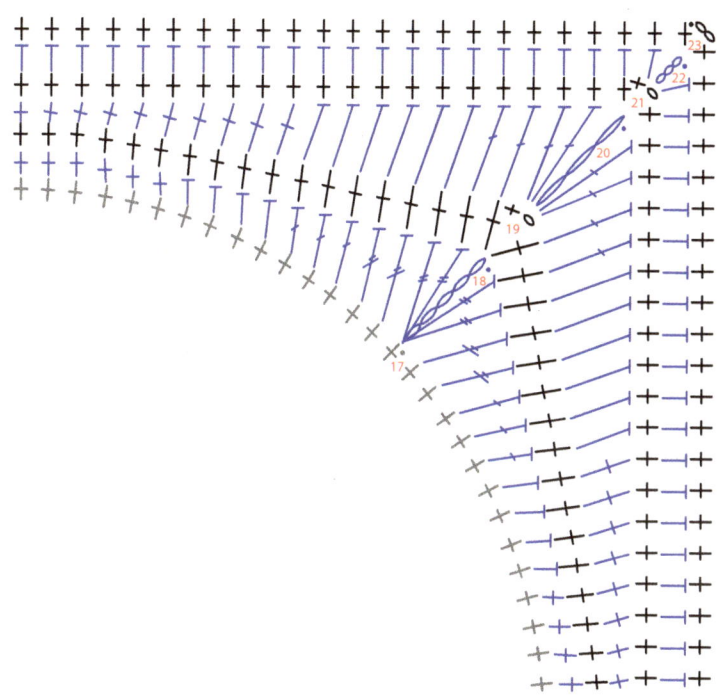

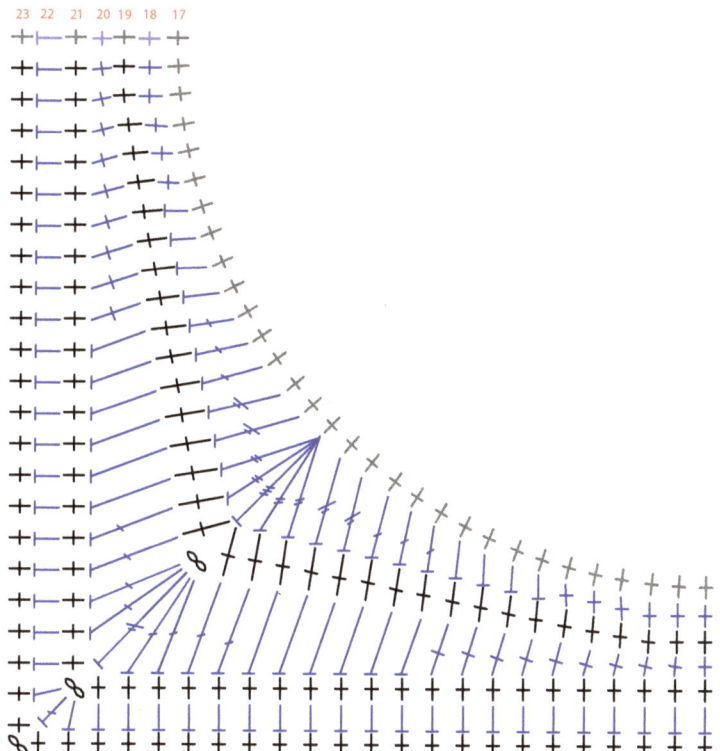

Kim

Kym

LARGE PATTERNS

Empyreal

Empyreal - related to highest heaven in the celestial sky.

 124 m / 136 yd

Begin with mc.

R1: ch2 (stch), 15htr, join with ss to 2nd ch of stch. {16 sts} [WS]

R2: turn, ch3 (stch), *ch1, tr in blo of next st, ch1**, tr in next st*, rep from * to * 6x & * to ** 1x, join with ss to 3rd ch of stch. {16 sts, 16 1-ch sps} [RS] from here on.

R3: dc in same st as ss, *dc in 1-ch sp**, dc in next st*, rep from * to * 14x & * to ** 1x, join with ss to first st. {32 sts}

R4: ch3 (stch), *ch2, dc in blo of next st, ch2**, tr in next st*, rep from * to * 14x & * to ** 1x, join with ss to 3rd ch of stch. {32 sts, 32 2-ch sps}

R5: dc in same st as ss, *ch3, skip (2-ch sp, 1 st & 2-ch sp)**, dc in next st*, rep from * to * 14x & * to ** 1x, join with ss to first st. {16 sts, 16 3-ch sps}

R6: dc in same st as ss, *3dc in 3-ch sp**, dc in next st*, rep from * to * 14x & * to ** 1x, join with ss to first st. {64 sts}

R7: ch3 (stch), *ch2, dc in blo of next st, ch2**, tr in next st*, rep from * to * 30x & * to ** 1x, join with ss to 3rd ch of stch. {64 sts, 64 2-ch sps}

R8: dc in same st as ss, *ch2, skip (2-ch sp, 1 st & 2-ch sp)**, dc in next st*, rep from * to * 30x & * to ** 1x, join with ss to first st. {32 sts, 32 2-ch sps}

R9: dc in same st as ss, *2dc in 2-ch sp**, dc in next st*, rep from * to * 30x & * to ** 1x, join with ss to first st. {96 sts}

R10: ch3 (stch), *ch2, dc in blo of next 2 sts, ch2**, tr in next st*, rep from * to * 30x & * to ** 1x, join with ss to 3rd ch of stch. {96 sts, 64 2-ch sps}

R11: dc in same st as ss, *ch3, skip (2-ch sp, 2 sts & 2-ch sp)**, dc in next st*, rep from * to * 30x & * to ** 1x, join with ss to first st. {32 sts, 32 3-ch sps}

R12: dc in same st as ss, *3dc in 3-ch sp**, dc in next st*, rep from * to * 30x & * to ** 1x, join with ss to first st. {128 sts}

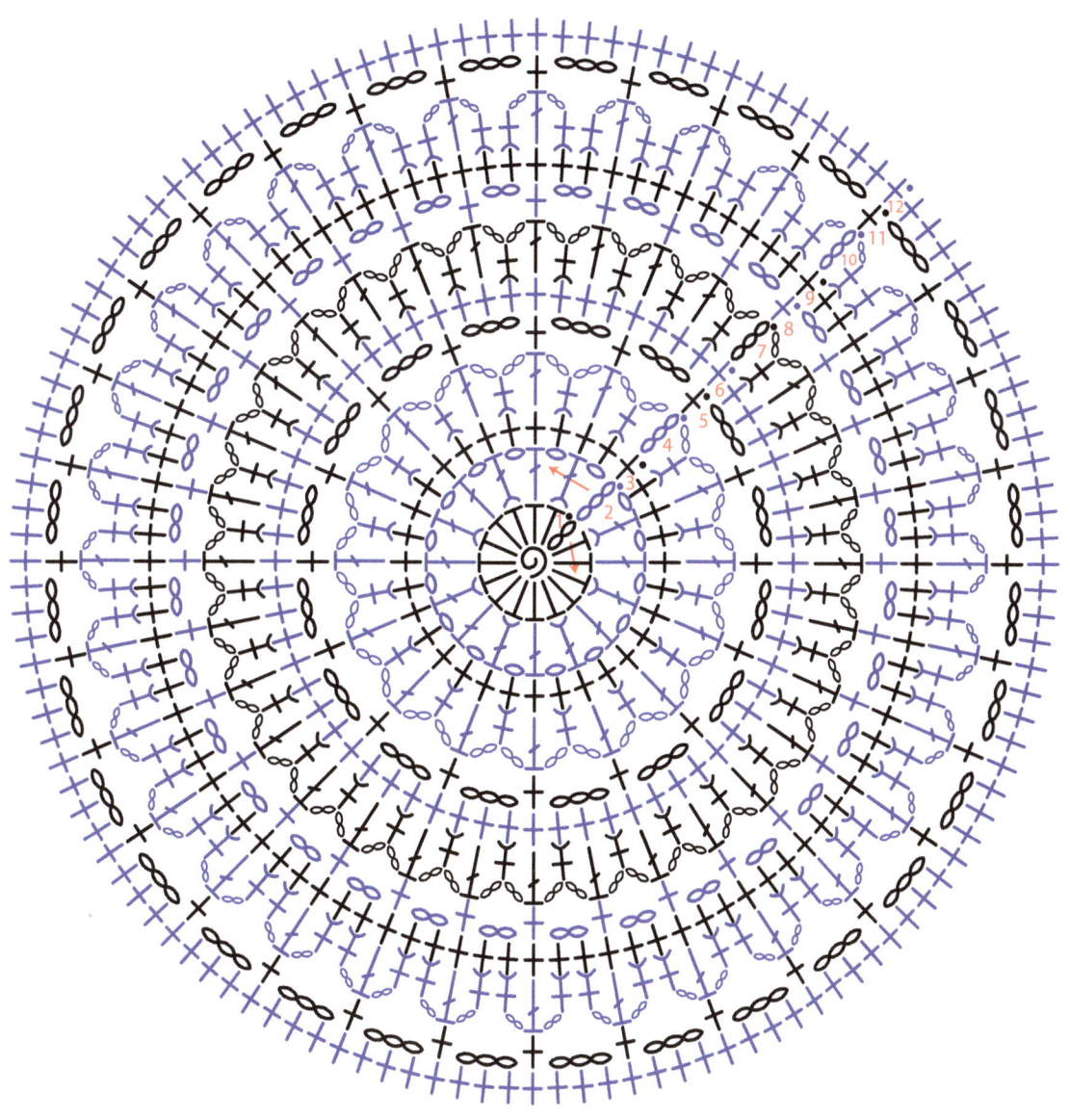

LARGE PATTERNS • 123

R13: ch4 (stch), dtr in same st as ss, *hdtr in blo of next st, hdtr in next st, tr in blo of next st, tr in next st, htr in blo of next st, htr in next st, 9x [dc in blo of next st, dc in next st], dc in blo of next st, htr in next st, htr in blo of next st, tr in next st, tr in blo of next st, hdtr in next st, hdtr in blo of next st**, (2dtr, ch2, 2dtr) in next st*, rep from * to * 2x & * to ** 1x, 2dtr in same st as first sts, ch1, join with dc to 4th ch of stch. {35 sts on each side; 4 2-ch cnr sps}

R14: ch3 (stch), *11x [ch2, dc in blo of next 2 sts, ch2, tr in next st], ch2, dc in blo of next 2 sts, ch2**, tr in 2-ch cnr sp*, rep from * to * 2x & * to ** 1x, join with ss to 3rd ch of stch. {35 sts, 24 2-ch sps on each side; 4 1-st cnrs}

R15: dc in same st as ss, *11x [ch2, skip (2-ch sp, 2 sts & 2-ch sp), dc in next st], ch2, skip (2-ch sp, 2 sts & 2-ch sp)**, (dc, ch2, dc) in next st*, rep from * to * 2x & * to ** 1x, dc in same st as first st, ch1, join with dc to first st. {13 sts, 12 2-ch sps on each side; 4 2-ch cnr sps}

R16: dc over joining dc, *12x [dc in next st, 2dc in 2-ch sp], dc in next st**, (dc, ch2, dc) in 2-ch cnr sp*, rep from * to * 2x & * to ** 1x, dc in same st as first st, ch1, join with dc to first st. {39 sts on each side; 4 2-ch cnr sps}

R17: ch3 (stch), *2x [tr in blo of next st, tr in next st], 2x [htr in blo of next st, htr in next st], 11x [dc in blo of next st, dc in next st], dc in blo of next st, 2x [htr in next st, htr in blo of next st], 2x [tr in next st, tr in blo of next st]**, (tr, ch2, tr) in 2-ch cnr sp*, rep from * to * 2x & * to ** 1x, tr in same sp as first st, ch1, join with dc to 3rd ch of stch. {41 sts on each side; 4 2-ch cnr sps}

R18: ch2 (stch), *20x [htr in blo of next st, htr in next st], htr in blo of next st**, (htr, ch2, htr) in 2-ch cnr sp*, rep from * to * 2x & * to ** 1x, htr in same sp as first st, ch1, join with dc to 2nd ch of stch. {43 sts on each side; 4 2-ch cnr sps}

R19: dc over joining dc, *21x [dc in blo of next st, dc in next st], dc in blo of next st**, (dc, ch2, dc) in 2-ch cnr sp*, rep from * to * 2x & * to ** 1x, dc in same sp as first st, ch2, join with ss to first st. Fasten off. {45 sts on each side; 4 2-ch cnr sps}

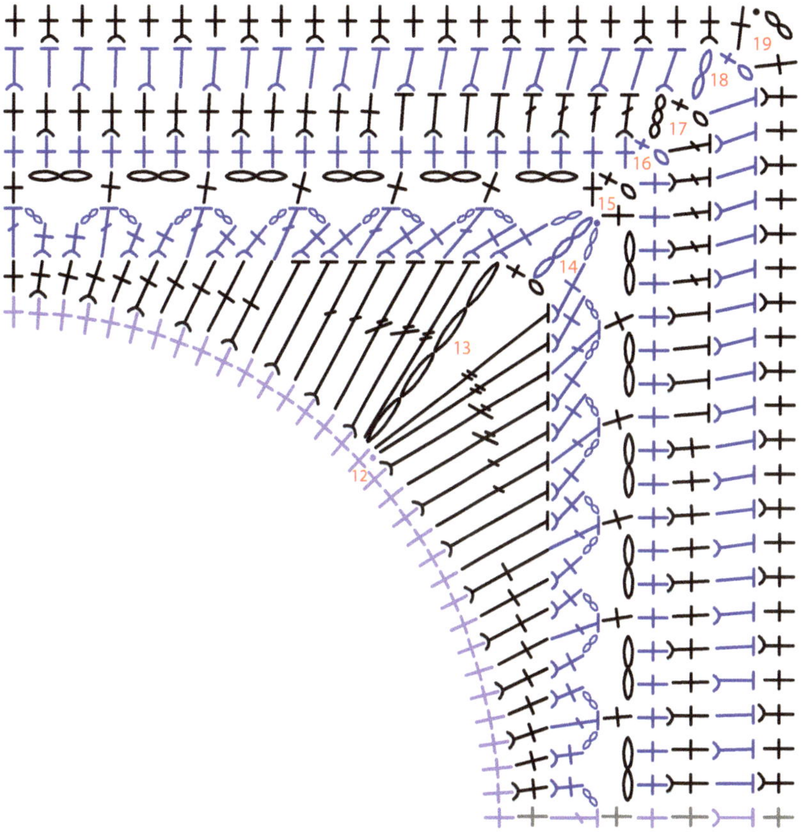

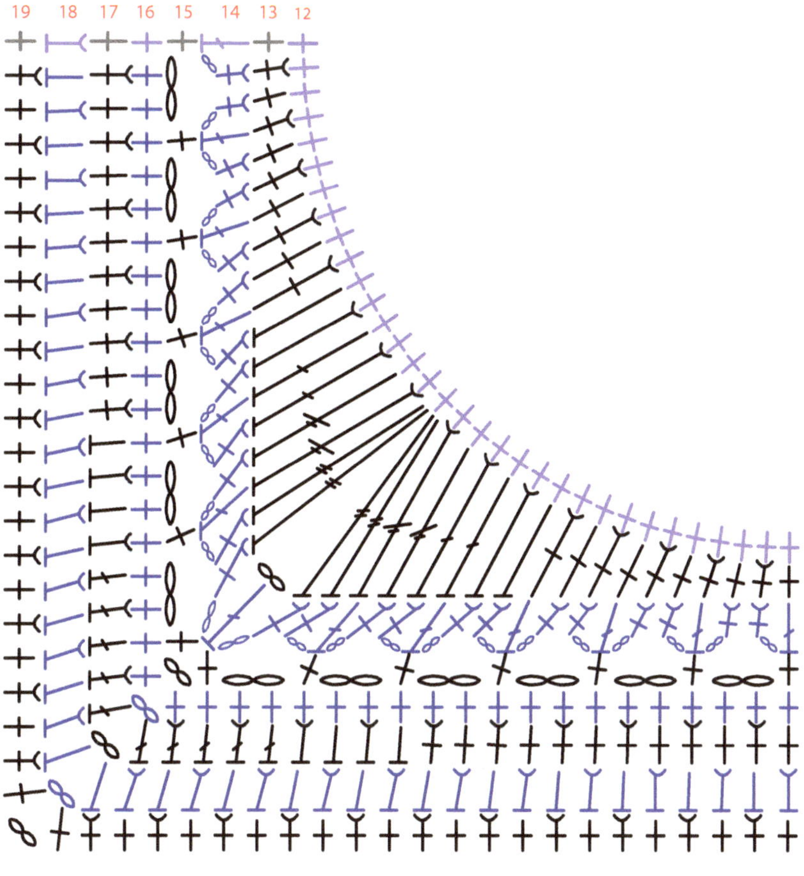

Kim

Kym

LARGE PATTERNS • 125

Picquant

Picots? No, they are not, though they look like them. So the name is not picots, but Picquant.

 131 m / 144 yd

Begin with mc.

R1: ch3 (stch), 2tr, *ch3**, 3tr*, rep from * to * 6x & * to ** 1x, join with ss to 3rd ch of stch. {24 sts, 8 3-ch sps}

R2: dc in same st as ss, dc in next 2 sts, *skip 3-ch sp**, dc in next 3 sts*, rep from * to * 6x & * to ** 1x, join with ss to first st. {24 sts} Pull 3-ch sps to front.

R3: ch3 (stch), tr in same st as ss, *(tr, ch3, tr) in next st, 2tr in next st, ch3**, 2tr in next st*, rep from * to * 6x & * to ** 1x, join with ss to 3rd ch of stch. {48 sts, 16 3-ch sps}

R4: dc in same st as ss, dc in next 2 sts, *skip 3-ch sp**, dc in next 3 sts*, rep from * to * 14x & * to ** 1x, join with ss to first st. {48 sts} Pull 3-ch sps to front.

R5: ch3 (stch), *(tr, ch3, tr) in next st, tr in next st, ch3**, tr in next st*, rep from * to * 14x & * to ** 1x, join with ss to 3rd ch of stch. {64 sts, 32 3-ch sps}

R6: dc in same sp as ss, dc in next st, *skip 3-ch sp**, dc in next 2 sts*, rep from * to * 30x & * to ** 1x, join with ss to first st. {64 sts} Pull 3-ch sps to front.

R7: dc in same st as ss, dc in next 63 sts, join with ss to first st. {64 sts}

R8: ch2 (stch), htr in next 63 sts, join with ss to 2nd ch of stch. {64 sts}

R9: dc in same st as ss, *dc in blo of next st**, dc in next st*, rep from * to * 30x & * to ** 1x, join with ss to first st. {64 sts}

R10: ch3 (stch), *2tr in next st**, tr in next st*, rep from * to * 30x & * to ** 1x, join with ss to 3rd ch of stch. {96 sts}

R11: dc in same st, *dc in blo of next 2 sts**, dc in next st*, rep from * to * 30x & * to ** 1x, join with ss to first st. {96 sts}

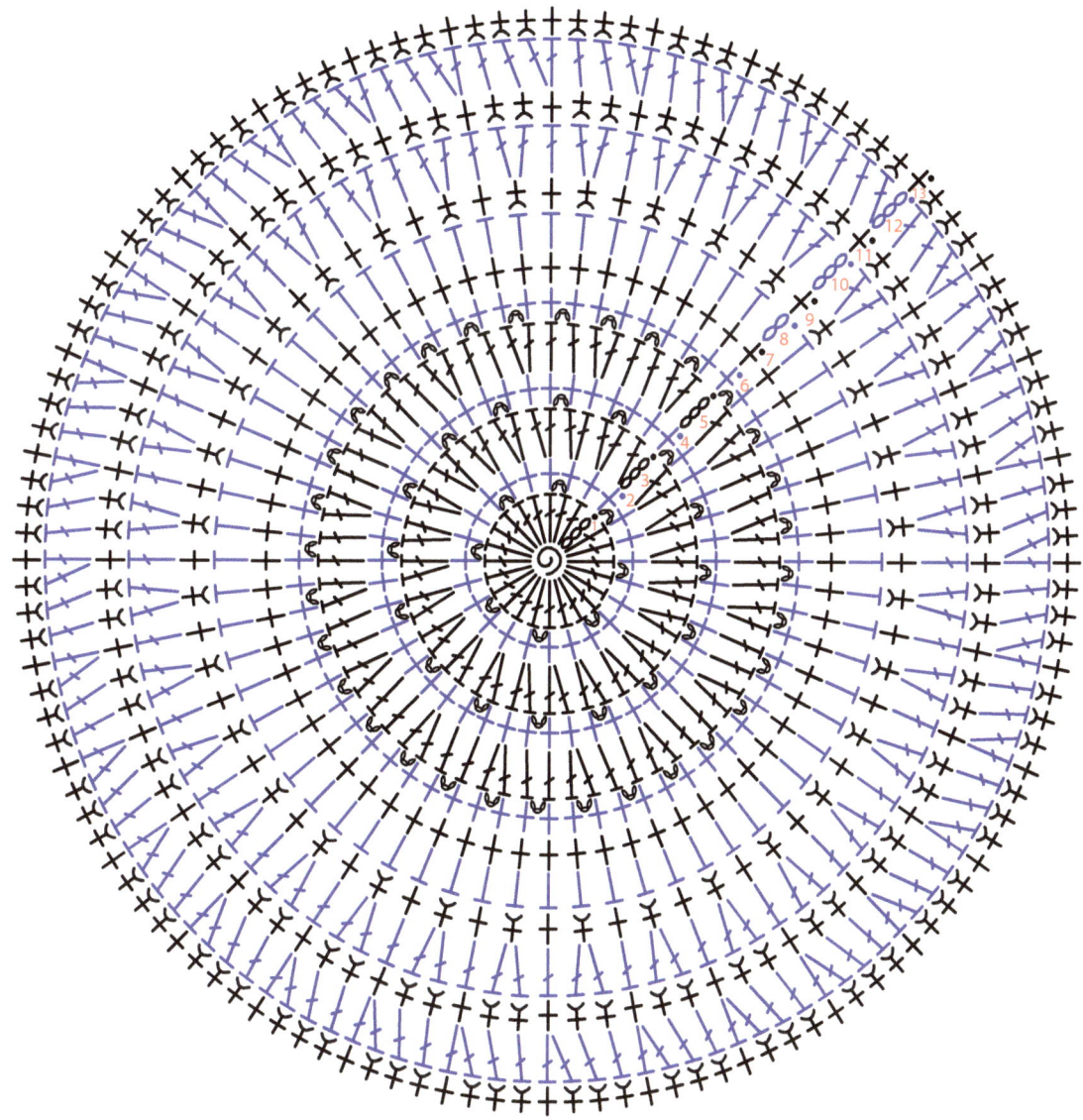

R12: ch3 (stch), tr in same st as ss, *tr in next 2 sts**, 2tr in next st*, rep from * to * 30x & * to ** 1x, join with ss to 3rd ch of stch. {128 sts}

R13: dc in same st as ss, *dc in blo of next 3 sts**, dc in next st*, rep from * to * 30x & * to ** 1x, join with ss to first st. {128 sts}

LARGE PATTERNS • 127

R14: ch5 (stch), trtr in same st as ss, *dtr in next 2 sts, hdtr in next 2 sts, tr in next 2 sts, htr in next 2 sts, dc in next 15 sts, htr in next 2 sts, tr in next 2 sts, hdtr in next 2 sts, dtr in next 2 sts**, (2trtr, ch2, 2trtr) in next st*, rep from * to * 2x & * to ** 1x, 2trtr in same st as first sts, ch1, join with dc to 5th ch of stch. {35 sts on each side; 4 2-ch cnr sps}

R15: ch3 (stch), *tr in next st, 3x [ch3, tr in next 3 sts], 5x [ch3, htr in next 3 sts], 3x [ch3, tr in next 3 sts], ch3, tr in next st**, (tr, ch2, tr) in 2-ch cnr sp*, rep from * to * 2x & * to ** 1x, tr in same sp as first st, ch1, join with dc to 3rd ch of stch. {37 sts, 12 3-ch sps on each side; 4 2-ch cnr sps}

R16: dc over joining dc, *dc in next 2 sts, 11x [skip 3-ch sp, dc in next 3 sts], skip 3-ch sp, dc in next 2 sts**, (dc, ch2, dc) in 2-ch cnr sp*, rep from * to * 2x & * to ** 1x, dc in same sp as first st, ch1, join with dc to first st. {39 sts on each side; 4 2-ch cnr sps} Pull 3-ch sps to front.

R17: dc over joining dc, *19x [dc in blo of next st, dc in next st], dc in blo of next st**, (dc, ch2, dc) in 2-ch cnr sp*, rep from * to * 2x & * to ** 1x, dc in same sp as first st, ch1, join with dc to first st. {41 sts on each side; 4 2-ch cnr sps}

R18: dc over joining dc, *dc in next 41 sts**, (dc, ch2, dc) in 2-ch cnr sp*, rep from * to * 2x & * to ** 1x, dc in same sp as first st, ch2, join with ss to first st. Fasten off. {43 sts on each side; 4 2-ch cnr sps}

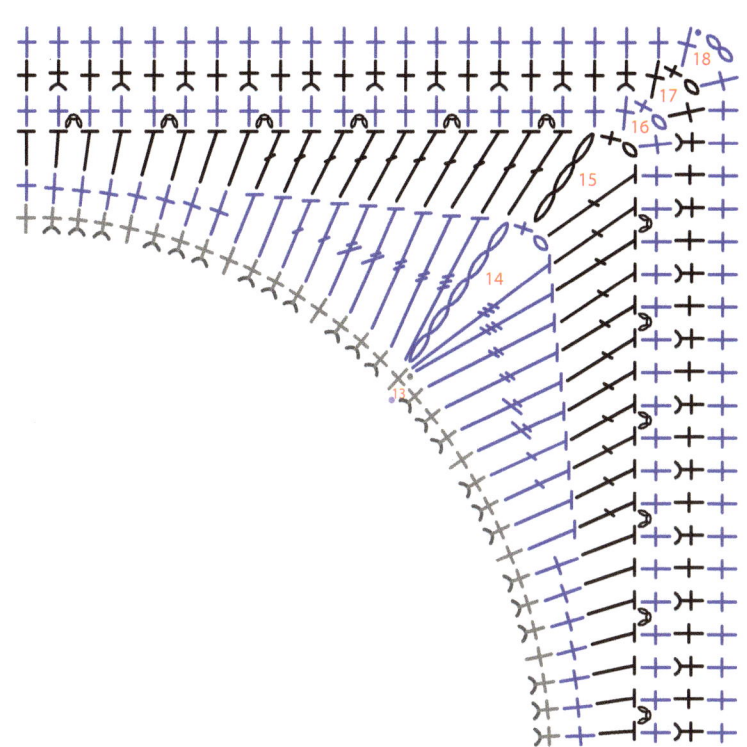

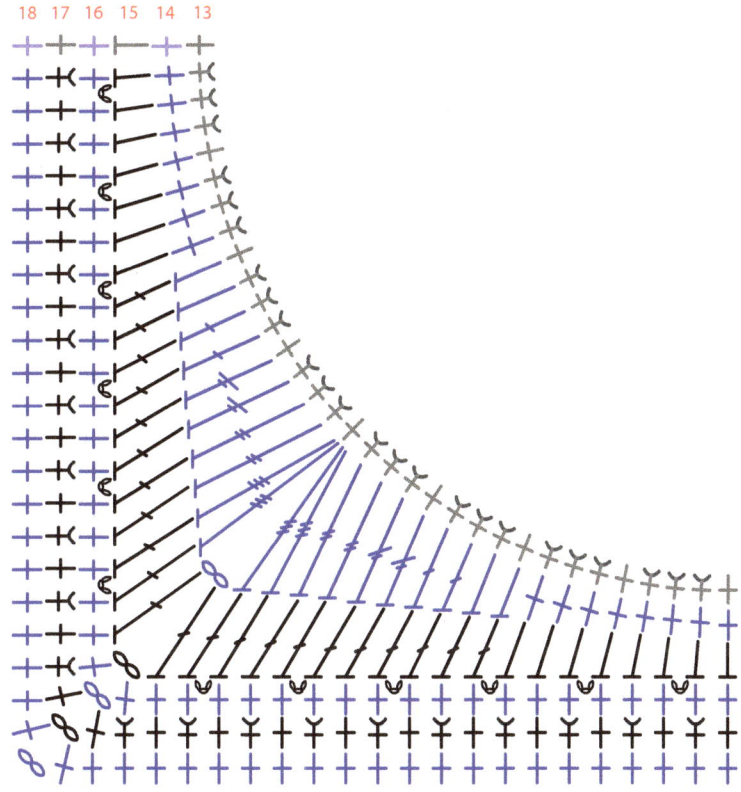

Kim

LARGE PATTERNS • 129

Sunbeams

Let the sunbeams shine down on you.

 141 m / 154 yd

Begin with mc.

R1: ch3 (stch), 15tr, join with ss to 3rd ch of stch. {16 sts}

R2: ch3 (stch), *ch1, 3trcl in next st, ch1**, tr in next st*, rep from * to * 6x & * to ** 1x, join with ss to 3rd ch of stch. {16 sts, 16 1-ch sps}

R3: ch3 (stch), *tr in 1-ch sp, ch2, skip 1 st, tr in 1-ch sp**, tr in next st*, rep from * to * 6x & * to ** 1x, join with ss to 3rd ch of stch. {24 sts, 8 2-ch sps}

R4: dc in same st as ss, dc in next st, *dc in 2-ch sp, fphdtr around R2 cl below, dc in same 2-ch sp**, dc in next 3 sts*, rep from * to * 6x & * to ** 1x, dc in next st, join with ss to first st. {48 sts}

R5: ch3 (stch), tr in next 47 sts, join with ss to 3rd ch of stch. {48 sts}

R6: ch3 (stch), *ch1, 3trcl in next st, ch1**, tr in next 2 sts*, rep from * to * 14x & * to ** 1x, tr in next st, join with ss to 3rd ch of stch. {48 sts, 32 1-ch sps}

R7: ch3 (stch), *tr in 1-ch sp, skip 1 st, tr in 1-ch sp**, tr in next 2 sts*, rep from * to * 14x & * to ** 1x, tr in next st, join with ss to 3rd ch of stch. {64 sts}

R8: dc in same st as ss, dc in next st, *fphdtr around R6 cl below**, dc in next 4 sts*, rep from * to * 14x & * to ** 1x, dc in next 2 sts, join with ss to first st. {80 sts}

R9: ch3 (stch), tr in next st, *2tr in next st**, tr in next 4 sts*, rep from * to * 14x & * to ** 1x, tr in next 2 sts, join with ss to 3rd ch of stch. {96 sts}

R10: ch3 (stch), tr in next 2 sts, *3trcl in next st**, tr in next 5 sts*, rep from * to * 14x & * to ** 1x, tr in next 2 sts, join with ss to 3rd ch of stch. {96 sts}

R11: ch3 (stch), tr in next 2 sts, *tr between last and next st, skip 1 st, tr between last and next st**, tr in next 5 sts*, rep from * to * 14x & * to ** 1x, tr in next 2 sts, join with ss to 3rd ch of stch. {112 sts}

R12: dc in same st as ss, dc in next 3 sts, *fphdtr around R10 cl below**, dc in next 7 sts*, rep from * to * 14x & * to ** 1x, dc in next 3 sts, join with ss to first st. {128 sts}

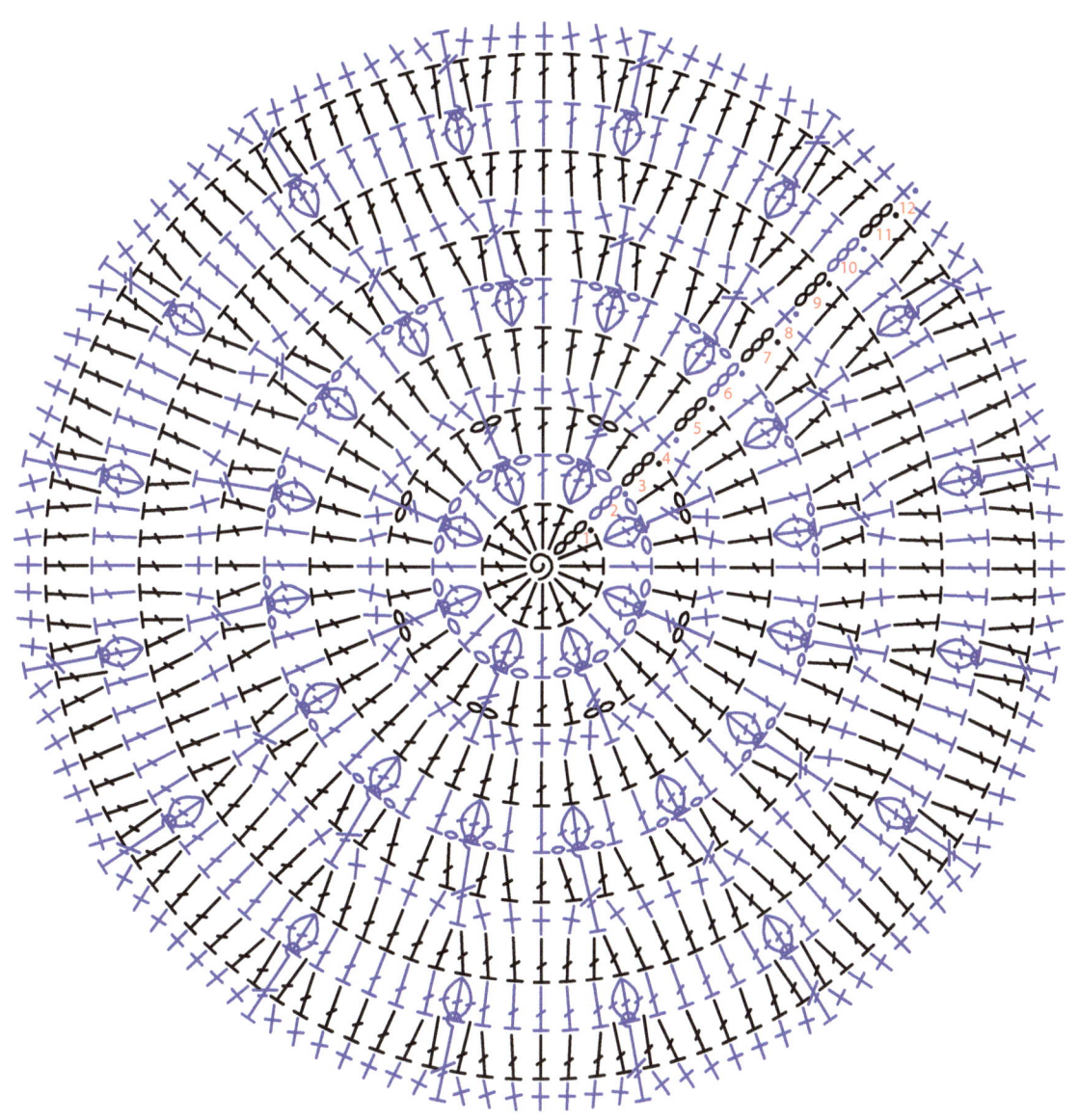

LARGE PATTERNS • 131

R13: ch5 (stch), trtr in same st as ss, *dtr in next 2 sts, hdtr in next 2 sts, tr in next 2 sts, htr in next 2 sts, dc in next 15 sts, htr in next 2 sts, tr in next 2 sts, hdtr in next 2 sts, dtr in next 2 sts**, (2trtr, ch2, 2trtr) in next st*, rep from * to * 2x & * to ** 1x, 2trtr in same st as first sts, ch1, join with dc to 5th ch of stch. {35 sts on each side; 4 2-ch cnr sps}

R14: ch2 (stch), htr over joining dc, *htr in next 12 sts, dc in next 11 sts, htr in next 12 sts**, (2htr, ch2, 2htr) in 2-ch cnr sp*, rep from * to * 2x & * to ** 1x, 2htr in same sp as first sts, ch1, join with dc to 2nd ch of stch. {39 sts on each side; 4 2-ch cnr sps}

R15: dc over joining dc, *13x [dc2tog over next 2 sts, dc in next st]**, (dc, ch2, dc) in 2-ch cnr sp*, rep from * to * 2x & * to ** 1x, dc in same sp as first st, ch1, join with dc to first st. {28 sts on each side; 4 2-ch cnr sps}

R16: ch3 (stch), tr over joining dc, *tr in next 28 sts**, (2tr, ch2, 2tr) in 2-ch cnr sp*, rep from * to * 2x & * to ** 1x, 2tr in same sp as first sts, ch1, join with dc to 3rd ch of stch. {32 sts on each side; 4 2-ch cnr sps}

R17: ch3 (stch), *31x [tr between next 2 sts], skip 1 st**, (tr, ch2, tr) in 2-ch cnr sp*, rep from * to * 2x & * to ** 1x, tr in same sp as first st, ch1, join with dc to 3rd ch of stch. {33 sts on each side; 4 2-ch cnr sps}

R18: dc over joining dc, *dc in next 33 sts**, (dc, ch2, dc) in 2-ch cnr sp*, rep from * to * 2x & * to ** 1x, dc in same sp as first st, ch2, join with ss to first st. Fasten off. {35 sts on each side; 4 2-ch cnr sps}

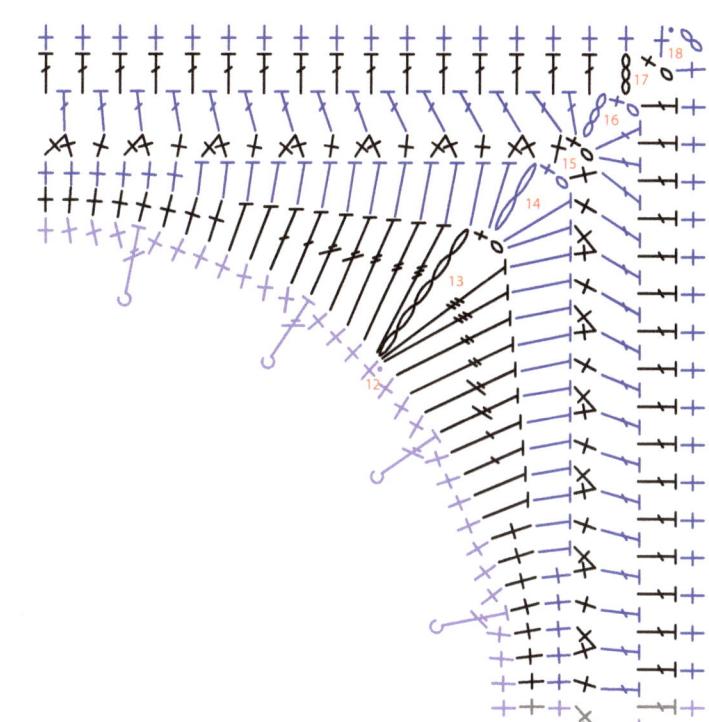

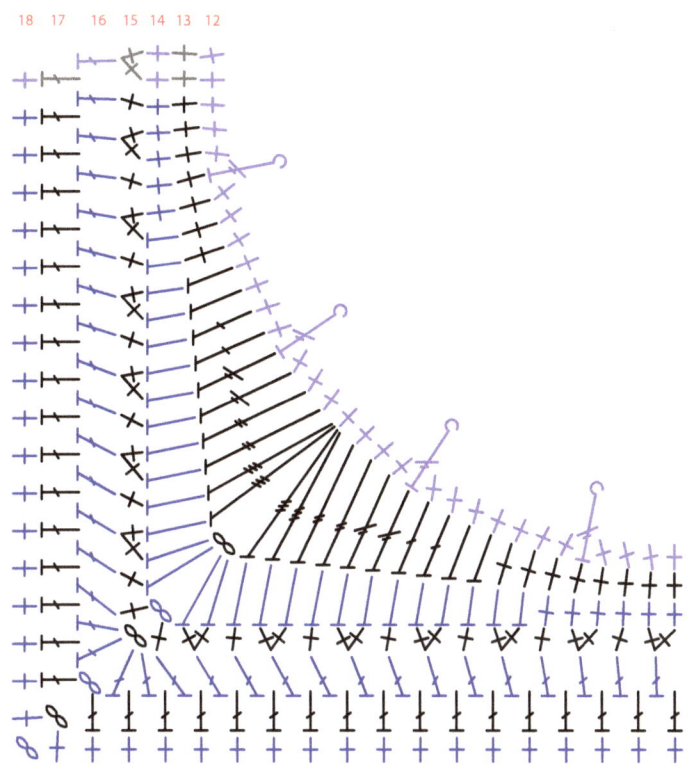

Kim

Kym

LARGE PATTERNS • 133

Big Octamerous

Hello big eight-sectioned granny square! The Wee Octamerous pattern is on page 60.

 143 m / 156 yd

Begin with mc.

R1: ch3 (stch), *ch1**, tr*, rep from * to * 6x & * to ** 1x, join with ss to 3rd ch of stch. {8 sts, 8 1-ch sps}

R2: ch3 (stch), *2tr in 1-ch sp**, tr in next st*, rep from * to * 6x & * to ** 1x, join with ss to 3rd ch of stch. {24 sts}

R3: skip same st as ss, *fpdtr around R1 st below, dc in next st, dc between last and next st, dc in next st, skip 1 st*, rep from * to * 7x, join with ss to first st. {32 sts}

R4: ch3 (stch), *ch1**, tr in next st*, rep from * to * 30x & * to ** 1x, join with ss to 3rd ch of stch. {32 sts, 32 1-ch sps}

R5: skip same st as ss, *fpdtr around R3 fp st below, 3x [dc in 1-ch sp, dc in next st], dc in 1-ch sp, skip 1 st*, rep from * to * 7x, join with ss to first st. {64 sts}

R6: ch3 (stch), tr in next 63 sts, join with ss to 3rd ch of stch. {64 sts}

R7: skip same st as ss, *fpdtr around R5 fp st below, dc in next 7 sts, skip 1 st*, rep from * to * 7x, join with ss to first st. {64 sts}

R8: ch3 (stch), tr in next 63 sts, join with ss to 3rd ch of stch. {64 sts}

R9: skip same st as ss, *fpdtr around R7 fp st below, 7x [dc between next 2 sts, skip 1 st]*, rep from * to * 7x, join with ss to first st. {64 sts}

R10: ch3 (stch), *2tr in next st**, tr in next st*, rep from * to * 30x & * to ** 1x, join with ss to 3rd ch of stch. {96 sts}

R11: skip same st as ss, *fpdtr around R9 fp st below, dc in next 11 sts, skip 1 st*, rep from * to * 7x, join with ss to first st. {96 sts}

R12: ch3 (stch), tr in next 95 sts, join with ss to 3rd ch of stch. {96 sts}

R13: skip same st as ss, *fpdtr around R11 fp st below, 11x [dc between next 2 sts, skip 1 st]*, rep from * to * 7x, join with ss to first st. {96 sts}

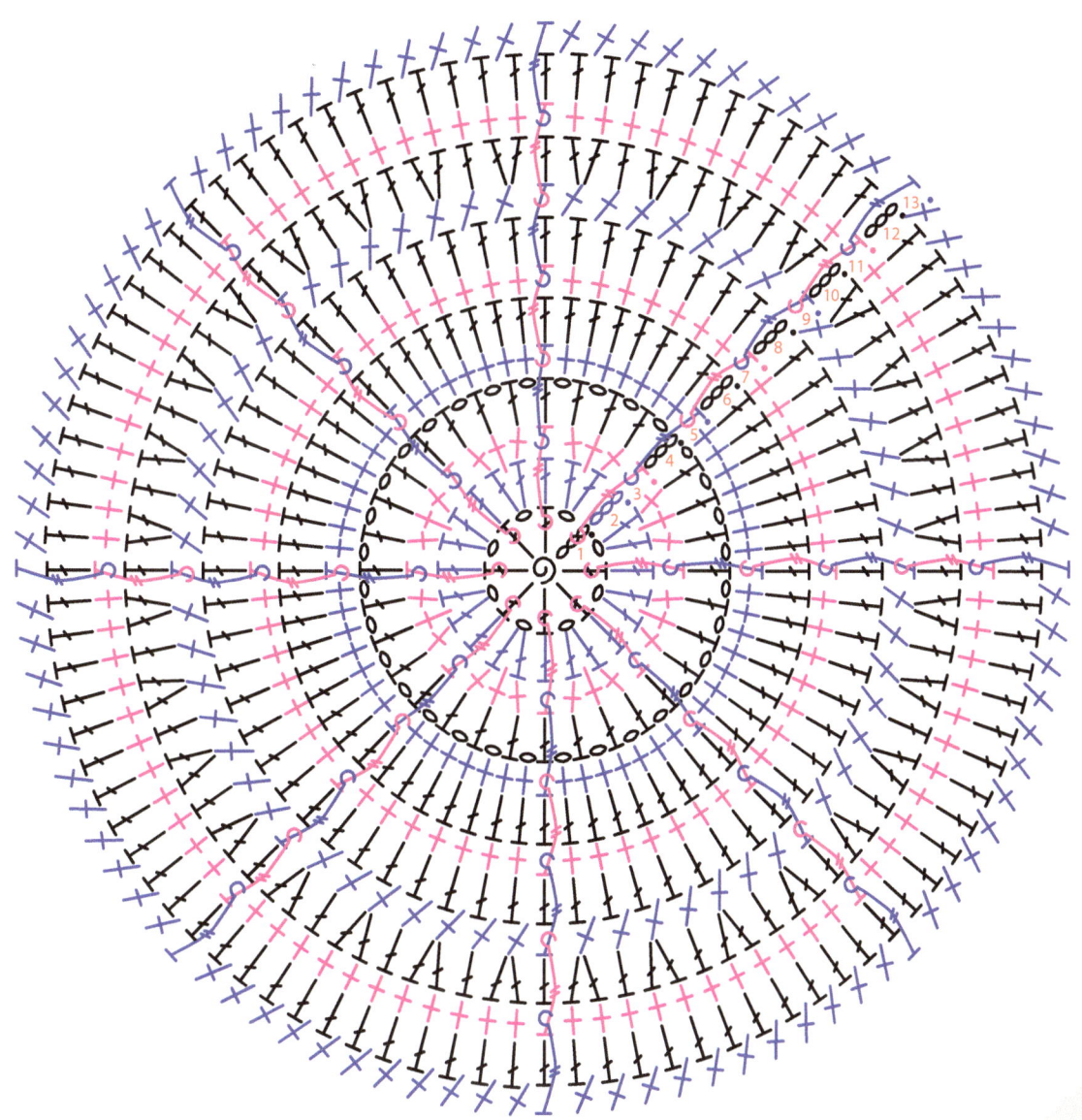

LARGE PATTERNS • 135

R14: ch4 (stch), 2dtr in same st as ss, *hdtr in next 2 sts, tr in next 2 sts, htr in next 2 sts, dc in next 11 sts, htr in next 2 sts, tr in next 2 sts, hdtr in next 2 sts**, 5dtr in next st*, rep from * to * 2x & * to ** 1x, 2dtr in same st as first sts, join with ss to 4th ch of stch. {23 sts on each side; 4 5-st cnrs}

R15: skip same st as ss, *fptrtr around R13 fp st below, htr in next 5 sts, dc in next 8 sts, fptr around R13 fp st below, skip 1 st, dc in next 8 sts, htr in next 5 sts, skip 1 st*, rep from * to * 3x, join with ss to first st. {27 sts on each side; 4 1-st cnrs}

R16: ch4 (stch), 2hdtr in same st as ss, *tr in next 27 sts**, (2hdtr, dtr, 2hdtr) in next st*, rep from * to * 2x & * to ** 1x, 2hdtr in same st as first sts, join with ss to 4th ch of stch. {27 sts on each side; 4 5-st cnrs}

R17: skip same st as ss, *fptrtr around R15 fp st below, 16x [dc between next 2 sts], skip 1 st, fphdtr around R15 fp st below, 16x [dc between next 2 sts], skip 1 st*, rep from * to * 3x, join with ss to first st. {33 sts on each side; 4 1-st cnrs}

R18: ch4 (stch), hdtr in same st as ss, *tr in next 33 sts**, (hdtr, dtr, hdtr) in next st*, rep from * to * 2x & * to ** 1x, hdtr in same st as first sts, join with ss to 4th ch of stch. {33 sts on each side; 4 3-st cnrs}

R19: skip same st as ss, *fptrtr around R17 fp st below, dc in next 17 sts, fphdtr around R17 fp st below, skip 1 st, dc in next 17 sts, skip 1 st*, rep from * to * 3x, join with ss to first st. {35 sts on each side; 4 1-st cnrs}

R20: ch3 (stch), 2htr in same st as ss, *dc in next 35 sts**, (2htr, tr, 2htr) in next st*, rep from * to * 2x & * to ** 1x, 2htr in same st as first sts, join with ss to 3rd ch of stch. {35 sts on each side; 4-5 st cnrs}

R21: dc in same st as ss, *dc in next 39 sts**, (dc, ch2, dc) in next st*, rep from * to * 2x & * to ** 1x, dc in same st as first st, ch2, join with ss to first st. Fasten off. {41 sts on each side; 4 2-ch cnr sps}

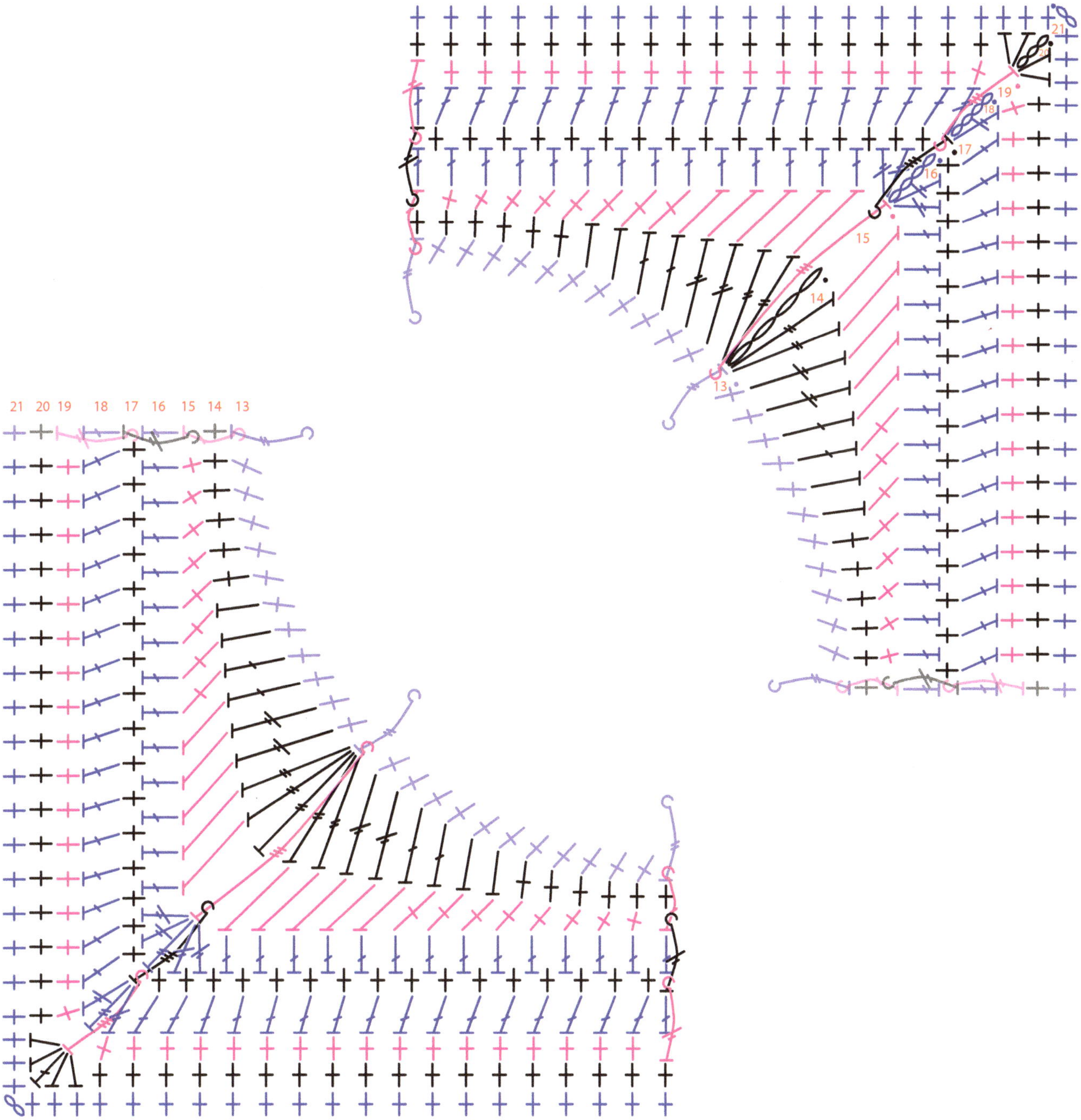

Kim

Kym

LARGE PATTERNS • 137

Cambric

This one uses techniques of linen stitch. Cambric is a lightweight, closely woven linen fabric first made in Cambrai, France.

 170 m / 186 yd

Begin with mc.

R1: ch3 (stch), *ch1, 3trcl, ch1**, tr*, rep from * to * 4x & * to ** 1x, join with ss to 3rd ch of stch. {12 sts, 12 1-ch sps}

R2: fpdc around same st as ss, *dc in 1-ch sp**, fpdc around next st*, rep from * to * 10x & * to ** 1x, join with ss to first st. {24 sts}

R3: ch3 (stch), *(tr, ch1, tr) in next st**, tr in next st*, rep from * to * 10x & * to ** 1x, join with ss to 3rd ch of stch. {36 sts, 12 1-ch sps}

R4: ch3 (stch), *fptr around next st, ch1, 3trcl in 1-ch sp, ch1, fptr around next st**, tr in next st*, rep from * to * 10x & * to ** 1x, join with ss to 3rd ch of stch. {48 sts, 24 1-ch sps} Will be ruffled.

R5: fptr around the 2 fp sts below at the same time skipping the same st as ss, *tr in 1-ch sp, fptr around next st, tr in 1-ch sp**, fptr around next 2 fp sts skipping the st between*, rep from * to * 10x & * to ** 1x, join with ss to first st. {48 sts}

R6: dc in same st as ss, *ch1**, dc in next st*, rep from * to * 46x & * to ** 1x, join with ss to first st. {48 sts, 48 1-ch sps}

R7: *dc in 1-ch sp, ch1**, skip 1 st*, rep from * to * 46x & * to ** 1x, join with ss to first st. {48 sts, 48 1-ch sps}

R8: *dc in 1-ch sp, ch1**, skip 1 st*, rep from * to * 46x & * to ** 1x, join with ss to first st. {48 sts, 48 1-ch sps}

R9: dc in same st as ss, *dc in 1-ch sp**, dc in next st*, rep from * to * 46x & * to ** 1x, join with ss to first st. {96 sts}

R10: ch3 (stch), tr in next st, *ch1**, tr in next 3 sts*, rep from * to * 30x & * to ** 1x, tr in next st, join with ss to 3rd ch of stch. {96 sts, 32 1-ch sps} Will be ruffled.

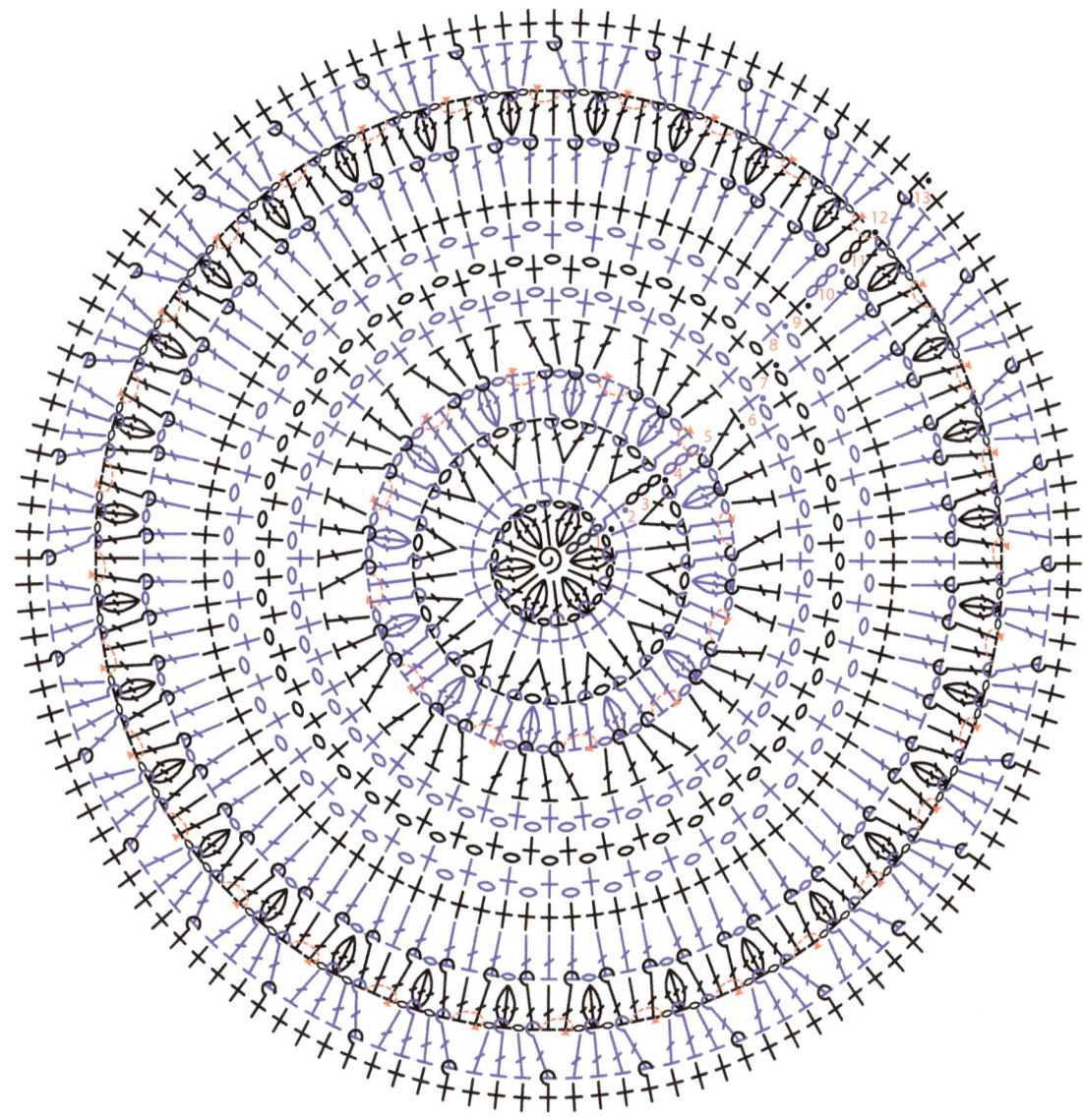

R11: ch3 (stch), *fptr around next st, ch1, 3trcl in 1-ch sp, ch1, fptr around next st** tr in next st*, rep from * to * 30x & * to ** 1x, join with ss to 3rd ch of stch. {128 sts} Will be very ruffled.

R12: fptr around the 2 fp sts below at the same time skipping the same st as ss, *tr in 1-ch sp, fptr around next st, tr in 1-ch sp**, fptr around next 2 fp sts skipping the st between*, rep from * to * 30x & * to ** 1x, join with ss to first st. {128 sts}

R13: fpdc around same st as ss, *dc in next 3 sts**, fpdc around next st*, rep from * to * 30x & * to ** 1x, join with ss to first st. {128 sts}

LARGE PATTERNS • 139

R14: ch4 (stch), 2x [ch1, dtr] in same st as ss, *ch1, skip 1 st, hdtr in next st, 2x [ch1, skip 1 st, tr in next st], ch1, skip 1 st, htr in next st, 7x [ch1, skip 1 st, dc in next st], ch1, skip 1 st, htr in next st, 2x [ch1, skip 1 st, tr in next st], ch1, skip 1 st, hdtr in next st, ch1, skip 1 st**, (4x [dtr, ch1], dtr) in next st*, rep from * to * 2x & * to ** 1x, 2x [dtr, ch1] in same st as first sts, join with ss to 4th ch of stch. {19 sts, 20 1-ch sps on each side; 4 1-st cnrs}

R15: dc in same st as ss, *19x [dc in 1-ch sp, ch1, skip 1 st], dc in 1-ch sp**, (dc, ch2, dc) in next st*, rep from * to * 2x & * to ** 1x, dc in same st as first st, ch1, join with dc to first st. {22 sts, 19 1-ch sps on each side; 4 2-ch cnr sps}

R16: dc over joining dc, *dc in next st, 19x [ch1, skip 1 st, dc in 1-ch sp], ch1, skip 1 st, dc in next st**, (dc, ch2, dc) in 2-ch cnr sp*, rep from * to * 2x & * to ** 1x, dc in same sp as first st, ch1, join with dc to first st. {23 sts, 20 1-ch sps on each side; 4 2-ch cnr sps}

R17: dc over joining dc, *dc in next 2 sts, 19x [dc in 1-ch sp, dc in next st], dc in 1-ch sp, dc in next 2 sts**, (dc, ch2, dc) in 2-ch cnr sp*, rep from * to * 2x & * to ** 1x, dc in same st as first st, ch1, join with dc to first st. {45 sts on each side; 4 2-ch cnr sps}

R18: ch3 (stch), *15x [ch1, tr3tog over next 3 sts], ch1**, (tr, ch2, tr) in 2-ch cnr sp*, rep from * to * 2x & * to ** 1x, tr in same sp as first st, ch1, join with dc to 3rd ch of stch. {17 sts, 16 1-ch sps on each side; 4 2-ch cnr sps}

R19: ch3 (stch), *fptr around next st, 15x [tr in 1-ch sp, (tr in, fptr around) next st], tr in 1-ch sp, fptr around next st**, (tr, ch2, tr) in 2-ch cnr sp*, rep from * to * 2x & * to ** 1x, tr in same sp as first st, ch1, join with dc to 3rd ch of stch. {50 sts on each side; 4 2-ch cnr sps}

R20: dc over joining dc, *dc in next 50 sts**, (dc, ch2, dc) in 2-ch cnr sp*, rep from * to * 2x & * to ** 1x, dc in same sp as first st, ch2, join with ss to first st. Fasten off. {52 sts on each side; 4 2-ch cnr sps}

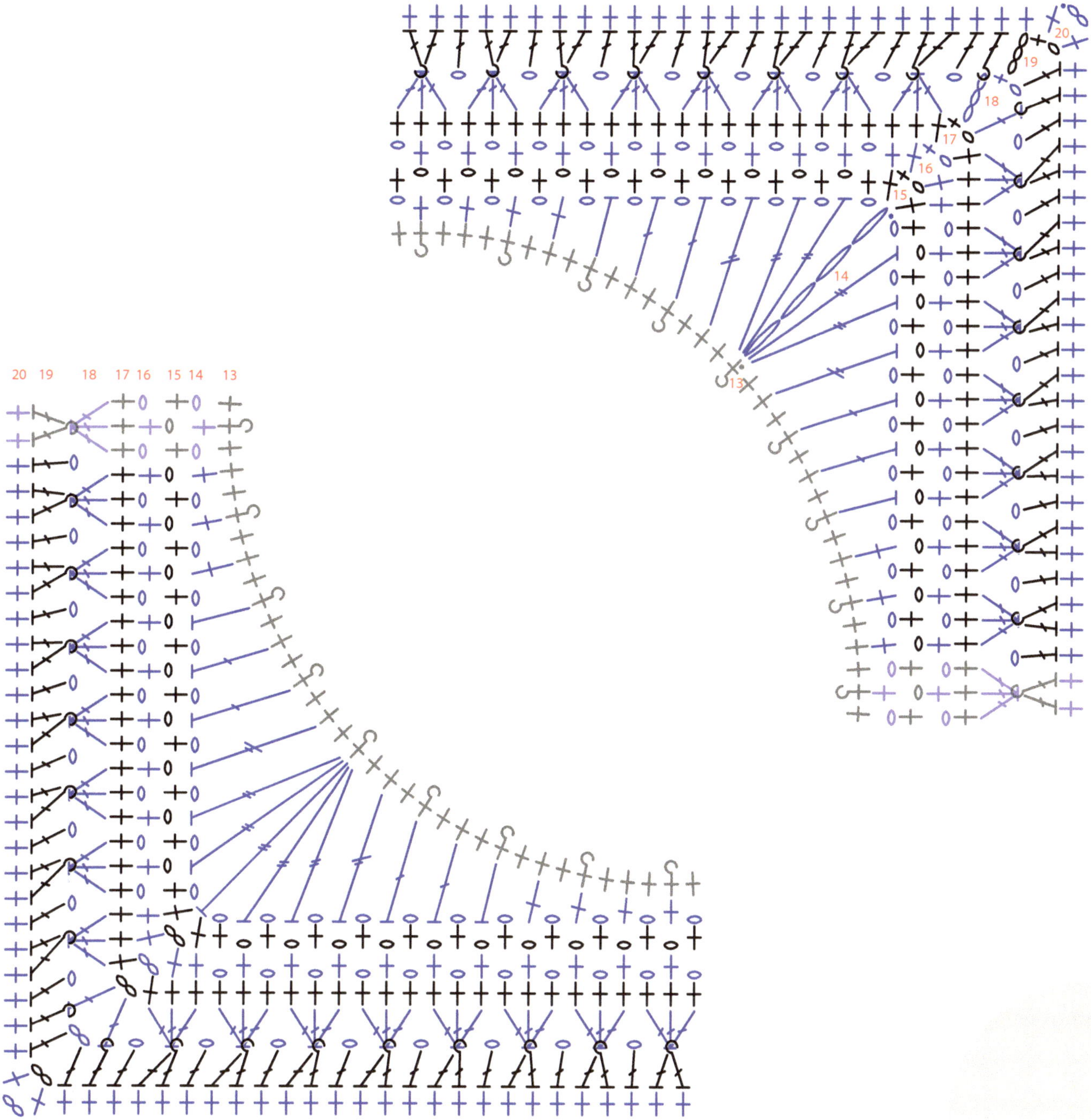

Kim

Kym

LARGE PATTERNS • 141

Grande Lavallière

A Lavallière is an ornamental pendant, usually jewelled, worn on a chain around the neck. It is a French word and as this is the largest of the three similar patterns, grande means large in French.

 179 m / 195 yd

Begin with mc.

R1: ch3 (stch), 15tr, join with ss to 3rd ch of stch. {16 sts}

R2: dc in same st as ss, *(dc, ch6, dc) in next st**, dc in next st*, rep from * to * 6x & * to ** 1x, join with ss to first st. {24 sts, 8 6-ch sps}

R3: ch3 (stch), tr in same st as ss, *tr2tog over next 2 sts pulling 6-ch sp to front**, 3tr in next st*, rep from * to * 6x & * to ** 1x, tr in same st as first sts, join with ss to 3rd ch of stch. {32 sts}

R4: dc in same st as ss, dc in next st, *dc in 6-ch sp of R2 and next st at the same time**, dc in next 3 sts*, rep from * to * 6x & * to ** 1x, dc in next st, join with ss to first st. {32 sts}

R5: (dc, ch6, dc) in same st as ss, *dc in next st**, (dc, ch6, dc) in next st*, rep from * to * 14x & * to ** 1x, join with ss to first st. {48 sts, 16 6-ch sps}

R6: tr2tog over same st as ss and next st pulling 6-ch sp to front, *3tr in next st**, tr2tog over next 2 sts pulling 6-ch sp to front*, rep from * to * 14x & * to ** 1x, join with ss to first st. {64 sts}

R7: dc in 6-ch sp of R5 and same st as ss at the same time, *dc in next 3 sts**, dc in 6-ch sp of R5 and next st at the same time*, rep from * to * 14x & * to ** 1x, join with ss to first st. {64 sts}

R8: (dc, ch6, dc) in same st as ss, *dc in next st**, (dc, ch6, dc) in next st*, rep from * to * 30x & * to ** 1x, join with ss to first st. {96 sts, 32 6-ch sps}

R9: tr2tog over same st as ss and next st pulling 6-ch sp to front, *tr in next st**, tr2tog over next 2 sts pulling 6-ch sp to front*, rep from * to * 30x & * to ** 1x, join with ss to first st. {64 sts}

R10: dc in 6-ch sp of R8 and same st as ss at the same time, *2dc in next st, dc in 6-ch sp of R8 and next st at the same time, dc in next st**, dc in 6-ch sp of R8 and next st at the same time*, rep from * to * 14x & * to ** 1x, join with ss to first st. {80 sts}

R11: (dc, ch6, dc) in same st as ss, *dc in next st**, (dc, ch6, dc) in next st*, rep from * to * 38x & * to ** 1x, join with ss to first st. {120 sts, 40 6-ch sps}

R12: tr2tog over same st as ss and next st pulling 6-ch sp to front, *tr in next st**, tr2tog over next 2 sts pulling 6-ch sp to front *, rep from * to * 38x & * to ** 1x, join with ss to first st. {80 sts}

R13: dc in 6-ch sp of R11 and same st as ss at the same time, *dc in next st**, dc in 6-ch sp of R11 and next st at the same time*, rep from * to * 38x & * to ** 1x, join with ss to first st. {80 sts}

LARGE PATTERNS

R14: ch5 (stch), 2dtr in same st as ss, *hdtr in next 2 sts, tr in next 2 sts, htr in next 2 sts, dc in next 7 sts, htr in next 2 sts, tr in next 2 sts, hdtr in next 2 sts**, (2dtr, trtr, 2dtr) in next st*, rep from * to * 2x & * to ** 1x, 2dtr in same st as first sts, join with ss to 5th ch of stch. {19 sts on each side, 4 5-st cnrs}

R15: dc in same st as ss, *dc in next 23 sts**, (dc, ch2, dc) in next st*, rep from * to * 2x & * to ** 1x, dc in same st as first st, ch1, join with dc to first st. {25 sts on each side; 4 2-ch cnr sps}

R16: dc over joining dc, *12x [dc in next st, (dc, ch6, dc) in next st], dc in next st**, (dc, ch2, dc) in 2-ch cnr sp*, rep from * to * 2x & * to ** 1x, dc in same sp as first st, ch1, join with dc to first st. {39 sts, 12 6-ch sps on each side; 4 2-ch cnr sps}

R17: ch3 (stch), tr over joining dc, *tr in next 2 sts, 12x [tr2tog over next 2 sts pulling 6-ch sp to front, tr in next st], tr in next st**, (tr, hdtr, tr) in 2-ch cnr sp*, rep from * to * 2x & * to ** 1x, tr in same sp as first sts, join with ss to 3rd ch of stch. {27 sts on each side; 4 3-st cnrs}

R18: dc in same st as ss, *dc in next 3 sts, 12x [dc in 6-ch sp of R16 and next st at the same time, dc in next st], dc in next 2 sts**, (dc, ch2, dc) in next st*, rep from * to * 2x & * to ** 1x, dc in same st as first st, ch1, join with dc to first st. {31 sts on each side; 4 2-ch cnr sps}

R19: dc over joining dc, *15x [(dc, ch6, dc) in next st, dc in next st], (dc, ch6, dc) in next st**, (dc, ch2, dc) in 2-ch cnr sp*, rep from * to * 2x & * to ** 1x, dc in same sp as first st, ch1, join with dc to first st. {49 sts, 16 6-ch sps on each side; 4 2-ch cnr sps}

R20: ch3 (stch), tr over joining dc, *tr in next st, 16x [tr2tog over next 2 sts pulling 6-ch sp to front, tr in next st]**, (tr, hdtr, tr) in 2-ch cnr sp*, rep from * to * 2x & * to ** 1x, tr in same sp as first sts, join with ss to 3rd ch of stch. {33 sts on each side; 4 3-st cnrs}

R21: dc in same st as ss, *dc in next 2 sts, 16x [dc in 6-ch sp of R19 and next st at the same time, dc in next st], dc in next st**, (dc, ch2, dc) in next st*, rep from * to * 2x & * to ** 1x, dc in same st as first st, ch1, join with dc to first st. {37 sts on each side; 4 2-ch cnr sps}

R22: dc over joining dc, *dc in next 37 sts**, (dc, ch2, dc) in 2-ch cnr sp*, rep from * to * 2x & * to ** 1x, dc in same sp as first st, ch2, join with ss to first st. Fasten off. {39 sts on each side; 4 2-ch cnr sps}

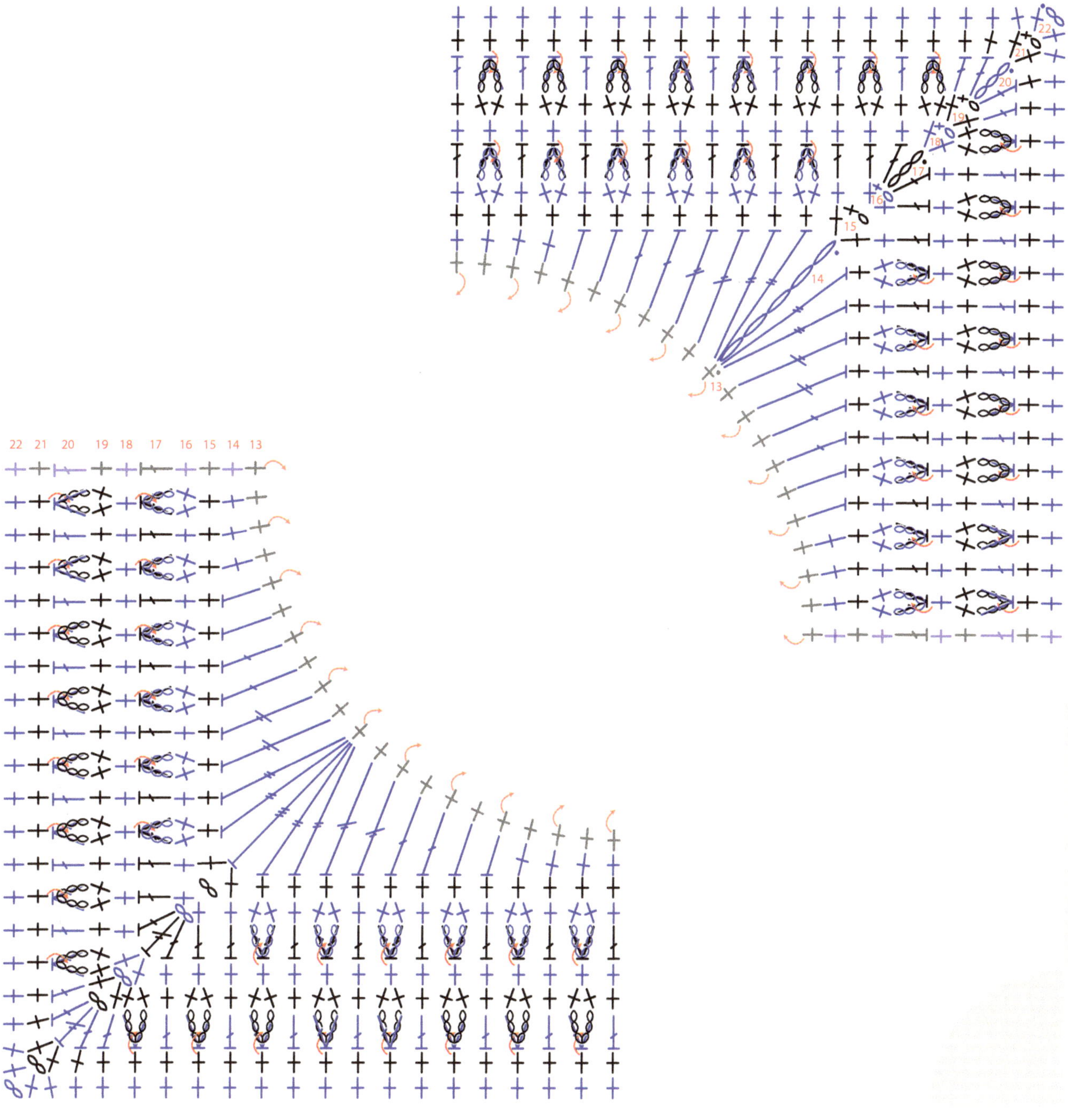

Kim

Kym

LARGE PATTERNS

Serry

Ranks of tall, tall stitches. Serry means to press or crowd together in ranks.

 117 m / 128 yd

Begin with mc.

R1: ch3 (stch), 11tr, join with ss to 3rd ch of stch. {12 sts}

R2: ch5 (stch), trtr in same st as ss, 2trtr in next 11 sts, join with ss to 5th ch of stch. {24 sts}

R3: 2dc in same st as ss, 2dc in next 23 sts, join with ss to first st. {48 sts}

R4: ch5 (stch), *skip 1 st, trtr in next st, trtr in skipped st**, trtr in next st*, rep from * to * 14x & * to ** 1x, join with ss to 5th ch of stch. {48 sts}

R5: 2dc in same st as ss, *dc between last and next st, fpdc around next 2 sts at the same time, dc between last and next st**, 2dc in next st*, rep from * to * 14x & * to ** 1x, join with ss to first st. {80 sts}

R6: ch5 (stch), trtr in next 79 sts, join with ss to 5th ch of stch. {80 sts}

R7: dc in same st as ss, dc in next 79 sts, join with ss to first st. {80 sts}

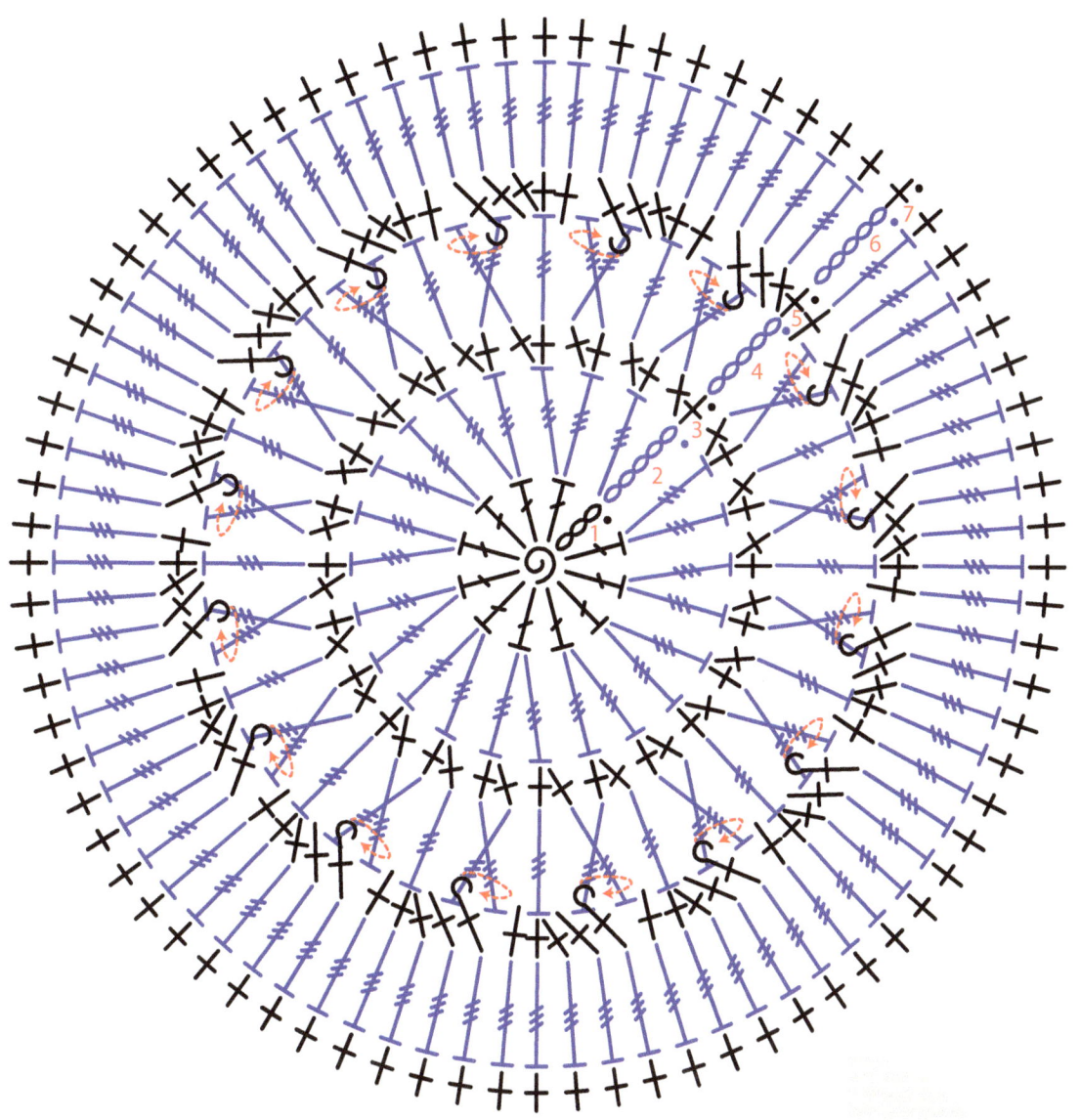

LARGE PATTERNS • 147

R8: ch5 (stch), trtr in same st as ss, *dtr in next 2 sts, hdtr in next 2 sts, tr in next 2 sts, htr in next 2 sts, dc in next 3 sts, htr in next 2 sts, tr in next 2 sts, hdtr in next 2 sts, dtr in next 2 sts**, (2trtr, ch2, 2trtr) in next st*, rep from * to * 2x & * to ** 1x, 2trtr in same st as first sts, ch1, join with dc to 5th ch of stch. {23 sts on each side; 4 2-ch cnr sps}

R9: 2dc over joining dc, *dc in next 23 sts**, (2dc, ch2, 2dc) in 2-ch cnr sp*, rep from * to * 2x & * to ** 1x, 2dc in same sp as first sts, ch1, join with dc to first st. {27 sts on each side; 4 2-ch cnr sps}

R10: ch5 (stch), *trtr in next 27 sts**, (trtr, ch2, trtr) in 2-ch cnr sp*, rep from * to * 2x & * to ** 1x, trtr in same sp as first st, ch1, join with dc to 5th ch of stch. {29 sts on each side; 4 2-ch cnr sps}

R11: dc over joining dc, *dc in next 29 sts**, (dc, ch2, dc) in 2-ch cnr sp*, rep from * to * 2x & * to ** 1x, dc in same sp as first st, ch1, join with dc to first st. {31 sts on each side; 4 2-ch cnr sps}

R12: ch5 (stch), *trtr in next 31 sts**, (trtr, ch2, trtr) in 2-ch cnr sp*, rep from * to * 2x & * to ** 1x, trtr in same sp as first st, ch1, join with dc to 5th ch of stch. {33 sts on each side; 4 2-ch cnr sps}

R13: dc over joining dc, *dc in next 33 sts**, (dc, ch2, dc) in 2-ch cnr sp*, rep from * to * 2x & * to ** 1x, dc in same sp as first st, ch2, join with ss to first st. Fasten off. {35 sts on each side; 4 2-ch cnr sps}

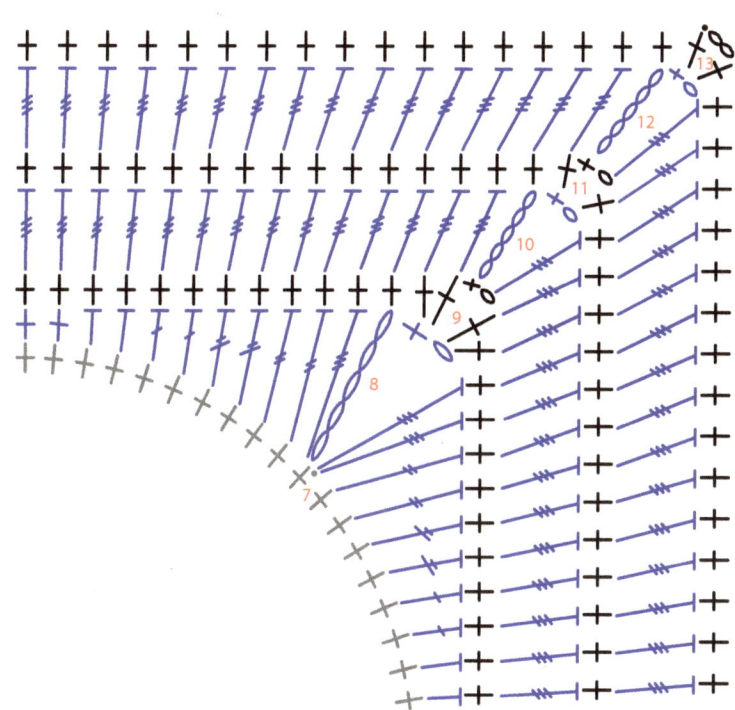

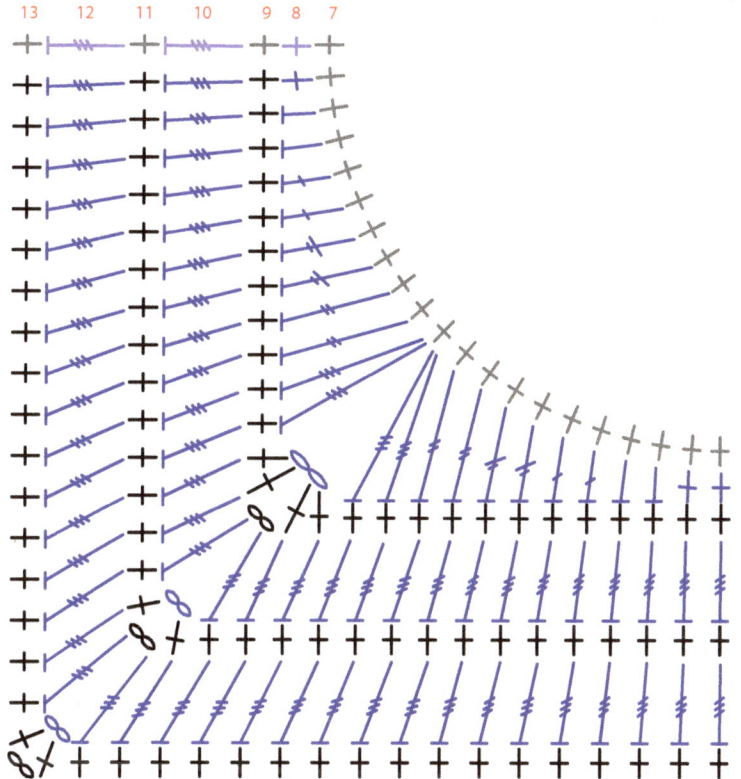

Kim

Kym

LARGE PATTERNS • 149

Camarilla

Groups, cabals, sects - or a Camarilla. The groups of stitches are surrounded by stitches - secret groups among the multitude.

 191 m / 209 yd

Begin with mc.

R1: ch3 (stch), 23tr, join with ss to 3rd ch of stch. {24 sts}

R2: *dc2tog over next 2 sts*, rep from * to * 11x, join with ss to first st. {12 sts}

R3: ch3 (stch), tr in same st as ss, 2tr in next 11 sts, join with ss to 3rd ch of stch. {24 sts}

R4: dc in same st as ss, *ch1, fpdc around next st, ch1**, dc in next st*, rep from * to * 10x & * to ** 1x, join with ss to first st. {24 sts, 24 1-ch sps}

R5: ch3 (stch), *tr in 1-ch sp, fptr around next st, tr in 1-ch sp**, tr in next st*, rep from * to * 10x & * to ** 1x, join with ss to 3rd ch of stch. {48 sts}

R6: ch4 (stch), 4dtrcl in same st as ss, ch1, fpdtr around same st as ss, *dtr in next st, fpdtr around next st, dtr in next st**, (fpdtr around, ch1, 5dtrcl in, ch1, fpdtr around) next st*, rep from * to * 10x & * to ** 1x, fpdtr around same st as first fp st, ch1, join with ss to 4dtrcl. {72 sts, 24 1-ch sps} Will be ruffled.

R7: fpdc around same st as ss & cl at the same time, *skip 1-ch sp, dc in next 5 sts, skip 1-ch sp**, fpdc around next st*, rep from * to * 10x & * to ** 1x, join with ss to first st. {72 sts} Will still be a little ruffled.

R8: skip same st as ss, *fptr2tog around 2 fp sts of R6 either side of cl below, dc in next 5 sts**, skip 1 st*, rep from * to * 10x & * to ** 1x, join with ss to first st. {72 sts} Pop cl to front between fp sts.

R9: ch3 (stch), tr in next 3 sts, *fpdtr around fp st of R6**, tr in next 6 sts*, rep from * to * 10x & * to ** 1x, tr in next 2 sts, join with ss to 3rd ch of stch. {84 sts}

R10: fptr around same st as ss, fptr around next 83 sts, join with ss to first st. {84 sts}

R11: fptr around same st as ss, fptr around next 83 sts, join with ss to first st. {84 sts}

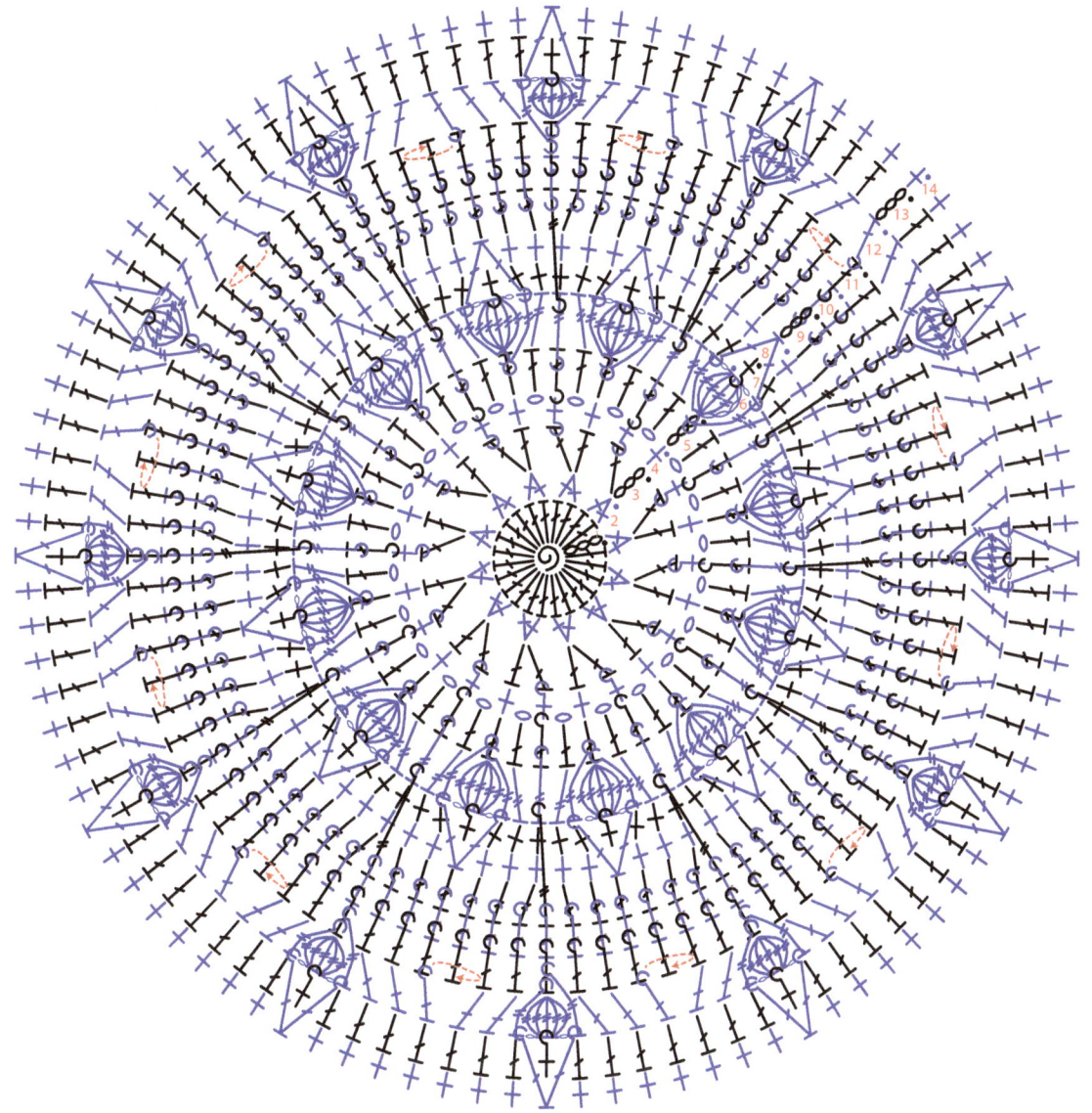

R12: fptr around same st as ss and next st at the same time, *tr in next 2 sts, (fpdtr around, ch1, 5dtrcl in, ch1, fpdtr around) next st, tr in next 2 sts**, fptr around next 2 sts at the same time*, rep from * to *10x & * to ** 1x, join with ss to first st. {96 sts, 24 1-ch sps}

R13: ch3 (stch), tr in next 3 sts, *skip 1-ch sp, fpdc around next st, skip 1-ch sp**, tr in next 7 sts*, rep from * to *10x & * to ** 1x, tr in next 3 sts, join with ss to 3rd ch of stch. {96 sts}

R14: dc in same st as ss, dc in next 3 sts, *fptr2tog around 2 fp sts of R12 either side of cl, skip 1 st**, dc in next 7 sts*, rep from * to *10x & * to ** 1x, dc in next 3 sts, join with ss to first st. {96 sts} Pop cl to front between fp sts.

LARGE PATTERNS • 151

R15: ch4 (stch), 4dtrcl in same st as ss, *ch1, hdtr in next st, tr in next 2 sts, htr in next 2 sts, dc in next 13 sts, htr in next 2 sts, tr in next 2 sts, hdtr in next st, ch1**, 5dtrcl in next st*, rep from * to * 2x & * to ** 1x, join with ss to 4dtrcl. {23 sts, 2 1-ch sps on each side; 4 1-st cnrs}

R16: fpdc around same st as ss & cl at the same time, *fptrtr around R14 st cl is in, tr in 1-ch sp, tr in next 23 sts, tr in 1-ch sp, fptrtr around R14 st cl is in**, fpdc around next st*, rep from * to * 2x & * to ** 1x, join with ss to first st. {27 sts on each side; 4 1-st cnrs} Pop cl to front between fp sts.

R17: ch4 (stch), 3dtr in same st as ss, *skip 1 st, fptr around next 25 sts, skip 1 st**, 7dtr in next st*, rep from * to * 2x & * to ** 1x, 3dtr in same st as first sts, join with ss to 4th ch of stch. {25 sts on each side; 4 7-st cnrs}

R18: skip same st as ss, *fptrtr around 2 fp sts of R16 either side of cl at the same time, dc in next 3 sts, fptr around next 25 sts, dc in next 3 sts**, skip 1 st*, rep from * to * 2x & * to ** 1x, join with ss to first st. {31 sts on each side; 4 1-st cnrs} Pop cl to front between fp sts.

R19: ch3 (stch), (fptr around, tr in) same st as ss, *fphdtr around next 3 sts of R17, skip 3 sts, fptr around next 25 sts, fphdtr around next 3 sts of R17, skip 3 sts**, (tr in, fptr around, tr in) next st*, rep from * to * 2x & * to ** 1x, join with ss to 3rd ch of stch. {31 sts on each side; 4 3-st cnrs}

R20: ch4 (stch), dtr2tog over next 2 sts, *2dtr in next st, 2hdtr in next st, tr in next 3 sts, htr in next 21 sts, tr in next 3 sts, 2hdtr in next st, 2dtr in next st**, dtr3tog over next 3 sts*, rep from * to * 2x & * to ** 1x, join with ss to dtr2tog. {35 sts on each side; 4 1-st cnrs}

R21: ch3 (stch), tr in same st as ss, *dc in next 3 sts, htr in next 4 sts, htr in lbv of next 21 sts, htr in next 4 sts, dc in next 3 sts**, (tr, hdtr, tr) in next st*, rep from * to * 2x & * to ** 1x, tr in same st as first sts, join with ss to 3rd ch of stch. {35 sts on each side; 4 3-st cnrs}

R22: ch2 (stch), *htr in next 4 sts, htr in lbv of next 29 sts, htr in next 4 sts**, (htr, ch2, htr) in next st*, rep from * to * 2x & * to ** 1x, htr in same st as first st, ch2, join with ss to 2nd ch of stch. Fasten off. {39 sts on each side; 4 2-ch cnr sps}

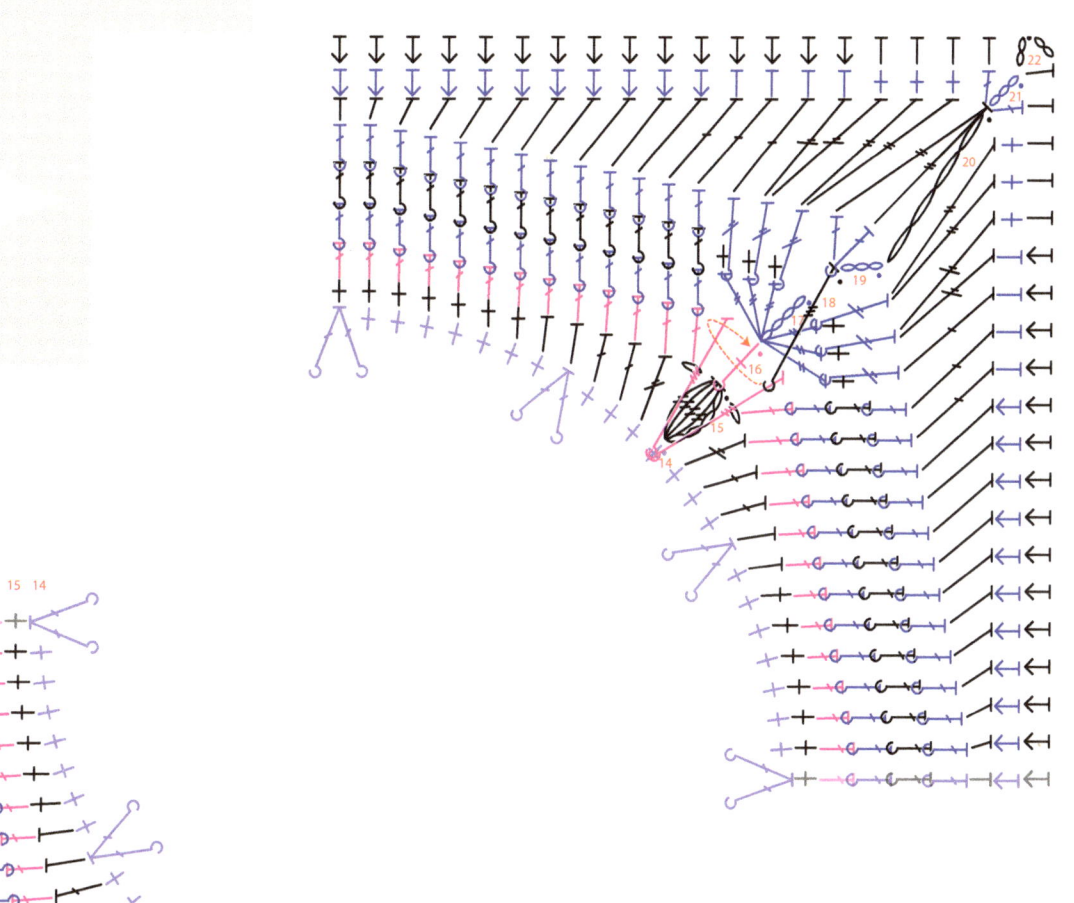

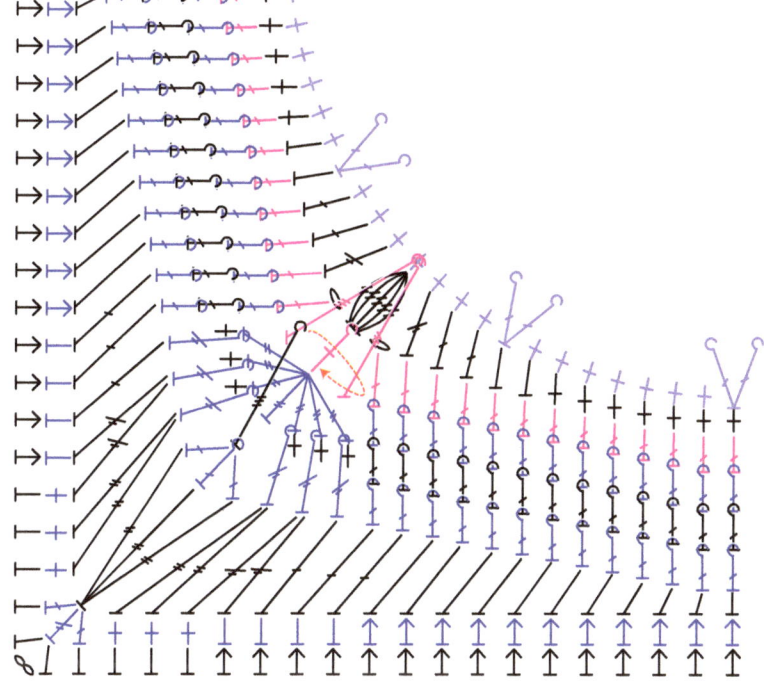

Kim

Kym

LARGE PATTERNS • 153

Stellate Stratified

Remember Stellate from the small pattern section? Well, this is Stellate Stratified. It's layered, as in strata layers of rock.

 188 m / 205 yd

Begin with mc.

R1: ch3 (stch), 15tr, join with ss to 3rd ch of stch. {16 sts}

R2: dc between same st as ss and next st, *ch1**, dc between next 2 sts*, rep from * to * 14x & * to ** 1x, join with ss to first st. {16 sts, 16 1-ch sps}

R3: ch3 (stch), tr2tog over (1-ch sp & next st), *ch2, dc in 1-ch sp, ch2**, tr3tog over (next st, 1-ch sp & next st)*, rep from * to * 6x & * to ** 1x, join with ss to top of tr2tog. {16 sts, 16 2-ch sps}

R4: dc in same st as ss, *ch5, skip (2-ch sp, 1 st & 2-ch sp)**, dc in next st*, rep from * to * 6x & * to ** 1x, join with ss to first st. {8 sts, 8 5-ch sps}

R5: ch3 (stch), *5tr in R3 st behind 5-ch sp**, tr in next st*, rep from * to * 6x & * to ** 1x, join with ss to 3rd ch of stch. {48 sts}

R6: dc in same st as ss, *ch3, pull 5-ch sp of R4 to the back through the st the 5tr are worked into, dc in that 5-ch sp, ch3, skip 5 sts**, dc in next st*, rep from * to * 6x & * to ** 1x, join with ss to first st. {16 sts, 16 3-ch sps}

R7: dc in same st as ss, *3dc in 3-ch sp**, dc in next st*, rep from * to * 14x & * to ** 1x, join with ss to first st. {64 sts}

R8: *fptr around R5 st below, 2tr in next 5 sts of R5*, rep from * to * 7x, join with ss to first st. (skip all R7 sts) {88 sts}

R9: dc in same st as ss, *tr in next 7 sts of R7 behind the 5tr of R5, skip 10 sts**, dc in next st*, rep from * to * 6x & * to ** 1x, join with ss to first st. {64 sts}

R10: skip same st as ss, *fptr around R8 fp st below, htr in next 3 sts, dc between middle 10 sts of R8 and next st at the same time, htr in next 3 sts**, skip 1 st*, rep from * to * 6x & * to ** 1x, join with ss to first st. {64 sts}

R11: dc in same st as ss, dc in next 63 sts, join with ss to first st. {64 sts}

R12: dc in same st as ss, *ch2, tr3tog over next 3 sts, ch2**, dc in next st*, rep from * to * 14x & * to ** 1x, join with ss to first st. {32 sts, 32 2-ch sps}

R13: NOTE: Don't work a false st. ch3 (stch), 4tr in same st as ss, *skip 2-ch sp, dc in next st, skip 2-ch sp**, 5tr in next st*, rep from * to * 14x & * to ** 1x, join with inv join to first true st. {96 sts}

R14: attach with stdg bptr around any R12 st with 5 sts in it, *(fptr, ch2, fptr) around next R12 st**, (bptr, ch2, bptr) around next R12 st*, rep from * to * 14x & * to ** 1x, bptr around same st as first sts, ch1, join with dc to first st. (skip all R13 sts) {64 sts, 32 2-ch sps}

R15: ch3 (stch), tr over joining dc, *skip 2 sts**, 3tr in 2-ch sp*, rep from * to * 30x & * to ** 1x, tr in same sp as first sts, join with ss to 3rd ch of stch. {96 sts}

R16: fptr around same st as ss, *skip 1 st, 2tr in next st, 3tr in next st, 2tr in next st, skip 1 st**, fptr around next st*, rep from * to * 14x & * to ** 1x, join with ss to first st. {128 sts}

R17: fphtr around same st as ss, *bphtr around next 7 sts**, fphtr around next st*, rep from * to * 14x & * to ** 1x, join with ss to first st. {128 sts}

R18: dc in same st as ss, dc in next 127 sts, join with ss to first st. {128 sts}

LARGE PATTERNS

R19: dc in same st as ss, dc in next 127 sts, join with ss to first st. {128 sts}

R20: ch5 (stch), 2trtr in same st as ss, *ch1, skip 1 st, dtr in next st, ch1, skip 1 st, hdtr in next st, ch1, skip 1 st, tr in next st, ch1, skip 1 st, htr in next st, 7x [ch1, skip 1 st, dc in next st], ch1, skip 1 st, htr in next st, ch1, skip 1 st, tr in next st, ch1, skip 1 st, hdtr in next st, ch1, skip 1 st, dtr in next st, ch1, skip 1 st**, 5trtr in next st*, rep from * to * 2x & * to ** 1x, 2trtr in same st as first sts, join with ss to 5th ch of stch. {15 sts, 16 1-ch sps on each side; 4 5-st cnrs}

R21: dc in same st as ss, *2x [dc between last and next st, dc in next st], 15x [dc in 1-ch sp, dc in next st], dc in 1-ch sp, 2x [dc in next st, dc between last and next st]**, (dc, ch2, dc) in next st*, rep from * to * 2x & * to ** 1x, dc in same st as first st, ch1, join with dc to first st. {41 sts on each side; 4 2-ch cnr sps}

R22: ch3 (stch), *skip 1 st, 9x [ch2, tr3tog over next 3 sts, ch2, dc in next st], ch2, tr3tog over next 3 sts, ch2, skip 1 st**, tr in 2-ch cnr sp*, rep from * to * 2x & * to ** 1x, join with ss to 3rd ch of stch. {19 sts, 20 2-ch sps on each side; 4 1-st cnrs}

R23: ch3 (stch), tr in same st as ss, *skip 2-ch sp, 9x [dc in next st, skip 2-ch sp, 3tr in next st, skip 2-ch sp], dc in next st, skip 2-ch sp**, 3tr in next st*, rep from * to * 2x & * to ** 1x, tr in same st as first sts, join with ss to 3rd ch of stch. {37 sts on each side; 4 3-st cnrs}

R24: dc in same st as ss, *dc in next st, 9x [ch1, fptr around R22 st, ch1, bptr around R22 st], ch1, fptr around R22 st, ch1, skip all R23 side sts up to last st, dc in last st of R23**, (dc, ch2, dc) in next st*, rep from * to * 2x & * to ** 1x, dc in same st as first st, ch1, join with dc to first st. {23 sts, 20 1-ch sps on each side; 4 2-ch cnr sps}

R25: dc over joining dc, *dc in next 2 sts, 19x [dc in 1-ch sp, dc in next st], dc in 1-ch sp, dc in next 2 sts**, (dc, ch2, dc) in 2-ch cnr sp*, rep from * to * 2x & * to ** 1x, dc in same sp as first st, ch1, join with dc to first st. {45 sts on each side; 4 2-ch cnr sps}

R26: dc over joining dc, *dc in blo of next 45 sts**, (dc, ch2, dc) in 2-ch cnr sp*, rep from * to * 2x & * to ** 1x, dc in same sp as first st, ch2, join with ss to first st. Fasten off. {47 sts on each side; 4 2-ch cnr sps}

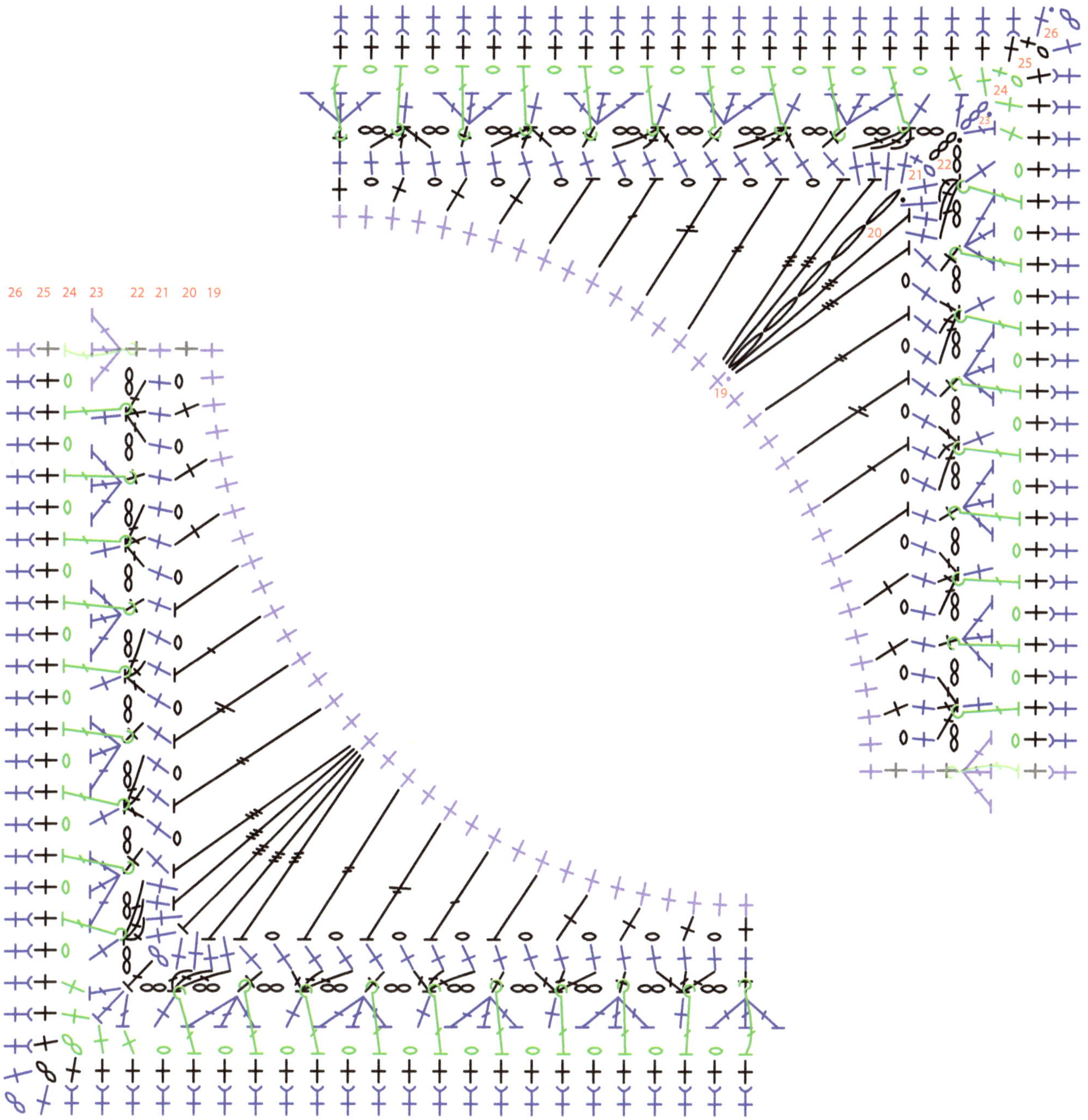

Kim

Kym

LARGE PATTERNS • 157

Extensions

The following six patterns can be used in two ways.

Each of these patterns will add enough to make any pattern up to the next size. For example, adding one to a small sized pattern will make it up to the medium size.

You can also use these patterns for borders for your projects.

Even/Odd stitch counts

Each pattern states whether an even, odd or any stitch count is needed. If you need one stitch different, skip a stitch at the start of each side, or work the last 2 stitches together on each side in the first round and all will be well.

Things to note for extending patterns

If using any of these patterns to make a granny square larger and using the same colour, end the last round of the square with "ch1, join with dc to first st/stch", then you will be able to continue.

If changing colour for the extension, end the granny square as in the pattern then attach the extension colour with the appropriate standing stitch. E.g., stdg dc if the pattern begins with a dc, stdg htr if it begins with ch2 (stch), or a stdg tr if it begins with ch3 (stch).

Things to note for using these patterns as borders

The borders will look better if you first work a round of double crochet as described on the extension pattern pages.

Special notes for the Withe pattern

To adjust the stitch count, use the last stitch of each side twice, by working a stitch in and a stitch around it.

When used as a border, this pattern will require blocking to sit flat. Some fibres block better than others, so use this border pattern with a fibre that will take blocking well – natural wool and cotton.

EXTENSIONS • 159

Kernel

One increment extension for an odd numbered stitch count

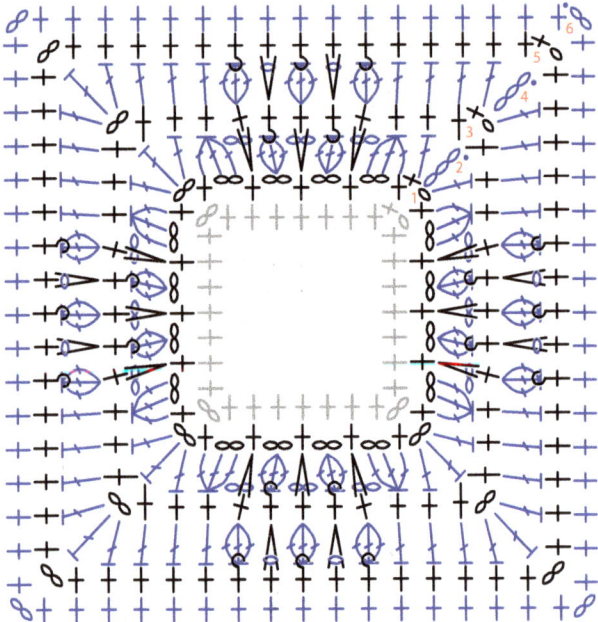

If using as a border, first add a round of dc with a st in every st, 2-ch sp and join with (dc, ch2, dc) corners, ch1, join with dc to first st.

R1: dc over joining dc, *along side x [ch2, skip 1 st, dc in next st], ch2, skip 1 st**, (dc, ch2, dc) in 2-ch cnr sp*, rep from * to * 2x & * to ** 1x, dc in same sp as first st, ch1, join with dc to first st.

R2: **tr3tog at start and end of side worked over 1 st and 2-ch sp – 1 leg in the st and 2 legs in the 2-ch sp**

ch3 (stch), tr over joining dc, *tr3tog over next st and 2-ch sp, along side x [ch2, skip 1 st, 3trcl in 2-ch sp], ch2, skip 1 st, tr3tog over 2-ch sp and next st**, 3tr in 2-ch cnr sp*, rep from * to * 2x & * to ** 1x, tr in same sp as first sts, join with ss to 3rd ch of stch.

R3: dc in same st as ss, *dc in next 2 sts, along side x [spike dc over 2-ch sp in skipped st of R1, fpdc around next st], spike dc over 2-ch sp in skipped st of R1, dc in next 2 sts**, (dc, ch2, dc) in next st*, rep from * to * 2x & * to ** 1x, dc in same st as first st, ch1, join with dc to first st.

R4: ch3 (stch), tr over joining dc, *tr in next 3 sts, along side x [3trcl in next st, ch1, skip 1 st], 3trcl in next st, tr in next 3 sts**, 3tr in 2-ch cnr sp*, rep from * to * 2x & * to ** 1x, tr in same sp as first sts, join with ss to 3rd ch of stch.

R5: dc in same st as ss, *dc in next 4 sts, along side x [fpdc around next st, spike dc over 1-ch sp in skipped st of R3], fpdc around next st, dc in next 4 sts**, (dc, ch2, dc) in next st*, rep from * to * 2x & * to ** 1x, dc in same st as first st, ch1, join with dc to first st.

R6: dc over joining dc, *dc in each st along side**, (dc, ch2, dc) in 2-ch cnr sp*, rep from * to * 2x & * to ** 1x, dc in same sp as first st, ch2, join with ss to first st. Fasten off.

Dornick

One increment extension for an odd numbered stitch count

If using as a border, first add a round of dc with a st in every st, 2-ch sp and join with (dc, ch2, dc) corners, ch1, join with dc to first st.

R1: ch3 (stch), *along side x [ch1, skip 1 st, tr in next st], ch1, skip 1 st**, (tr, ch2, tr) in 2-ch cnr sp*, rep from * to * 2x & * to ** 1x, tr in same sp as first st, ch1, join with dc to first st.

R2: dc over joining dc, *dc in next st, along side x [dtr in st skipped in R1 behind R2, ch1, skip (1-ch sp & 1 st)], dtr in last st skipped in R1, dc in last st**, (dc, ch2, dc) in 2-ch cnr sp*, rep from * to * 2x & * to ** 1x, dc in same sp as first st, ch1, join with dc to first st.

R3: dc over joining dc, *dc in next 2 sts, along side x [tr in 1-ch sp of R1 and in next st of R2 at the same time, ch1, skip 1-ch sp], tr in last 1-ch sp of R1 and last dtr of R2 at the same time, dc in last 2 sts**, (dc, ch2, dc) in 2-ch cnr sp*, rep from * to * 2x & * to ** 1x, dc in same sp as first st, ch1, join with dc to first st.

R4: dc over joining dc, *dc in next 3 sts, ch1, skip 1 st, along side x [tr in 1-ch sp of R2 behind R3, ch1, skip (1-ch sp & 1 st)], dc in last 3 sts**, (dc, ch2, dc) in 2-ch cnr sp*, rep from * to * 2x & * to ** 1x, dc in same sp as first st, ch1, join with dc to first st.

R5: dc over joining dc, *dc in next 4 sts, along side x [ch1, skip 1-ch sp, tr in 1-ch sp of R3 and next st of R4 at the same time], ch1, skip 1-ch sp, dc in last 4 sts**, (dc, ch2, dc) in 2-ch cnr sp*, rep from * to * 2x & * to ** 1x, dc in same sp as first st, ch1, join with dc to first st.

R6: dc over joining dc, *dc in next 5 sts, along side x [spike dc into the 2 1-ch sps of R4 & R5 at the same time, dc in next st], spike dc into the 2 1-ch sps of R4 & R5 at the same time, dc in last 5 sts**, (dc, ch2, dc) in 2-ch cnr sp*, rep from * to * 2x & * to ** 1x, dc in same sp as first st, ch1, join with dc to first st.

R7: dc over joining dc, *dc in each st along side**, (dc, ch2, dc) in 2-ch cnr sp*, rep from * to * 2x & * to ** 1x, dc in same sp as first st, ch2, join with ss to first st. Fasten off.

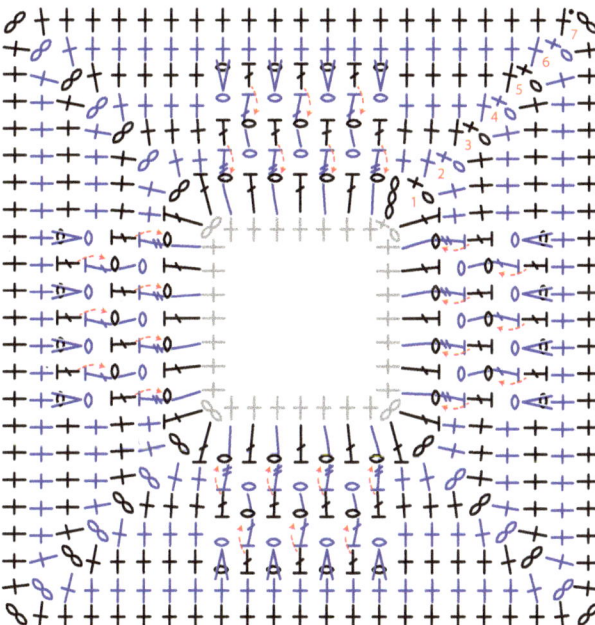

EXTENSIONS

Sideline

One increment extension for any stitch count

If using as a border, first add a round of dc with a st in every st, 2-ch sp and join with (dc, ch2, dc) corners, ch1, join with dc to first st.

R1: dc over joining dc, *dc in each st along side**, (dc, ch2, dc) in 2-ch cnr sp*, rep from * to * 2x & * to ** 1x, dc in same sp as first st, ch1, join with dc to first st.

R2: ch2 (stch), *htr in blo of each st along side**, (htr, ch2, htr) in 2-ch cnr sp*, rep from * to * 2x & * to ** 1x, htr in same sp as first st, ch1, join with dc to 2nd ch of stch.

R3: ch2 (stch), *htr in lbv of each st along side**, (htr, ch2, htr) in 2-ch cnr sp*, rep from * to * 2x & * to ** 1x, htr in same sp as first st, ch1, join with dc to 2nd ch of stch.

R4: ch2 (stch), *htr in blo of each st along side**, (htr, ch2, htr) in 2-ch cnr sp*, rep from * to * 2x & * to ** 1x, htr in same sp as first st, ch1, join with dc to 2nd ch of stch.

R5: dc over joining dc, *dc in lbv of each st along side**, (dc, ch2, dc) in 2-ch cnr sp*, rep from * to * 2x & * to ** 1x, dc in same sp as first st, ch1, join with dc to first st.

R6: dc over joining dc, *skip 1 st, dc in each st along side**, (dc, ch2, dc) in 2-ch cnr sp*, rep from * to * 2x & * to ** 1x, dc in same sp as first st, ch2, join with ss to first st. Fasten off.

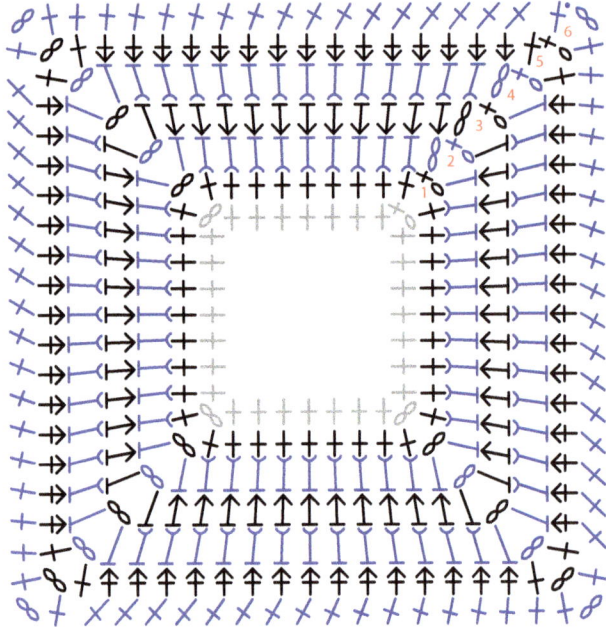

162 • EXTENSIONS

Binary

One increment extension for an even numbered stitch count

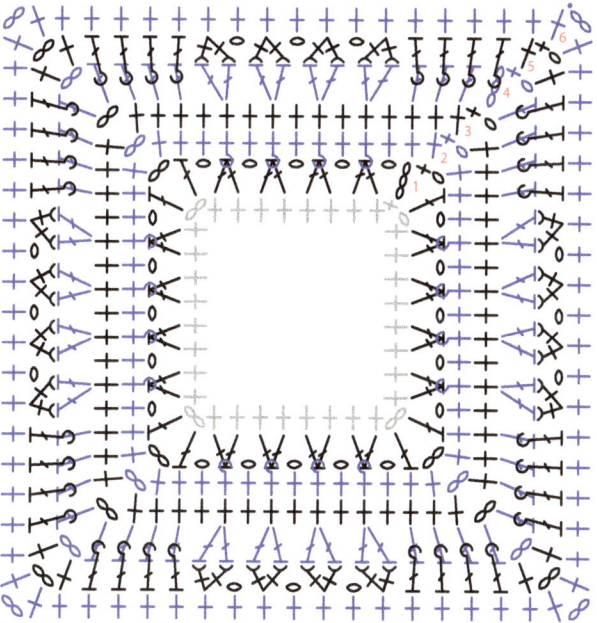

If using as a border, first add a round of dc with a st in every st, 2-ch sp and join with (dc, ch2, dc) corners, ch1, join with dc to first st.

R1: ch3 (stch), *along side x [ch1, tr2tog over next 2 sts], ch1**, (tr, ch2, tr) in 2-ch cnr sp*, rep from * to * 2x & * to ** 1x, tr in same sp as first st, ch1, join with dc to first st.

R2: dc over joining dc, *dc in next st, along side x [dc in 1-ch sp, fpdc around next st], dc in 1-ch sp, dc in last st**, (dc, ch2, dc) in 2-ch cnr sp*, rep from * to * 2x & * to ** 1x, dc in same sp as first st, ch1, join with dc to first st.

R3: dc over joining dc, *dc in each st along side**, (dc, ch2, dc) in 2-ch cnr sp*, rep from * to * 2x & * to ** 1x, dc in same sp as first st, ch1, join with dc to first st.

R4: ch3 (stch), *tr in next 3 sts, along side x [skip 1 st, 2tr in next st], skip 1 st, tr in last 3 sts**, (tr, ch2, tr) in 2-ch cnr sp*, rep from * to * 2x & * to ** 1x, tr in same sp as first st, ch1, join with dc to 3rd ch of stch.

R5: dc over joining dc, *fptr around next 4 sts, along side x [dc2tog in blo over next 2 sts, ch1], dc2tog in blo over next 2 sts, fptr around last 4 sts**, (dc, ch2, dc) in 2-ch cnr sp*, rep from * to * 2x & * to ** 1x, dc in same sp as first st, ch1, join with dc to first st.

R6: dc over joining dc, *dc in next 6 sts, along side x [dc in 1-ch sp, dc in next st], dc in 1-ch sp, dc in last 6 sts**, (dc, ch2, dc) in 2-ch cnr sp*, rep from * to * 2x & * to ** 1x, dc in same sp as first st, ch2, join with ss to first st. Fasten off.

Withe

One increment extension for an odd numbered stitch count

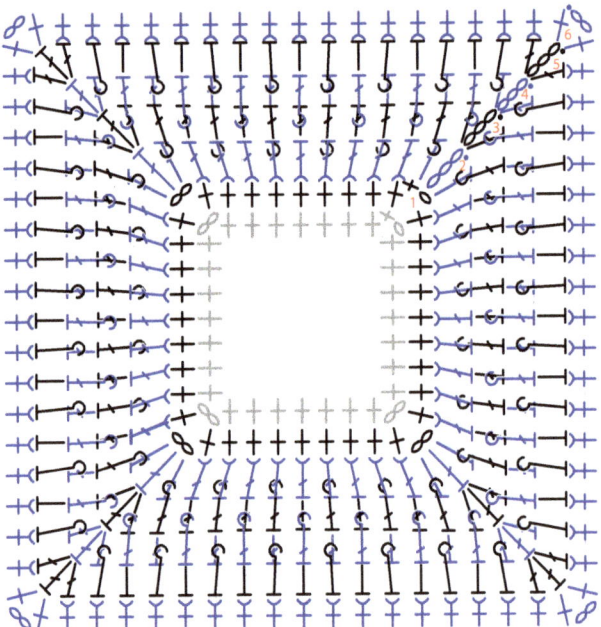

If using as a border, first add a round of dc with a st in every st, 2-ch sp and join with (dc, ch2, dc) corners, ch1, join with dc to first st.

R1: dc over joining dc, *dc in each st along side**, (dc, ch2, dc) in 2-ch cnr sp*, rep from * to * 2x & * to ** 1x, dc in same sp as first st, ch1, join with dc to first st.

R2: ch3 (stch), tr over joining dc, *tr in blo of each st along side**, 3tr in 2-ch cnr sp*, rep from * to * 2x & * to ** 1x, tr in same sp as first sts, join with ss to 3rd ch of stch.

R3: ch3 (stch), tr in same st as ss, *along side x [fptr around next st, tr in next st], fptr around next st**, 3tr in next st*, rep from * to * 2x & * to ** 1x, tr in same st as first sts, join with ss to 3rd ch of stch.

R4: ch3 (stch), tr in same st as ss, *along side x [fptr around next st, tr in next st], fptr around next st**, 3tr in next st*, rep from * to * 2x & * to ** 1x, tr in same st as first sts, join with ss to 3rd ch of stch.

R5: ch3 (stch), tr in same st as ss, *along side x [fphtr around next st, htr in next st], fphtr around next st**, 3tr in next st*, rep from * to * 2x & * to ** 1x, tr in same st as first sts, join with ss to 3rd ch of stch.

R6: dc in same st as ss, *dc in blo of each st along side**, (dc, ch2, dc) in next st*, rep from * to * 2x & * to ** 1x, dc in same st as first st, ch2, join with ss to first st. Fasten off.

Please see notes on page 158 if using this pattern as a border.

Right-about

One increment extension for any stitch count

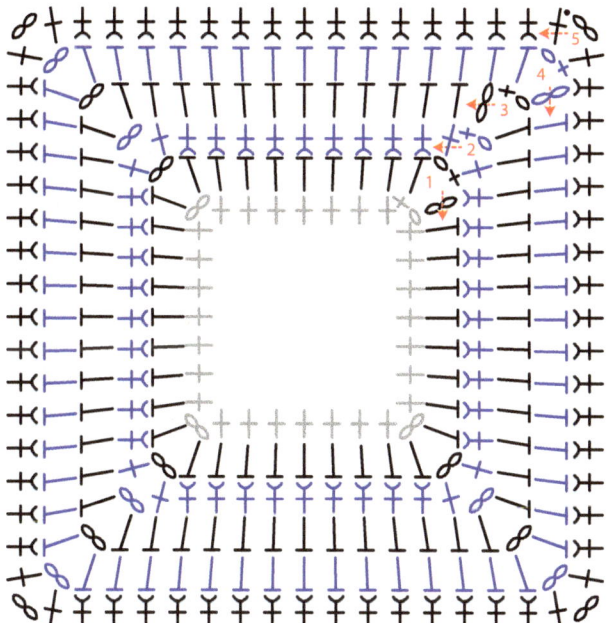

If using as a border, first add a round of dc with a st in every st, 2-ch sp and join with (dc, ch2, dc) corners, ch1, join with dc to first st.

R1: turn, ch2 (stch), *htr in each st along side**, (htr, ch2, htr) in 2-ch cnr sp*, rep from * to * 2x & * to ** 1x, htr in same sp as first st, ch1, join with dc to first st. [WS]

R2: turn, dc over 1-ch sp, *dc in blo of each st along side**, (dc, ch2, dc) in 2-ch cnr sp*, rep from * to * 2x & * to ** 1x, dc in same sp as first st, ch1, join with dc to first st. [RS]

R3: ch2 (stch), *htr in each st along side**, (htr, ch2, htr) in 2-ch cnr sp*, rep from * to * 2x & * to ** 1x, htr in same sp as first st, ch1, join with dc to 2nd ch of stch. [RS]

R4: turn, ch2 (stch), *htr in each st along side**, (htr, ch2, htr) in 2-ch cnr sp*, rep from * to * 2x & * to ** 1x, htr in same sp as first st, ch1, join with dc to 2nd ch of stch. [WS]

R5: turn, dc over 1-ch sp, *dc in blo of each st along side**, (dc, ch2, dc) in 2-ch cnr sp*, rep from * to * 2x & * to ** 1x, dc in same sp as first st, ch2, join with ss to first st. Fasten off. [RS]

EXTENSIONS • 165

Projects

Stellar Trivets
Pg 168

Tippit
Pg 170

Malachite
Pg 172

Beacon Wrap
Pg 174

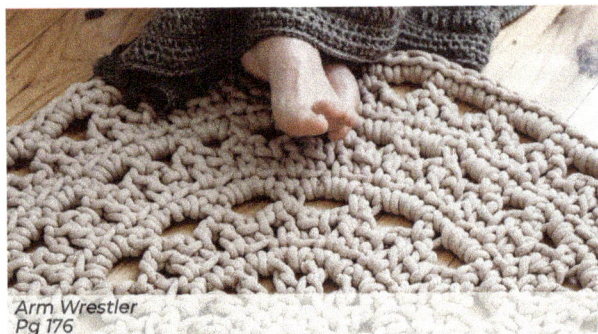

Arm Wrestler
Pg 176

Beachcomber
Pg 180

Viminalis
Pg 182

Keepsake
Pg 178

Vinyl Revival
Pg 184

Sweet Shop
Pg 186

Compendium
Pg 190

PROJECTS • 167

Stellar Trivets

Pattern used:	Stellate Stratified, page 154
Yarn:	Quince & Co Whimbrel
Fibre:	Organic cotton
Weight:	10 ply/aran/worsted
Yardage:	165 metres/180 yards per 100 grams
Hook:	5 mm
Size:	Small 16 cm/6.5 in across Large 28 cm/11 in across

Colours:	No. of skeins:	Amount used:
Starboard 702	1	100 grams
Pelagic 729	1	90 grams

Make

To make the small trivet:

Using Pelagic, make Rounds 1-11 of Stellate Stratified twice. Fasten each off at the end of Round 11.

To make the large trivet:

First circle: Using Starboard, make Rounds 1-19 of Stellate Stratified.

Second circle: Make Rounds 1-19 of Stellate Stratified using these colours:

Rounds 1-9	Starboard
Rounds 10-16	Pelagic
Rounds 17-19	Starboard

Join

Use Pelagic to join the small trivet and Starboard to join the large one. Holding the 2 circles wrong sides together, attach with a slip stitch to a stitch of both circles. Work a double crochet through both loops of each stitch around the circles. End with an invisible join to the first true stitch.

PROJECTS TO MAKE • 169

Tippit

Pattern used: Swirlygig, page 108
Yarn: Leachim Wool
Fibre: 100% Poll Merino wool
Weight: 4 ply/sock/fingering
Yardage: 400 metres/437 yards per 100 grams
Hook: 4 mm
Size: 48 cm deep, 96 cm around/19 in deep, 38 in around

Colours:	No. of skeins:	Amount used:
Mountain Blue	3	290 grams

Make

Make 18 Swirlygig squares.

Cowl: 6 x 3 cylinder

Join

Join into a 6 x 3 rectangle using the whip st in blo on back join from page 14. Then join the two short edges in the same manner.

Edging

Attach with slip stitch to any st, ch1, dc in each (st, ch-sp & join) around, join with inv join to first st. Repeat on opposite edge.

PROJECTS TO MAKE • 171

Malachite

Patterns used: Little Avens, page 50
Little Bluet, page 52
Large Bluet, page 92
Large Avens, page 88

Yarn: Louie and Lola Hand Dyed Yarn

Fibre: 100% Cormo Wool

Weight: 4 ply/sock/fingering

Yardage: 365 metres/400 yards per 100 grams

Hook: 4.5 mm

Size: 41 x 216 cm/16 x 85 in

Colours:	No. of skeins:	Amount used:
Friendlies Beach	1	15 grams
Swansea	1	60 grams
St Helens	2	150 grams
Franklin River	2	200 grams

Make

No. of squares:	Pattern:	Rounds:	Colour:
8	Little Bluet	Rounds 1-2	Swansea
		Rounds 3-5	St Helens
		Rounds 6-8	Franklin River
7	Little Avens	Rounds 1-2	Swansea
		Rounds 3-5	St Helens
		Rounds 6-8	Franklin River
6	Large Bluet	Rounds 1-2	Friendlies Beach
		Rounds 3-5	Swansea
		Rounds 6-10	St Helens
		Rounds 11-14	Franklin River
6	Large Avens	Rounds 1-2	Friendlies Beach
		Rounds 3-5	Swansea
		Rounds 6-10	St Helens
		Rounds 11-14	Franklin River

Join

Join according to the schematic using the dc on back join from page 14.

Edging and Chain Fringe

NOTE: if you are not keen on the fringe, work the short edges the same as the long edges, with (dc, ch2, dc) in each 2-ch cnr sp.

chfr: ch18, dc in 4th ch from hook, 2x [ch6, skip 5 ch, dc in next ch], ch2

R1: Attach Franklin River with stdg dc to any 2-ch cnr sp before a long edge, *dc in each (st, 2-ch sp & join) along edge**, (dc, ch2, dc) in 2-ch cnr sp*, rep from * to * 2x & * to ** 1x, dc in same sp as first st, ch1, join with dc to first st.

R2: dc over joining dc, *dc in blo of each st along side, dc in 2-ch cnr sp, chfr, 38x [dc in next st, chfr, skip 1 st], dc in next st, chfr*, dc in 2-ch cnr sp, rep from * to * 1x, join with ss to first st. Fasten off.

Large Avens	Little Avens	Large Bluet	Large Avens	Little Bluet	Little Avens	Little Bluet	Large Bluet	Large Avens	Little Bluet	Large Bluet
	Little Bluet			Little Avens	Little Bluet	Little Avens			Little Avens	
Large Bluet	Little Avens	Large Avens	Large Bluet	Little Bluet	Little Avens	Little Bluet	Large Avens	Large Bluet	Little Bluet	Large Avens

PROJECTS TO MAKE • 173

Beacon Wrap

Pattern used: Fresnel, page 34

Yarn: Skein Sisters Fabulous Sock

Fibre: 80% Australian extra fine superwash merino, 20% nylon

Weight: 4 ply/sock/fingering

Yardage: 400 metres/437 yards per 100 grams

Hook: 3.5 mm

Size: 88 x 107 cm/35 x 42 in

Colour:	Number of skeins:	Amount used:
Red Rattler	6 - 7	600 grams

Make

Make 80 Fresnel squares.

Join

Join into two 4 x 10 rectangles using the dc on back join from page 14.

Join 4 squares along the long side of each rectangle according to the schematic.

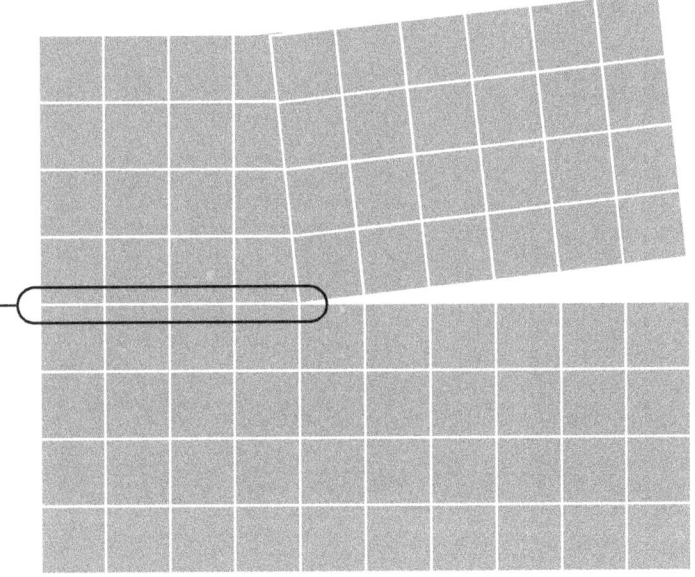

Border

R1: Attach with a stdg dc to any 2-ch corner sp, *dc in each (st, 2-ch sp & join) along side**, (dc, ch2, dc) in 2-ch cnr sp*, rep from * to * 5x & * to ** 1x, dc in same sp as first st, ch1, join with dc to first st.

NOTE: At the inside join of the 2 rectangles, skip the 2-ch sps either side of the join.

R2: dc over joining dc, *dc in blo of each st along side**, (dc, ch2, dc) in 2-ch cnr sp*, rep from * to * 5x & * to ** 1x, dc in same sp as first st, ch2, join with ss to first st. Fasten off.

See pages 19 & 166 for other ways to wear the Beacon Wrap.

PROJECTS TO MAKE • 175

Arm Wrestler

Pattern used: Empyreal, page 122
Yarn: Bobbiny Braided Cord
Fibre: Recycled cotton, polyester core
Weight: 9 mm thick
Yardage: 100 metres/108 yards per 1,200 grams
Hook: 16 mm
Size: 94 cm/37 in across

Colour:	No. of skeins:	Amount used:
Biscuit	3	2,800 grams

Make

Take this project slowly, taking breaks and supporting the work on a table as it gets very heavy very quickly.

Make rounds 1 to 12 of the Empyreal pattern. Fasten off.

Tip: Use a 5-6 mm hook to help weave in the ends.

If using on a smooth floor, add some hot glue dots on the back for some stability.

Keepsake

Pattern used: Coffer, page 22
Yarn: Fiddlesticks WREN
Fibre: 100% cotton
Weight: 8 ply/DK/light worsted
Yardage: 125 metres/137 yards per 50 grams
Hook: 4 mm
Size: 90 x 90 cm/35.5 x 35.5 in

Colours:	No. of balls:	Amount used:
Ivory W003	3 - 4	150 grams
Butter W004	1 - 2	50 grams
Ice Blue W023	2	75 grams
Sky W024	2	60 grams
Nil W032	2	85 grams

Make

No. of squares:	Pattern:	Rounds:	Colour:
25	Coffer	Round 1	Butter
		Round 2	Nil
		Round 3	Sky
		Round 4	Ivory
		Round 5	Butter
		Round 6	Ivory
		Round 7	Nil
		Round 8	Ivory
		Round 9	Ice Blue

Join

Join according to the schematic using Ice Blue and the dc on back join from page 14.

Border

Add the Sideline border from page 162. Ignore the note about if using as border. Work R1 side sts into each stitch, chain space and join.

Round 1	Ice Blue
Round 2	Butter
Round 3	Ivory
Round 4	Nil
Round 5	Ice Blue
Round 6	Sky

Beachcomber

Pattern used: Sand Dollar, page 104
Yarn: Hobbii Rainbow Cotton 8/6
Fibre: 100% cotton
Weight: 8 ply/DK/light worsted
Yardage: 105 metres/114 yards per 50 grams
Hook: 4.5 mm
Size: 122 x 122 cm/48 x 48 in

Colours:	No. of balls:	Amount used:
Light Blue 27	3 - 4	150 grams
Pastel Pink 42	3	140 grams
Pastel Yellow 53	3	140 grams
Mist 97	10	450 grams

Make

No. of squares:	Pattern:	Rounds:	Colour:
9	Sand Dollar	Rounds 1-8	Light Blue
		Rounds 9-12	Mist
8	Sand Dollar	Rounds 1-8	Pastel Pink
		Rounds 9-12	Mist
8	Sand Dollar	Rounds 1-8	Pastel Yellow
		Rounds 9-12	Mist

Join

Join according to the schematic using the dc on back join from page 14.

Border

R1: Attach with stdg dc to any 2-ch cnr sp, *dc in each (st, 2-ch sp & join) along side**, (dc, ch2, dc) in 2-ch cnr sp, rep from * to * 2x & * to ** 1x, dc in same sp as first st, ch1, join with dc to first st. {159 sts on each side; 4 2-ch cnr sps}

R2: ch3 (stch), tr over joining dc, *skip 1 st, 31x [tr in next 3 sts, ch2, skip 2 sts], tr in next 3 sts**, (2tr, ch2, 2tr) in 2-ch cnr sp*, rep from * to * 2x & * to ** 1x, 2tr in same sp as first sts, ch1, join with dc to 3rd ch of stch. {100 sts & 31 2-ch sps on each side; 4 2-ch cnr sps}

R3: ch3 (stch), tr over joining dc, *tr in next 5 sts, 30x [2tr in 2-ch sp, tr in next 3 sts], 2tr in 2-ch sp, tr in next 5 sts**, (2tr, ch2, 2tr) in 2-ch cnr sp*, rep from * to * 2x & * to ** 1x, 2tr in same sp as first sts, ch1, join with dc to 3rd ch of stch. {166 sts on each side; 4 2-ch cnr sps}

R4: dc over joining dc, *dc in blo of next 166 sts**, (dc, ch2, dc) in 2-ch cnr sp*, rep from * to * 2x & * to ** 1x, dc in same sp as first st, ch2, join with ss to first st. Fasten off. {168 sts on each side; 4 2-ch cnr sps}

Pastel Pink	Light Blue	Pastel Yellow	Light Blue	Pastel Pink
Light Blue	Pastel Yellow	Pastel Pink	Pastel Yellow	Light Blue
Pastel Yellow	Pastel Pink	Light Blue	Pastel Pink	Pastel Yellow
Light Blue	Pastel Yellow	Pastel Pink	Pastel Yellow	Light Blue
Pastel Pink	Light Blue	Pastel Yellow	Light Blue	Pastel Pink

PROJECTS TO MAKE • 181

Viminalis

Yarn: Tarndwarncoort Wool
Fibre: 100% Polwarth wool
Weight: 8 ply/DK/light worsted
Yardage: 192 metres/210 yards per 100 grams
Hook: 6 mm
Size: 127 x 127 cm/50 x 50 in

Colours:	No. of balls:	Amount used:
Manna Gum	14	1,400 grams

Since 1840, the Dennis family have grown wool and developed the Polwarth breed at Tarndwarncoort to suit their environment in south-east Australia. The natural colour of the Polwarth sheep farm matches the two-toned bark of the endemic Manna Gum tree creating a subtle variation and depth in spun yarn.

Betwixt & Binary	HAL 9000	Wee Oct. & Kernel	Zinderella	Esker & Withe
Swirlygig	Ataraxia & Sideline	Large Bluet	Wellspring & Right-about	Settings
Passionflower & Kernel	Sand Dollar	Cincture & Dornick	33 1/3	Begirt & Sideline
Moyenne Lavallière	Ipheion & Right-about	Carnassial	Gyre & Binary	Large Avens
Sprocket & Withe	Radiance Squared	Octad & Kernel	Corolla	Fresnel & Dornick

Make

Small Patterns:	Page:	Plus Extension:	Page:
Ataraxia	20	Sideline	162
Sprocket	26	Withe	164
Begirt	30	Sideline	162
Cincture	32	Dornick	161
Fresnel	34	Dornick	161
Gyre	36	Binary	163
Ipheion	38	Right-about	165
Octad	40	Kernel	160
Betwixt	44	Binary	163
Esker	48	Withe	164
Passionflower	54	Kernel	160
Wee Octamerous	60	Kernel	160
Wellspring	64	Right-about	165
Medium Patterns:			**Page:**
Settings			68
33 1/3			72
Carnassial			76
Corolla			80
HAL 9000			84
Large Avens			88
Large Bluet			92
Moyenne Lavallière			96
Radiance Squared			100
Sand Dollar			104
Swirlygig			108
Zinderella			112

Join

Join according to the schematic using the dc on back through blo join from page 14.

Border

Use the Dornick pattern on page 161 as the border.

Vinyl Revival

Patterns used: 45, page 28
33 1/3, page 72
78, page 118

Yarn: Bendigo Woollen Mills Cotton

Fibre: 100% cotton

Weight: 4 ply/sock/fingering

Yardage: 670 metres/732 yards per 200 grams

Hook: 3.5 mm

Size: 107 x 107 cm/42 x 42 in

Colours:	No. of balls:	Amount used:
Denim 871	3	500 grams
Parchment 816	2	380 grams

Make

No. of squares:	Pattern:	Rounds:	Colour:
22	45	Rounds 1-6	Denim
		Rounds 7-10	Parchment
8	33 1/3	Rounds 1-10	Denim
		Rounds 11-16	Parchment
6	78	Rounds 1-16	Denim
		Rounds 17-23	Parchment

Join

Join according to the schematic using the dc on back join from page 14.

Border

R1: Using Parchment, attach yarn with a stdg dc to any 2-ch cnr sp, *dc in each (st, 2-ch sp & join) along side**, (dc, ch2, dc) in 2-ch cnr sp*, rep from * to * 2x & * to ** 1x, dc in same sp as first st, ch1, join with dc to first st.

R2: dc over joining dc, *dc in each st along side**, (dc, ch2, dc) in 2-ch cnr sp*, rep from * to * 2x & * to ** 1x, dc in same sp as first st, ch2, join with ss to first st. Fasten off.

R3: Using Denim, attach with stdg tr to any 2-ch cnr sp, *tr in each st along side**, (tr, ch2, tr) in 2-ch cnr sp*, rep from * to * 2x & * to ** 1x, tr in same sp as first st, ch2, join with ss to first st. Fasten off.

R4: Using Parchment, attach with stdg dc to any 2-ch cnr sp, *dc in each st along side**, (dc, ch2, dc) in 2-ch cnr sp*, rep from * to * 2x & * to ** 1x, dc in same sp as first st, ch1, join with dc to first st.

R5: dc over joining dc, *dc in each st along side**, (dc, ch2, dc) in 2-ch cnr sp*, rep from * to * 2x & * to ** 1x, dc in same sp as first st, ch2, join with ss to first st. Fasten off.

PROJECTS TO MAKE • 185

Sweet Shop

Patterns used: Petite Lavallière, page 56
Moyenne Lavallière, page 96
Grande Lavallière, page 142

Yarn: Berroco Pima 100

Fibre: 100% cotton

Weight: 8 ply/DK/light worsted

Yardage: 200 metres/219 yards per 100 grams

Hook: 4 mm

Size: 120 x 120 cm/47 x 47 in

Colours:	No. of skeins:	Amount used:
Colour 1		
Wisteria 8403	12	1,150 grams
Colour 2		
Day Lily 8414 (Day)	1	70 grams
Chrysanthemum 8431 (Chrys)	1	70 grams
Zinnea 8429 (Zin)	1	70 grams
Dianthus 8419 (Dia)	1	70 grams
Chive 8415 (Chi)	1	70 grams

Make

Pattern:	No. of squares:	Colour 2:
Petite Lavallière	4	Day Lily
	4	Chrysanthemum
	5	Zinnea
	5	Dianthus
	4	Chive

Rounds:	Colour:
Rounds 1 - 2	Wisteria
Round 3	Colour 2
Round 4	Wisteria
Round 5	Colour 2
Round 6	Wisteria
Round 7	Colour 2
Rounds 8-10	Wisteria

Pattern:	No. of squares:	Colour 2:
Moyenne Lavallière	1	Day Lily
	1	Chrysanthemum
	2	Zinnea
	2	Dianthus
	2	Chive

Rounds:	Colour:
Round 1	Wisteria
Round 2	Colour 2
Round 3	Wisteria
Round 4	Colour 2
Round 5	Wisteria
Round 6	Colour 2
Round 7	Wisteria
Round 8	Colour 2
Round 9	Wisteria
Round 10	Colour 2
Rounds 11-16	Wisteria

Pattern:	No. of squares:	Colour 2:
Grande Lavallière	1	Day Lily
	1	Chrysanthemum
	1	Zinnea
	1	Dianthus
	2	Chive

Rounds:	Colour:
Rounds 1-2	Wisteria
Round 3	Colour 2
Round 4	Wisteria
Round 5	Colour 2
Round 6	Wisteria
Round 7	Colour 2
Round 8	Wisteria
Round 9	Colour 2
Round 10	Wisteria
Round 11	Colour 2
Round 12	Wisteria
Round 13	Colour 2
Rounds 14-22	Wisteria

Dia	Zin	Day	Chi	Zin
Chi				Dia
Zin	Chrys	Chi	Dia	Zin	Day
Dia					Chrys
Chrys	Chi	Day	Dia	Zin	Chrys	Chi	Zin
Day	Dia	Zin	Chi	Day	Dia
Zin	Chi	Dia	Chrys	Chi
Chrys				Day

Join

Join according to the schematic using the dc on back join from page 14.

Border

Attach Wisteria with stdg dc to any 2-ch cnr sp, *dc in each (st, 2-ch sp & join) along side**, (dc, ch2, dc) in 2-ch cnr sp*, rep from * to * 2x & * to ** 1x, dc in same sp as first st, ch1, join with dc to first st.

Use the Binary pattern on page 163 as the border.

Rounds 1-2	Wisteria
Round 3	Day Lily
Round 4	Wisteria
Round 5	Chive
Round 6	Chrysanthemum

Compendium

Patterns used: All

Small Version:

Yarn:	Bendigo Woollen Mills Cotton
Fibre:	100% cotton
Weight:	4 ply/sock/fingering
Yardage:	670 metres/732 yards per 200 grams
Hook:	3.5 mm
Size:	110 x 128 cm/43 x 50 in

Colours:	Number of balls:	Amount used:
Buttercream	5	950 grams

PROJECTS TO MAKE • 191

Medium Version:

Yarn:	Bendigo Woollen Mills Cotton
Fibre:	100% cotton
Weight:	8 ply/DK/light worsted
Yardage:	485 metres/530 yards per 200 grams
Hook:	4.5 mm
Size:	148 x 158 cm/58 x 62 in

Colours:	Number of balls:	Amount used:
Parchment	8	1,600 grams

Layout for all Compendium Blankets. Placement of the individual squares is up to you.

PROJECTS TO MAKE • 193

Large Version:

Yarn:	Bendigo Woollen Mills Cotton
Fibre:	100% cotton
Weight:	10 ply/aran/worsted
Yardage:	360 metres/393 yards per 200 grams
Hook:	5.5 mm
Size:	162 x 180 cm/64 x 71 in

Colours:	Number of balls:	Amount used:
Parchment	6	1,200 grams
Denim	6	1,100 grams

Make

Make 1 of each square in this book. For the large version, use Denim for all circles and square off with Parchment.

Join

Join with your preferred method from page 14 according to the schematic on page 192.

I used dc on back for small and large versions, and the dc in blo on back for the medium version.

Joining tip: See page 13 for help how to join this project.

Border

Use any of the extension patterns on pages 160 to 165 as a border.

I used Withe for the small version, Kernel for the medium version and Binary for the large version.

Design Your Own Projects

I want you to play with these granny squares to make your own fun. Here are some tips to help you design your own project.

What do you want to make?

Think about who it is for, the size it needs to be and a rough shape you want it to be. Square? Rectangular?

Which squares do you want to use?

Maybe you want to use just the one pattern over and over? Or one of each size? Or a mix of all sizes.

There are three different sized patterns in this book. Each size up increases by the same increment. For example, if you are using an 8 ply/DK/Light worsted yarn, the size goes up by 3 inches for each size. If you are using 4 ply/sock/fingering, the size increment is 2.5 inches for each size. If you are using 10 ply/aran/worsted, the size increases by 3.5 inches.

There are also six patterns you can use to add one increment to any of the patterns, extending them to the next size up if you need to for your layout. These extensions can also be used as borders for your projects.

On page 199 you will find a project planner page you can copy to help with your layout ideas. Print it a few times then cut it up to play with possible layouts. You can download it from the Helpful Links page as well.

Have a look at the projects I made to get some ideas how to mix and match the squares.

- In the Viminalis blanket, I made all the medium squares, then 13 of the small squares with an extension, so the blanket has 25 squares the same size.
- The Compendium blankets, I used every pattern of every size, no extensions.
- The Keepsake and Beachcomber blankets, I used one pattern only.

There are so many options open to you.

Once you have decided on your layout, write down how many of each pattern you need, including details of any that you are extending. Decide on a border to finish it off with.

DESIGN YOUR OWN PROJECTS • 197

Which yarn and how much do you need?

Which fibre and yarn?

Your yarn choice will be based on many things. Is the yarn fit for purpose? Is there a budget for the project? Are there environmental considerations? Does the recipient have any fibre allergies? What colour or colours will you use?

How much yarn?

The amount of yarn needed listed on the pattern pages, stated in metres/yards, is for the 8 ply/DK/light worsted yarn I used. The amount needed in other yarn weights is listed on page 200.

Compare the metres or yards per gram ratio of your yarn of choice to the weights listed. If it is less metres or yards per gram, you will need more, and if it is more, you will need less.

If your tension is different to mine, that will also impact the amount of yarn needed. If you crochet looser than me, you will need more. If you crochet tighter, you will need less. Make a pattern to see how your tension compares to mine.

Using more than one colour?

If using many colours, use the overall yardage as a guide. To be more precise, make a sample square of average size for your project in your yarn and colour choice. Weigh either the yarn balls or square as you go, to work out how much of each colour you will use. Work out rough percentages of each colour used and use those figures to work out how much you will need overall. My tip is to add extra of the colours used most at the end of patterns, particularly if you are using the larger sizes patterns.

Extra yarn for joining and border

Using your layout plan, work out how much yarn you need. Add 10-15% more for joining and the border. The larger your project, the more you will need for the finishing.

Project Planner

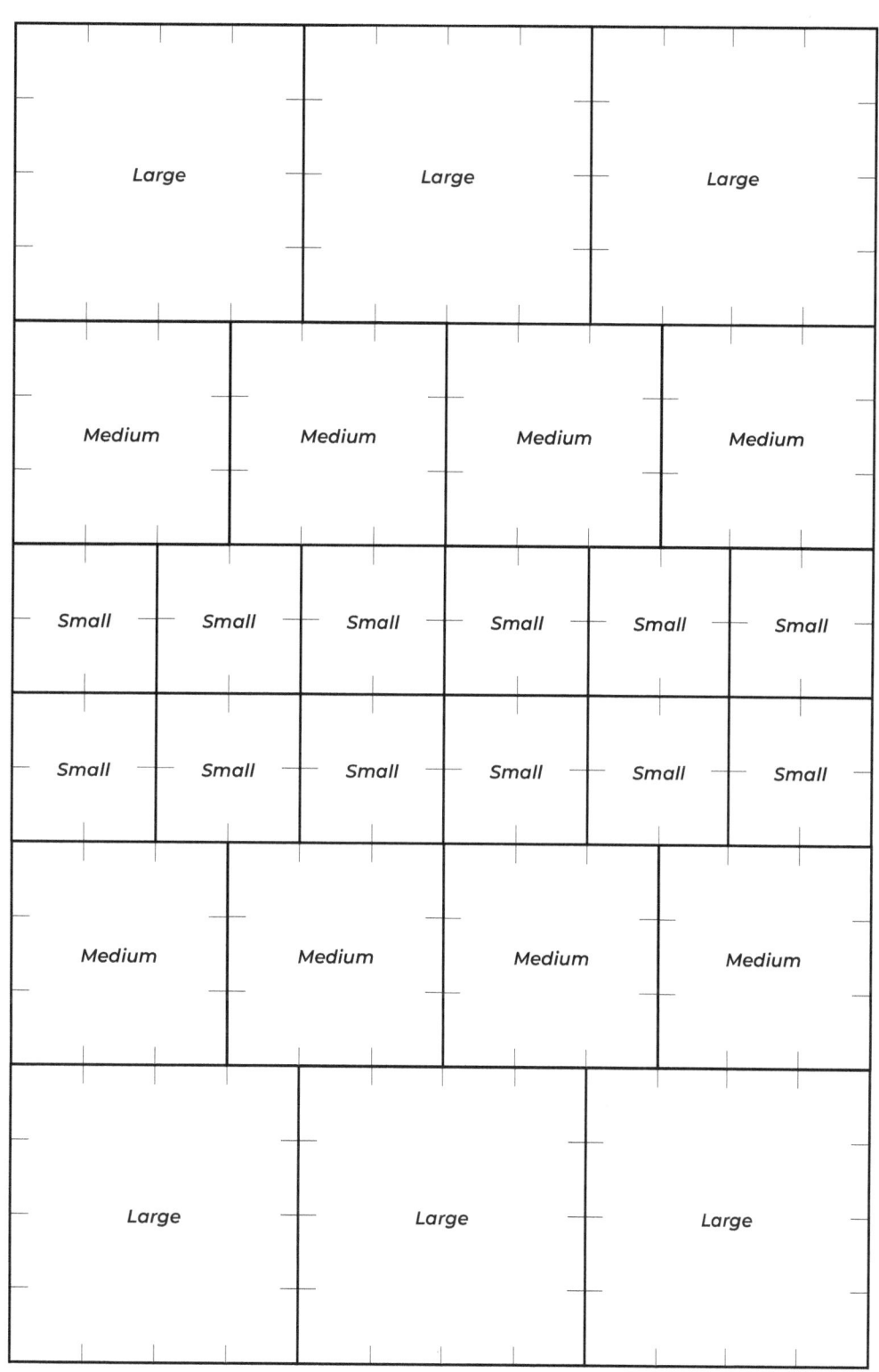

DESIGN YOUR OWN PROJECTS • 199

Yardage and Stitch Counts

I used Bendigo Woollen Mills cotton to make the sample squares. Compare the metres per gram ratio for this yarn as listed here to your yarn to help you work out your yarn needs. This is discussed on pages 6 and 198.

Bendigo Woollen Mills Cotton
4 ply/sock/fingering: 3.35 metres per gram
8 ply/DK/light worsted: 2.43 metres per gram
10 ply/aran/worsted: 1.8 metres per gram

Small Squares	Stitch Count	4 ply		8 ply		10 ply	
		Metres	Yards	Metres	Yards	Metres	Yards
45	22	37	41	44	48	48	53
Ataraxia	21	26	28	31	34	34	38
Begirt	23	30	33	36	39	39	42
Betwixt	18	28	30	32	35	36	39
Cincture	19	28	30	31	34	35	38
Coffer	22	29	32	35	38	41	45
Covey	23	37	41	42	46	47	51
Ecliptic	22	31	33	37	40	41	45
Esker	24	39	43	42	46	46	51
Fresnel	21	33	37	42	46	43	47
Gyre	20	38	42	42	46	48	53
Ipheion	23	29	32	34	37	38	42
Little Avens	20	30	33	37	40	37	41
Little Bluet	20	30	33	36	40	37	41
Octad	21	27	30	32	35	36	39
Passionflower	21	38	41	45	49	50	54
Petite Lavallière	21	35	38	41	45	46	50
Stellate	21	49	53	54	59	61	67
Stelliform	23	27	30	34	37	38	42
Spider web	21	35	39	41	44	45	49
Sprocket	23	29	32	34	38	38	42
Wee Octamerous	23	35	39	41	44	45	49
Wellspring	19	36	39	42	46	47	52
Totals:		756	828	885	966	976	1070

Medium Squares	Stitch Count	4 ply		8 ply		10 ply	
		Metres	Yards	Metres	Yards	Metres	Yards
33 1/3	34	84	92	102	112	111	121
Carnassial	34	78	86	94	103	103	112
Corolla	33	77	84	92	101	102	111
HAL 9000	29	78	85	92	101	100	109
Large Avens	34	71	78	84	91	93	101
Large Bluet	34	70	76	84	92	91	99
Moyenne Lavallière	33	88	96	107	117	115	126
Radiance Squared	32	64	70	77	84	76	83
Sand Dollar	29	59	65	70	77	78	85
Settings	31	58	63	70	77	75	82
Swirlygig	31	62	68	83	91	89	98
Zinderella	34	78	85	94	102	101	111
Totals:		867	948	1049	1148	1134	1238

Large Squares	Stitch Count	4 ply		8 ply		10 ply	
		Metres	Yards	Metres	Yards	Metres	Yards
78	45	162	177	193	211	213	233
Big Octamerous	41	112	123	143	156	147	161
Camarilla	39	165	180	191	209	215	235
Cambric	52	140	153	170	186	187	204
Empyreal	45	105	115	124	136	137	150
Grande Lavallière	39	150	164	179	195	201	220
Picquant	43	107	117	131	144	133	146
Serry	35	98	107	117	128	134	147
Stellate Stratified	47	162	177	188	205	209	228
Sunbeams	35	116	127	141	154	156	171
Totals:		1317	1441	1577	1724	1732	1895

Glossary

Abbreviations

	cnr	corner	
	R	round	
	rep	repeat	
	sp/s	space/s	
	st/s	stitch/es	
	stch	starting chain	Used in place of the first st in a round. Is included in stitch count.
	stdg	standing	Attach yarn to your hook with a slip knot then work the stitch indicated as normal.
	yo	yarn over	Wrap yarn over hook from back to front.

Stitches

•	ss	slip stitch	Insert hook into st or sp indicated, yo and pull through st or sp and loop on hook.
○	ch	chain	Yarn over, pull through loop on hook.
+	dc	double crochet	Insert hook into st or sp indicated, yo, pull loop to front, yo, pull through both loops on hook.
T	htr	half treble crochet	Wrap yarn around hook, insert hook into st or sp indicated, yo, pull loop to front (3 loops on hook), yo, pull through all 3 loops on hook.
T	tr	treble crochet	Wrap yarn around hook, insert hook into st or sp indicated, yo, pull loop to front (3 loops on hook), 2x [yo, pull through 2 loops on hook].
T	hdtr	half double treble crochet	Wrap yarn around hook twice, insert hook into st or sp indicated, yo, pull loop to front (4 loops on hook), yo, pull through 2 loops (3 loops on hook), yo, pull through all 3 loops on hook.
T	dtr	double treble crochet	Wrap yarn around hook twice, insert hook into st or sp indicated, yo, pull loop to front (4 loops on hook), 3x [yo, pull through 2 loops].
T	trtr	triple treble crochet	Wrap yarn around hook three times, insert hook into st or sp indicated, yo, pull loop to front (5 loops on hook), 4x [yo, pull through 2 loops].

Techniques

⌒	blo	back loop only	Insert hook into the back loop only of the st indicated.
⌣	flo	front loop only	Insert hook into the front loop only of the st indicated.
	bp	back post	Insert hook around the post of the st indicated from the back. Can be applied to any st.
	fp	front post	Insert hook around the post of the st indicated from the front. Can be applied to any st.
		behind	The bend in the post of the stitch shows it is worked behind previous round/s.
		in front	The bend in the post of the stitch shows it is worked in front of previous round/s.
	chfr	chain fringe	ch18, dc in 4th ch from hook, 2x{ch6, skip 5 ch, dc in next ch}, ch2
	cl	cluster	Numerous sts worked together as one st in the st or sp indicated. Begin the type of st indicated as many times as instructed. Work each st of the cl up to before the last yo and pull through 2 loops on hook, then yo and pull though all loops on hook. Could be any number of any kind of st. e.g. 4trcl, 5dtrcl, 3htrcl and worked as fp or bp.
ᴐ	inv join	invisible join	Cut yarn after completing last st of round. Pull tail up through the last st, thread tail onto needle, insert needle under "v" of first true st of the round and back through the centre of the last st, and through the lbv of the last st. Pull tight enough to form a "v" on top of the stch, weave end away.
	lbv	loop behind v	The third loop or back bump of a st on the back. It's located under the back loop of a st. Any st can be worked into lbv, including cl and tog sts.
	mc	magic circle	Method used to begin a square. Wrap yarn around a few fingers, forming a loop, insert your hook into the centre and pull the working yarn through, ch1 to secure. Work R1 sts into the ring, pull the tail to close the ring once all sts have been made and secure by weaving the end in well.
		at the same time	Shows where to place your hook when gathering sts from a previous round into one.
	tog	together	Numerous sts worked together as one st over a number of sts or sps as indicated. Work the specified number of sts up to before the last yo and pull through 2 loops on hook, then yo and pull though all loops on hook. "tog" will be followed by "over next # sts". It can be done with different numbers and types of sts. E.g. tr5tog over next 5 sts, dc2tog over next 2 sts. Can be worked as fp or bp.
←		turn	Turn the square and work on the other side.

GLOSSARY • 203

Yarn Information

Bendigo Woollen Mills

4, 8 & 10 ply cotton
Used for the Vinyl Revival and Compendium projects and some of the alternate colour samples.

https://www.bendigowoollenmills.com.au/

Berroco

Pima 100 cotton
Used for the Sweet Shop project.

https://berroco.com/

Bobbiny

9 mm braided cord
Used for the Arm Wrestler project.

https://shop.bobbiny.com/en/

Fyberspates

Vivacious 4 ply wool
Used for some of the alternate colour samples.

https://fyberspates.com/

Great Southern Yarn

5 ply SRS Merino
Used for some of the alternate colour samples.

https://greatsouthernyarn.com/

Hobbii

Rainbow cotton 8/6
Used for the Beachcomber project.

https://hobbii.com/

Leachim

4 ply wool
Used for the Tippet project.

https://www.leachimwool.com.au/

Louie and Lola

Cormo DK wool base
Used for the Malachite project.

https://www.louieandlolayarns.com.au/

Quince & Co

Wimbrel cotton worsted
Used for the Stellar Trivets project.

https://quinceandco.com/

Scheepjes

Catona cotton
Used for some of the alternate colour samples.

https://www.scheepjes.com/en/

Skein Sisters

Fabulous Sock
Used for the Beacon Wrap project.

https://www.skeinsisters.com.au/

Tarndwarncoort

Tarndwarncoort wool
Used for the Viminalis project.

https://www.tarndie.com/

Tex yarns

Fiddlesticks WREN & Bellissimo Orchard
Fiddlesticks WREN used for the Keepsake project, and Bellissimo Orchard used for some of the alternate colour samples.

https://texyarns.com/

Helpful Links

Head to this page on my blog,
https://shelleyhusbandcrochet.com/corners-and-curves-helpful-links/,
and use the password CCHELPLINKS to find all the following information:

Explanations of:

- How to read my patterns
- Seamless crochet tips
- How to work a stitch over a joining stitch

Links to my YouTube channel for:

- Stitch and Technique Playlist (short videos of most stitches and techniques used in the book)
- Seamless Crochet Tips (joining with a stitch and working over a joining stitch)
- How to work a standing stitch
- How to work a false stitch instead of a starting chain
- How to work a magic circle (and weave in the end well)
- A simple join (dc join)

Downloads:

- Glossary
- Project planner
- Alternate colour yarn details (yarn used and which rounds for which colours)
- Left-handed charts

If you are still having any trouble, please don't hesitate to reach out. You can email me from my website, **shelleyhusbandcrochet.com**.

Digital download

Scan the QR code to download the digital version of Corners and Curves.

Thank You

Corners and Curves has been in the making for 2 long years. And there are many folks who have helped me bring my tenth book to life.

Thanks, Michelle Lorimer, for your awesome graphic design – we know what to do now, don't we?

Thank you, Jo O'Keefe, for once again capturing the projects so well. Thank you to the wonderful Mel Macilwain for modelling the projects.

Thank you, Kelly Lonergan, for your fabulous technical editing and proofreading. Love your eagle eyes! Thanks to Amy Gunderson, for being there once more to make all the charts so beautifully.

Thank you, Kim Siebenhausen and Kym Craswell, for your most excellent colour play with all the granny squares. And Kim for making the Keepsake and Sweet Shop blankets, and Kym for making the Beacon wrap for me.

My pattern testing team were stellar as usual, testing all the patterns and charts, sometimes more than once or twice. Thank you, Anna M, Anne P, Bonita D, Chantelle D, Chris W, Diana L, Gretchen C, Jennifer F, Jenny H, Judy H, Keri-An R, Lyn M, Marion VS, Meghan M, Melissa R, Michelle M, Monica D, Nicole H, Pam F, Paulina S, Rita S, Ruth B, Samantha T, Sharon L, Shona C, Stephanie A, Tammy RP, Teresa J, Terrii L, Tharana R, and Ursula U.

I had a lot of wonderful yarn support for this book. Thank you, Bendigo Woollen Mills, for supplying the yarn for me to make all of the pattern samples and all the projects made with their cotton. Thank you, Tex Yarns, for the yarn for the Keepsake Blanket. Thank you, Hobbii, for the yarn to make the Beachcomber blanket. Thank you, Berroco Yarns, for the Sweet Shop blanket yarn. Thank you, Skein Sisters, for the Beacon Wrap yarn. Thank you, Tarndwarncoort, for the Viminalis blanket yarn. Thank you, Great Southern Yarns, for the yarn for some of the square samples. So many wonderful yarns!

To everyone else who has played a role in this book's creation, thank you from the bottom of my crochet hook to my biggest ball of yarn! Your contributions, big and small, are deeply appreciated.

I will end with a heartfelt thank you to you, dear granny square lover. It's you who keeps me going with your wonderful support in so many ways. I hope you enjoy playing with Corners and Curves.

xx Shelley

About the Author

Shelley Husband is a designer, author, and serious supporter of making crocheting easy and enjoyable. While Shelley learned crocheting as a child, it took her almost 40 years to crochet her next granny square — and she hasn't stopped since.

Soon after that square, Shelley realised she had a new design in mind, and then another, and…well, let's just say, there's no slowing the new designs that continue to have her granny square community buzzing.

From her first book, Granny Square Flair, winning UK's Best Crochet Book in 2019, to this, her tenth book, Shelley enjoys giving her community what they want. Now with an App, online group, and regular workshops across the country, Shelley loves getting the curious hooked on granny squares!

Old and new crocheters fall in love with the way Shelley designs patterns to be practical to grow their crochet confidence, one square at a time.

When Shelley's not running a retreat, working a workshop, or designing the next book from her hook, she's enjoying the land she loves and lives on in Gunditjmara Country (also known as Narrawong in Southwest Victoria, Australia).

If you haven't joined her community already, and you are crochet curious, you're most welcome to look her up on the socials @spincushions.

Other Books
by Shelley Husband

Granny Square Academy
Learn all there is to know about making granny squares, including how to read patterns.

Granny Square Academy 2
Expand your granny square knowledge with instructions for more advanced stitches and techniques.

Granny Square Flair
50 written and charted granny square patterns and 11 project ideas to make with them.

Beneath the Surface
A beginner friendly pattern, with lots of extra support including video links.

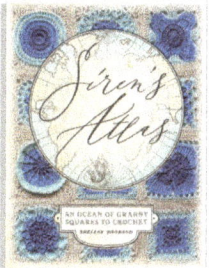

Siren's Atlas
64 written and charted granny square patterns for adventurous crocheters.

Granny Square Patchwork
40 written and charted granny square patterns of 6 sizes and 12 projects to make with them.

Dotty Spotty
Classic circle-to-square granny square fun.

Nimue Crochet Blanket
A crochet quest of epic proportions with very detailed help including video links.

The Cove
A pick your path pattern inspired by coastal adventures.

Buy my books direct in my online shop or at most online book retailers around the world. Visit my pattern shop for digital patterns galore.

shop.shelleyhusbandcrochet.com

OTHER BOOKS BY SHELLEY HUSBAND

www.ingramcontent.com/pod-product-compliance
Lightning Source LLC
Chambersburg PA
CBHW061805290426
44109CB00031B/2940